# JOHN DEWEY BETWEEN PRAGMATISM AND CONSTRUCTIVISM

# JOHN DEWEY BETWEEN PRAGMATISM AND CONSTRUCTIVISM

*Edited by*
LARRY A. HICKMAN
STEFAN NEUBERT
KERSTEN REICH

FORDHAM UNIVERSITY PRESS    NEW YORK    2009

### Library of Congress Cataloging-in-Publication Data

John Dewey between pragmatism and constructivism / edited by
Larry A. Hickman, Stefan Neubert, Kersten Reich.—1st ed.
p.   cm.
Includes bibliographical references and index.
ISBN 978-0-8232-3018-1 (cloth : alk. paper)
1. Dewey, John, 1859–1952.   2. Pragmatism.
3. Constructivism (Philosophy)   I. Hickman, Larry A., 1942–
II. Neubert, Stefan.   III. Reich, Kersten.
B945.D44J56   2009
191—dc22      2008043321

Printed in the United States of America
11 10 09   5 4 3 2 1
First edition

# Contents

# Preface

During the past few decades Pragmatist studies, and especially Dewey scholarship, have begun to enjoy broad international impact. Because of its potential for developing socially oriented versions of constructivism, Pragmatism is increasingly accepted as relevant to many contemporary discourses. More specifically, many contemporary constructivists are particularly attuned to Dewey's penetrating criticism of traditional epistemology, which offers rich alternatives for understanding processes of learning and education, knowledge and truth, and experience and culture. Dewey insisted that philosophy and science are always embedded in contexts of cultural practice. His version of Pragmatism therefore provides important perspectives on the world of action and interaction, especially as those processes relate to participation in democratic institutions.

It is against this background that we present this volume of contributions from American and German Dewey scholars. A result of cooperation between the Center for Dewey Studies at Southern Illinois University Carbondale and the Dewey Center at the University of Cologne, Germany, and building on the success of a conference held at the University of Cologne in 2001, it provides an excellent example of the international character of Pragmatist studies.

As a part of their exploration of the many points of contact between classical Pragmatism and contemporary constructivism, its contributors turn their attention to theories of interaction and transaction, communication and culture, learning and education, community and democracy, theory and practice, and inquiry and methods.

The volume contains three parts. Part I provides a basic survey of John Dewey's Pragmatism and its implications for contemporary constructivism. In Chapter 1, Larry A. Hickman presents an overview of Dewey's life and work. In Chapter 2, Stefan Neubert describes the main themes of Dewey's approach. In Chapter 3, Kersten Reich outlines some of the most important developments in contemporary constructivism and demonstrates their connections to Pragmatism.

Part II provides an elaboration of the essays in Part I by examining the theoretical implications of the connections between Deweyan Pragmatism and contemporary constructivism. In Chapter 4, Kenneth W. Stikkers discusses the problematic reception of Pragmatism in Europe, especially Germany, in the early twentieth century. His focus is Max Scheler's complex reaction to the works of Charles Sanders Peirce and William James as their versions of Pragmatism relate to Scheler's own sociology of knowledge. Stikkers discusses some of the reasons German scholars have been slow to engage Dewey's ideas, and he demonstrates some of the ways in which problems of translation still affect international studies in Pragmatism.

In Chapter 5, Jim Garrison introduces his own constructivist reading of Dewey's work by establishing a line of development between Dewey's pathbreaking 1896 essay on the reflex arc and the social constructivism explicit in his later works. Garrison demonstrates the relevance of classical Pragmatism to current issues in the philosophy of education, highlighting key theoretical and conceptual components of the cultural construction of meanings, truth claims, and identities.

Kersten Reich, in Chapter 6, explicates the distinction among observers, participants, and agents from the perspective of the Cologne program of interactive constructivism. He demonstrates numerous connections between constructivism and Dewey's Pragmatic theory of inquiry. Dewey, for example, had already distinguished spectators, agents, and participants, even though he did not articulate those distinctions in a systematic way. Reich thus builds upon Dewey's insights, suggesting ways in which a constructivist theory of observation can enrich contemporary Pragmatist arguments.

Larry A. Hickman reminds us in Chapter 7 of some main traits of classical Pragmatism and their potential as critical tools for contemporary discussions about Pragmatism and constructivism. He explores the vitality of Pragmatist thought and the usefulness of its basic tenets as resources for philosophic criticism. He is particularly interested in what he terms the problems of "cognitive relativism" in postmodern and neo-Pragmatist discourses (such as one finds in the work of Richard Rorty and others). From this standpoint he poses critical questions for the Cologne program of interactive constructivism. Hickman argues for a strong rearticulation of Dewey's instrumentalism and experimentalism and emphasizes its relevancy for our current situation.

In Chapter 8 Stefan Neubert discusses some of the central theoretical perspectives on culture and cultural practices implied in Pragmatism and interactive constructivism. He compares basic conceptual tools and interpretive approaches and shows that Dewey's work continues to provide fundamental resources in this field. In this connection, he provides a brief introduction to theories of discourse and power and discusses some implications for current controversies regarding multiculturalism. He argues that Dewey's Pragmatism and the Cologne program of interactive constructivism share a robust interest in culture and cultural diversity.

Chapter 9 in Part III presents a lively exchange among the contributors, in which they challenge one another and defend their own positions and perspectives. As they clarify their differences and seek common ground, they articulate concepts such as power, truth, relativism, inquiry, and democracy from Pragmatist and interactive constructivist vantage points, in ways designed to render the preceding essays even more accessible. In our view, this concluding discussion demonstrates both the enduring relevance of classical Pragmatism and the challenge of its reconstruction from the perspective of the Cologne program of interactive constructivism.

*Acknowledgments*

Special thanks are due to Davidson Films for permission to publish a revised version of the script for the video "John Dewey: His Life and Work." Special thanks also go to Dewey Center editors James Down-hour and Karen Mylan for their many contributions to the production of this volume.

# Abbreviations

T he *Collected Works of John Dewey* is referenced in this volume through the use of abbreviations. The following includes the complete bibliographical information for these works and the abbreviations with which they are referenced.

The standard, critical (print) edition of Dewey's works, *The Collected Works of John Dewey, 1882–1953*, was edited by Jo Ann Boydston and her staff at *Center for Dewey Studies*, Southern Illinois University Carbondale (USA) and published by Southern Illinois University Press. It consists of the following three sections:

*The Early Works* (EW 1–5): 1882–1898. Carbondale and Edwardsville: Southern Illinois University Press.

*The Middle Works* (MW 1–15): 1899–1924. Carbondale and Edwardsville: Southern Illinois University Press.

*The Later Works* (LW 1–17): 1925–1953. Carbondale and Edwardsville: Southern Illinois University Press.

This edition contains the following volumes (dates of publication refer to the paperback edition):

EW 1 (1882–1888): Includes essays and *Leibniz's New Essays Concerning Human Understanding*. Introduction by L. E. Hahn, 1975.

EW 2 (1887): *Psychology*. Introduction by H. W. Schneider, 1975.

EW 3 (1889–1892): Includes essays, reviews, and *Outlines of a Critical Theory of Ethics*. Introduction by S. M. Eames, 1975.

EW 4 (1893–1894): Includes essays, reviews, and *The Study of Ethics: A Syllabus*. Introduction by W. A. R. Leys, 1975.

EW 5 (1895–1898): Includes essays, reviews, and miscellany. Introduction by W. R. McKenzie, 1975.

MW 1 (1899–1901): Includes essays, reviews, miscellany and *The School and Society*. Introduction by J. R. Burnett, 1983.

MW 2 (1902–1903): Includes essays, reviews, miscellany, *The Child and the Curriculum*, and *Studies in Logical Theory*. Introduction by S. Hook, 1983.

MW 3 (1903–1906): Includes essays, reviews, and miscellany. Introduction by D. Rucker, 1983.

MW 4 (1907–1909): Includes essays, reviews, and *Moral Principles in Education*. Introduction by L. E. Hahn, 1983.

MW 5 (1908): *Ethics*. Introduction by C. L. Stevenson, 1978.

MW 6 (1910–1911): Includes essays, reviews, miscellany, and *How We Think*. Introduction by H. S. Thayer and V. T. Thayer, 1985.

MW 7 (1912–1914): Includes essays, reviews, and miscellany. Introduction by R. Ross, 1985.

MW 8 (1915): Includes essays, reviews, miscellany, *German Philosophy and Politics*, and *Schools of To-Morrow*. Introduction by S. Hook, 1985.

MW 9 (1916): *Democracy and Education*. Introduction by S. Hook, 1985.

MW 10 (1916–1917): Includes essays, reviews, and miscellany. Introduction by L. E. Hahn, 1985.

MW 11 (1918–1919): Includes essays, reviews, and miscellany. Introduction by O. Handlin and L. Handlin, 1988.

MW 12 (1920): Includes essays, reviews, miscellany, and *Reconstruction in Philosophy*. Introduction by R. Ross, 1988.

MW 13 (1921–1922): Includes essays, reviews, and miscellany. Introduction by R. Ross, 1988.

MW 14 (1922): *Human Nature and Conduct*. Introduction by M. G. Murphey, 1988.

MW 15 (1923–1924): Includes essays, reviews, and miscellany. Introduction by C. Cohen, 1988.

LW 1 (1925): *Experience and Nature*. Introduction by S. Hook, 1988.

LW 2 (1925–1927): Includes essays, reviews, miscellany, and *The Public and Its Problems*. Introduction by J. Gouinlock, 1988.

LW 3 (1927–1928): Includes essays, reviews, miscellany, and "Impressions of Soviet Russia." Introduction by D. Sidorsky, 1988.

LW 4 (1929): Includes essays, reviews, miscellany, and *The Quest for Certainty*. Introduction by S. Toulmin, 1988.

LW 5 (1929–1930): Includes essays, reviews, miscellany, and *The Sources of a Science of Education, Individualism, Old and New,* and *Construction and Criticism*. Introduction by P. Kurtz, 1988.

LW 6 (1931–1932): Includes essays, reviews, miscellany, and reports. Introduction by S. Ratner, 1989.

LW 7 (1932): *Ethics* (Revised Edition). Introduction by A. Edel and E. Flower, 1989.

LW 8 (1933): Includes contributions to *Encyclopedia of the Socieal Sciences*, contributions to *The Educational Frontier*, and *How We Think* (Revised Edition). Introduction by R. Rorty, 1989.

LW 9 (1933–1934): Includes essays, reviews, miscellany, contributions to *People's Lobby Bulletin*, and *A Common Faith*. Introduction by M. R. Konvitz, 1989.

LW 10 (1934): *Art as Experience*. Introduction by A. Kaplan, 1989.

LW 11 (1935–1937): Includes essays, reviews, miscellany, *Liberalism and Social Action*, contributions to the *Leon Trotsky Inquiry*, and contributions to *Social Frontier*. Introduction by J. J. McDermott, 1991.

LW 12 (1938): *Logic: The Theory of Inquiry*. Introduction by E. Nagel, 1991.

LW 13 (1938–1939): Includes essays, reviews, miscellany, *Experience and Education*, *Freedom and Culture*, and *Theory of Valuation*. Introduction by S. M. Cahn, 1991.

LW 14 (1939–1941): Includes essays, reviews, and miscellany. Introduction by R. W. Sleeper, 1991.

LW 15 (1942–1948): Includes essays, reviews, and miscellany. Introduction by L. S. Feuer, 1991.

LW 16 (1949–1952): Includes essays, reviews, typescripts, and *Knowing and the Known*. Introduction by T. Z. Lavine, 1991.

LW 17 (1885–1953): Includes miscellaneous writings. Introduction by S. Hook, 1991.

*The Collected Works*, 1882–1953: *Index*.

In order to ensure uniform citation, the line breaks and pagination of the print edition have been preserved in *The Collected Works of John Dewey, 1882–1953: The Electronic Edition*, edited by Larry A. Hickman (Charlottesville, Va.: InteLex Corp., 1996).

# JOHN DEWEY BETWEEN PRAGMATISM AND CONSTRUCTIVISM

PART ONE

# DEWEY BETWEEN PRAGMATISM AND CONSTRUCTIVISM

# ONE

# JOHN DEWEY: HIS LIFE AND WORK
Larry A. Hickman

I n 1929 John Dewey declared in a newsreel clip:

> I am not here to knock going to college. If a young person has the opportunity to do so and has the character and intelligence to take advantage of it, it is a good thing. But going to college is not the same thing as getting an education, although the two are often confused. A boy or a girl can go to college and get a degree and not much more. On the other hand, a boy or a girl in a factory, shop or store can get an education without a degree, if they have the ambition. They have to work hard, want to learn, be observing (keep their ears and eyes open), talk to those wiser than themselves and set aside some time every day for reading. They have to struggle harder than those that go to college. But the struggle, if they make the effort, will give them power. They get their education from contact with the realities of life and not just from books.

With some minor editorial changes, this chapter is the script of the video "John Dewey: His Life and Work," written and narrated by Larry A. Hickman (Davidson

Dewey was already seventy when this newsreel footage, in which he distinguished education from mere schooling, was shot. It was rather a surprising position for a famous professor to take in the mass media of the day. After all, he was in his forty-fifth year of university teaching and had already written more than a dozen books. He would live another twenty-two years and publish eleven more books. What this little newsreel clip reveals is Dewey's remarkable ability to envision possibilities beyond his own experience, his faith in the intelligence of average citizens, and his openness to the use of new technologies.[1] These qualities were to be profoundly important in his scholarly writings and his involvement in human affairs.

During his long and productive life, Dewey wrote widely about psychology, philosophy, art, and social issues. To give you an introduction to this wealth of material, I will focus on three general topics that are recurring themes in his work. These do *not* cover all of the many subjects that Dewey discussed, but I hope they will inspire you to delve more deeply into his work. The themes I am pursuing are: (1) his concept of the purpose and process of human learning; (2) his understanding of truth as a process, instead of something absolute and unchanging; and (3) his faith in democracy as the only means of social organization that can foster individual fulfillment, and its implications for education and the arts.

Like all of us, Dewey was profoundly influenced by the historical and technical changes of his times. In the course of his ninety-two years he witnessed dramatic changes in almost every aspect of human life. When he was born, on October 20, 1859, Abraham Lincoln had not yet been elected president. The Civil War was only a storm cloud on the horizon. He died during the presidency of Dwight D. Eisenhower after two horrific world wars, one ended by an atomic bomb. At the time of Dewey's birth, most Americans were dependent on wind, water, and wood technologies. During that year, 1859, America drilled its first oil well, which led to technologies on which we all now

Films 2001). It can be ordered through Davidson Films Inc., 668 March Street, San Luis Obispo CA 93401. For further information see http://www.davidsonfilms.com.

depend. Also during 1859, Charles Darwin's culture-shattering work *The Origin of Species* was published. This book was to have a major influence on Dewey's thought.

John Dewey was born in Burlington, Vermont, the third of four sons of Archibald Sprague Dewey and Lucina Artemesia Rich Dewey. During the Civil War his father, a grocer by trade, served in the First Vermont Cavalry as a quartermaster. It is almost certain that the young John Dewey witnessed the devastation of that war when the family joined Archibald at his post in northern Virginia in 1864. In 1867, the family returned together to Burlington. The Burlington of Dewey's youth was a center of immigration and industrialization. The ethnic, class, and religious diversity young Dewey experienced there may have helped prepare him for the diverse cultures he would seek out during the rest of his life, both in urban America and abroad.

Dewey studied philosophy at the University of Vermont, graduating in 1879. He continued his study of philosophy during the next few years, even while he was employed as a high school teacher in the boom town of Oil City, Pennsylvania. In 1882, he entered the new doctoral program at Johns Hopkins University, where he studied logic, new experimental psychology, and neo-Hegelian philosophy. After completing his doctorate two years later, he accepted a teaching position at the University of Michigan in Ann Arbor.

During Dewey's decade in Michigan, his personal life changed dramatically. He met and fell in love with an intelligent, socially progressive student named Harriet Alice Chipman. The two were married in 1886 and would eventually have seven children. Alice Dewey's involvement in progressive causes such as securing the vote for women and defending the rights of ethnic minorities had a great influence on John Dewey's growing awareness of social injustice.

The course of Dewey's intellectual life also underwent major changes during his years in Ann Arbor. He began to reject most of the claims of traditional metaphysics and to develop a Pragmatic notion of truth. During this period Dewey was greatly influenced by William James's *Principles of Psychology*, published in 1890. James thought of habits as active forces in human life, and he treated belief as a kind of habit. In his view, beliefs, as well as other types of habits, are really rules for action. They are identifiable in terms of the results they produce. James's new "dynamic" psychology was exactly what Dewey had been looking for to advance his own theories about how we learn.

In 1894 the recently founded University of Chicago appointed Dewey as head of its department of philosophy, which included psychology and pedagogy, or what we now call education. Dewey would excel in all three disciplines. By 1905, at the age of forty-six, he had served as president of both the *American Psychological Association* and the *American Philosophical Association*, and he was one of America's best-known educators.

Dewey's association in Chicago with social reformer Jane Addams and his involvement with Hull House, where she administered community services, provided him with firsthand knowledge of the poverty and despair of the hundreds of thousands of immigrants who were attempting to make their living in Chicago during the 1890s.[2] Although the Deweys were only in Chicago for ten years, those were crucial years for their lives and work. Both Deweys were thoroughly involved in the education of their own children and close observers of their learning processes. These experiences, and John's experiments in psychology, led him in 1896 to found an elementary school that would serve as a laboratory for the university's new Department of Education.

### Analysis of Human Learning

Earlier I said that Darwin's *Origin of Species* had been a major influence on Dewey's thought. Dewey took one of Darwin's central concepts and applied it to the fields of psychology and philosophy. This was the idea that species are not fixed, but constantly undergoing change.[3] (We will return to this idea in a moment, when we discuss Dewey's notion of truth.) Dewey combined this idea of the tendency of organisms to adapt with the observation that the existence of living organisms is rhythmic, alternating between phases of imbalance and equilibrium. In 1896 Dewey worked out some of the consequences of these ideas in an article entitled "The Reflex Arc Concept in Psychology" (EW 5:96–109). This watershed essay was to have a major impact on the fields of philosophy, psychology, and education, and even now, more than one hundred years later, it is still the subject of extensive interest and discussion.

The basic idea of the reflex arc went back at least as far as René Descartes in the seventeenth century. Descartes had developed a mechanical model, according to which an external impulse, say from a burned foot, activates a kind of cord or cable attached to the brain. The brain then activates another cable attached to the foot, thus completing the reflex arc. In his *Principles of Psychology*, published in 1890, William James sought to improve this traditional reflex arc model, which he thought was too mechanical. First, James replaced Descartes' image of a man next to a fire with the more modern image of a child reaching for a candle. According to the old mechanical model that James was seeking to improve, a child sees a candle: that is the stimulus. She reaches for the flame: that is the response. The flame burns the child's finger: that's another stimulus. And the child withdraws her hand: that's another response. In both sequences of the child's behavior, the seeing / reaching and the feeling-the-burn / withdrawing-the-hand, there was said to be an arc from the *external* stimulation of the sense organs to a response set up by the *internal* working of the child's brain.

James attempted to improve this model by emphasizing the associations produced in the child's mind and the new habit they produced. In this case, the new habit was the child's withdrawing her hand in the presence of a flame. James replaced the mechanical stimulus-response model of Descartes with an organic model, according to which new associations are formed. These associations were said to be in the mind.

But Dewey was still not convinced. He thought the reflex arc model was fatally flawed because it amounted, as he put it, to "a series of jerks" (EW 5:99) that were unable to account for the rich coordination of situations and processes that make up even the simplest of human learning experiences. His own analysis of this learning experience begins, not with a stimulus that is *external* to the organism, but with a stimulus that is a coordinated act involving the sensory and motor actions of the child and the context in which the situation occurs. The context includes such things as the child's past experiences, the environment in which the event takes place, and her level of engagement, or how involved she is in the experience. *All* of these factors shape the episode and the learning that takes place, or doesn't, as a result of it.

For Dewey, as it would be later for Jean Piaget, learning is not a series of truncated arcs, but a circuit of imbalance and restored equilibrium. The learner is not an inactive recipient of experience but an active player within it, bringing with her a set of behaviors and expectations from past events. Dewey's analysis, as he later elaborated in his five-step analysis of effective learning, would go like this:

1. Emotional response: A child in a state of equilibrium, say playing with a familiar toy, comes upon something unexpected. Her equilibrium is disturbed. The situation is now unstable and this instability triggers an emotional response.

2. Definition of problem: The child attempts to make the situation more stable by applying lessons learned from past experiences—the new situation calls for exploration, just as previous ones have. This phase of learning involves an intellectual response.

3. Formation of hypothesis: Now that the problem has been defined as something that requires exploration, the child uses a familiar method—she reaches for the candle.

4. Testing / experimenting: Her reach for the candle is a test of the proposed solution. In the past, she has grasped objects in order to become better acquainted with them. But now, her attempt to apply this familiar solution results in a burned finger.

5. Application: If the burn sensation is sufficient to prevent further exploration, the child has completed the circuit of learning. She now knows about the effect of flame on fingers, and has thus added a new

circle of adjustment to her understanding of the world. The problematic situation has been resolved. As an organism, she is once again in a state of equilibrium.

If the burn is *not* sufficient to prevent further exploration, the experiment starts all over again until the lesson is learned and equilibrium is restored.

Dewey's analysis of the classic situation of the candle and child illuminates several points critical to an understanding of his work: Dewey insists that learning always begins in the middle of things. The learner is not a blank slate upon which ideas are to be written. Nor is her mind a file cabinet, into which facts are to be filed away. Each learner is a living *organism* with her own history, needs, desires, and, perhaps most importantly, her own interests. As we saw in the newsreel clip, Dewey thought that learning takes place outside, as well as inside, the school room.

It is in the context of the University of Chicago Elementary School that Dewey's ideas about learning received their most rigorous tests. This school, also known as the "Laboratory School," was opened in 1896, the same year that Dewey published his "Reflex Arc" article. From 1901 until 1904, Alice would serve as its principal. The Laboratory School was a laboratory in fact as well as in name. Dewey never intended it to be a model that other schools should follow, nor would he feel that there ever would be a school that would be the perfect model. In his view, education always reflects the circumstances of the times and students involved and should evolve as these elements change.

Dewey's educational ideas were, in part, a rejection of the rote, curriculum-driven approach to learning that was the standard methodology of his day. But he also rejected the opposite concept, the exaggerated "child-centered" approach that uncritically follows the impulses and uninformed interests of the child. Unfortunately, Dewey's term "progressive education" has too frequently been used as a disparaging phrase to describe such educational practices—practices that involve what Dewey rejected as "plan-less improvisation."

In Dewey's view, the challenge of education should be to integrate the educational subject matter with the talents and interests of the learner. As we will see, Dewey often overcame either / or dichotomies by looking beyond the conflicts they represented. At the Lab School, children learned traditional academic subjects such as arithmetic, reading, and science, but they were also taught skills such as weaving, carpentry, cooking, and gardening. These practical skills were presented as examples of problem-solving. But they were also taught as embodiments of more abstract forms of knowledge, and as providing important tools for further discoveries.

If education is adjustment within an environment, as Dewey thought,[4] then it is the *whole* person that adjusts, and not just the function or aspect of the organism we call the intellect. Deborah Meier, principal of the Mission Hill School in Boston, who has been a force for widening the scope of traditional education, comments on the relevance of Dewey's ideas for educational practice:

> Once we recognize that academia is but one form of intellectual life, we can begin to imagine other possibilities. Other possibilities don't mean that all traditional disciplines are unimportant to us; quite the opposite, they force us to ask how such disciplines are relevant to our inquiries. What determines what we study, the driving criteria, should be the demands of a democratic citizenry, not the requirements of academia.
>
> Our school, Mission Hill, a public school in Boston, serves 164 students between the ages of five and fourteen. Dewey's five-step analysis of the process of inquiry applies to how our students go about their learning.
>
> 1. Emotional response: For instance, a sixth–seventh grade class is studying support and structure as a part of physical science. The entire school has been studying ancient Greece and these children were intrigued that slim pillars held up enormous loads. This curiosity about the nature of material strength and function led to further explorations.
>
> 2. Definition of problem: Their teacher challenged them to build a structure eleven inches high that would hold a heavy load

using only 100 index cards. The children had to realize the task involved modifying their materials. An important task of education, I feel, is to expand the ways one can look at a situation. What are the elements of a problem that are important and which are extraneous?

3. Formation of hypothesis: They then applied their previous knowledge of the strength of columns and formulated plans to build their structures. Their ability to make a useful hypothesis evolved from their knowledge base and experience of how columns work.

4. Testing / experimenting: These students then subjected their hypothesis to testing, in this case with quite dramatic results. In other situations, the testing involves collecting data or with imaginary "dramatic rehearsals," to use Dewey's terminology for "what if" thinking.

5. Application: The final application of knowledge sometimes comes immediately, in other situations later. Our students aren't all going to become structural engineers, but we feel this kind of problem solving prepares them for reasoned inquiry in other situations and preparation for the more theoretical physics they will encounter a few years later in high school. Learning to apply the methodology of reasoned inquiry to scientific, social and artistic situations has been the great legacy of civilization and one that is basic to a democracy.

Of course Dewey's five-step description of how we go about solving problems and learning is not meant to be a kind of cookie cutter, stamping out uniform experiences. Each episode of learning is unique. As Deborah Meier reminded us, every sequence of learning begins and ends with an emotional response. The very first step in inquiry is felt need, and the very last step is a feeling of satisfaction or completion. Between these steps we do intellectual work such as defining problems and forming and testing hypotheses. Taken as a whole, this organic rhythm of doubt, followed by struggle and then recovery of equilibrium, is precisely what Dewey offered more than a century ago as an alternative to the reflex model of learning. Despite

Dewey's enormous influence, however, some well-known educational theorists still accept the basic premise of the reflex arc model. These people think of learning as a mechanical process, measurable by standardized tests, that has very little to do with the emotional life of the learner.

## The Nature of Truth

This brings us to Dewey's view of the nature of truth. Some philosophers, whom we might call absolutists, have argued that there are statements forever absolute and unchanging. Moral laws, such as the Ten Commandments; physical laws, such as the speed of light; and mathematical equations, such as "10 divided by 3 = $3^{1}/_{3}$ . . ." are often cited as examples of such certainties. Other philosophers, often termed relativists, have argued that there is no such thing as objective truth. Whatever works for a particular culture or individual is true for that culture or individual. If it feels good, do it.

Typically, Dewey found something of value in both of these extreme views, even though he rejected their central claims. Drawing on his analysis of reflex arc, he argued that truth is neither absolute nor arbitrary. A belief is true when it is the product of objective experimental inquiry. But inquiry may lead to different truths in different situations. Dewey's reflex arc research led him to the conclusion that truth depends on factors such as interest, habit, and context. If the child had not been interested in the bright light, or if she had not had the habit of touching things in order to learn about them, she would never have discarded the old truth in favor of the new one. There would have been no learning.

Dewey argued that moral laws, physical laws, and even mathematical laws are true only as *regulative principles*. Regulative principles are principles that shape our behavior, all things being equal. They are general rules of action that have been so thoroughly refined over time that it is highly unlikely they need to be revised. In general, for example, touching objects is usually a good way to find out about them. When we attempt to apply such principles, however, we often find that the actual conditions create exceptions.

Moral truths, for example, such as the regulative principle "Do not kill," are subject to exceptions such as the defense of one's person, family, or country. Physical truths, such as "the speed of light is 186,000 miles per second," may also have exceptions. In 1999, for example, a Harvard physicist slowed the speed of light to 17 meters per second (Hau 1999; Browne 1999) in her laboratory. Several months later, she was able to stop it altogether! Along with the rest of us, Dewey would probably have been surprised at this particular result. Even so, he had already provided a place for it in his theory of truth. The same can be said of mathematical truths. Take the well-known equation that says "10 divided by 3 equals $3\frac{1}{3}$. . . ." Dewey argued that this equation is only a guide, and not an absolute truth. Its application is subject to the pressure of real events. For example, you cannot divide ten children into three equal groups. The best you can do is to get two groups with three and one with four, not three groups with $3\frac{1}{3}$ each.

Sometimes, even well-established regulative principles undergo dramatic change. Before Galileo, for example, most astronomers thought the earth was the center of the universe. Now, of course, it is a truth, or to use Dewey's term, a regulative principle, of astronomy that the earth revolves around the Sun. Will that truth ever change? Probably not. But Dewey argued that if our knowledge is to grow, we must always be open to new experiences. Up until 1999, for example, it seemed inconceivable that the speed of light could ever be modified.

As for the relativists who think that truth is just arbitrary or accidental, Dewey realized that they are correct in the sense that cultural practices *are* different in different parts of the world, and that each of us has our own unique perspective. But he also argued that carefully designed experiments, whether they be in the arts, sciences, or humanities, can produce objective truths. Even though such truths may change over time, they are validated at the time that the experiments are completed, and we may proceed with confidence until faced with new and conflicting data.

Dewey's Pragmatic theory of truth, therefore, rejected the common idea that truth is the correspondence between a statement or idea and some fact or state of affairs in "reality." In his view, truth is neither discovered, as the absolutists claimed, nor invented, as the relativists claimed. It is instead *constructed* as a byproduct of the process of solving problems. This conception of truth is basic to the philosophical tradition called Pragmatism with which Dewey is often identified.

The central idea of Pragmatism is that the meaning or truth of an idea lies in its possible consequences. Dewey thought that truth is like the fit between a key and a lock. There is no absolute key that fits all locks, and not just any arbitrary key will do if you want to open a particular lock. If we want to make a key to fit the lock, there are objective conditions that must be taken into consideration. Dewey thought that his Pragmatic model of truth was applicable, not only to the construction of better outcomes in the natural sciences, but also to experimentation in every area of human life, including social and political institutions.

### Faith in Democracy

By 1905, Dewey had left Chicago to accept a position at Columbia University in New York City. His appointments were in the department of philosophy and at Teachers College. He would remain at Columbia until his retirement at age eighty in 1939. During his extensive travels during the 1920s and '30s, Dewey turned his attention more and more to understanding the relationship between the ideals of democracy and cultural diversity. He visited Mexico, China, Japan, Turkey, and the Soviet Union, in addition to many countries in Western Europe. Wherever he went, he was keen to discover whether local institutions, such as schools, promoted democratic forms of association and the growth of individuals.

This was a time of great political upheaval, most acutely represented by the rise of Fascism in Italy and Germany and Communism in the Soviet Union. Unlike some of his academic colleagues, Dewey was drawn to neither ideology. He continued to affirm his faith in democratic ideals, even as he criticized the failure of the American political system to fully realize these goals. One person who knew Dewey at this time is Louise Rosenblatt, who was to become an important voice for the teaching of literature:

> Of course those were the days in the '30s when fascist ways of thinking were becoming very apparent both abroad and at home, so that the need to protect and develop democracy became increasingly important. And it certainly motivated Dewey and the rest of us who were concerned with education as a force for democracy. . . . Dewey's writings are a constant meditation in one way or another on the idea of democracy as a way of life, and not just a set of ideas. . . . It's that ability to think about the consequences of, to imagine the consequences of your actions, your decisions and to place yourself in the place of others who would be affected by it that a person who is a member of a democracy must possess. The power of imagination, that ability to resist self-interest, and the ability to resist the either/or point of view, those were ideas that were very much Dewey's and certainly ones that I tried in my humble way to apply in the field of the teaching of reading.

Dewey had been thinking about these matters for most of his public life. Earlier, in his 1916 book *Democracy and Education* (MW 9), he had written that there were two requirements for democracy. One requirement is that social control could not be imposed from above, by kings or despots or even an enlightened elite. It is instead a recognition of mutual interests by all the people involved. Another requirement is that people and the systems they create to live together must be flexible and open to readjustments as circumstances change. In Dewey's view, democracy is not based on a particular political system but on the continuing commitment of each individual to work to make his or her own life, as well as the lives of his or her fellow citizens, as full and rewarding as possible. In 1939, with Europe as already engaged in war and the forces of Fascism advancing, Dewey, now eighty years old, wrote: "The democratic faith in human equality is belief that every human being, independent of the quantity or range of his personal endowment, has a right to equal opportunity with every other person for development of whatever gifts he has" (LW 14:226f).

For Dewey, the development of an individual's gifts is a life-long process. At its best, it involves an application of the pattern of inquiry that we have discussed, an appreciation of the flexible and corrigible nature of truth as Dewey characterized it, and the support of democratic social and political institutions. The aim of education for Dewey is to enable individuals to continue growing throughout their entire lives. Schools must prepare people for more than simply making a living. They must create the desire for richer, more meaningful experiences. They must provide the tools by means of which the viewpoints of others can be understood and conflicts resolved.

Dewey thought that promotion of the arts played an essential role in the attainment of these goals. He had long rejected the idea that cognitive or intellectual knowing was the only way of experiencing. He had always emphasized the emotional and aesthetic components of successful inquiry. As much as he valued spoken and written language, he also highly valued the arts. He thought that music, dance, painting, design, and drama were important ways of exploring and communicating the richness of human experiences.

Fairly late in life, at the age of seventy-five, he addressed these issues in his book *Art as Experience* (LW 10). It combined two of his major themes. The first was his democratic vision of a society in which all people could develop their talents and be enriched by the talents of others. The second was the importance of the aesthetic dimension of human life. We all live in a sea of experiences, but not all of them are of equal value. Some of them excite more interest than others. Like the child and the candle, we sometimes follow through; we sometimes interact with portions of our environment in ways that make our experiences more meaningful. When this happens, Dewey says, we have "*an* experience." One of the ways that we remain open to new experiences is by making and enjoying works of art. Art helps us learn to focus our senses, to hone our sensory powers. It also provides an important means of communication among the many diverse individuals and groups that make up our global village.

Dewey thought that even where there is no common language, music and the visual arts can help us communicate across cultures. Music and the other arts are "universal languages." He wrote: "the work of art operates to deepen and to raise to great clarity that sense of an enveloping undefined whole that accompanies every normal experience. This whole is then felt as an expansion of ourselves. . . . [W]e are citizens of this vast world beyond ourselves, and any intense realization of its presence with and in us brings a peculiarly satisfying sense of unity in itself and with ourselves" (LW 10:199).

During his long life, Dewey continued to insist that even in the face of the most difficult of circumstances there are still opportunities for enhanced meaning and growth. Despite the cruel losses of two beloved children, harsh criticism of his work, the death of his wife, Alice, in 1927, and dismay at the horrors of the Great Depression and two World Wars, he continued to face the future with great hope. He continued to be active as a philosopher and social critic even after his ninetieth birthday. In 1946, almost two decades after the death of Alice, Dewey married Roberta Lowitz Grant. He was then eighty-seven; she was forty-two. Shortly thereafter, the couple adopted two young children in whom he delighted. Dewey died at his apartment in New York City on June 1, 1952.

Although Dewey's influence waned during the decades that followed his death, his ideas have enjoyed a remarkable resurgence of interest since the mid-1980s. Today, his work is held in high regard by philosophers, historians, political scientists, sociologists, educators, and others. Even though his theory of learning and his promotion of the method of intelligence are still resisted in some quarters, they continue to enrich educational systems around the world. His Pragmatic theory of truth as a process of discovery honors the experimental and creative aspects of human experience. And his conception of democracy as "a belief in the ability of human experience to generate the aims and methods by which further experience shall grow in ordered richness" (LW 4:229) seems as fresh and compelling today as when it was first articulated more than a half century ago. As more and more countries attempt democratic forms of government, Dewey's vision of democratic forms of life, and his awareness of the capacities of all humans to think, feel, and create are becoming increasingly important.

In 1949, on the occasion of his ninetieth birthday, Dewey was hailed by the *New York Times* as "America's Philosopher." Their tribute is as appropriate now as it was then.

# TWO

# PRAGMATISM: DIVERSITY OF SUBJECTS IN DEWEY'S PHILOSOPHY AND THE PRESENT DEWEY SCHOLARSHIP

Stefan Neubert

## Diversity of Subjects in Dewey's Works

In addition to the information already given by Larry A. Hickman in Chapter 1, I wish to examine some central philosophical topics from the impressive richness of Dewey's works and the comprehensive body of his writings, which fill thirty-seven volumes in the critical edition of the *Collected Works*. I will confine my comments to a brief discussion of each topic, highlighting its importance as an element within Dewey's overall philosophical approach. It is obvious that any such attempt necessarily involves a simplification of more complex affairs that can be only touched on here. The reader will be provided with references to some of Dewey's most important writings on each topic as a starting point for more extensive studies.

### "Experience" as a Philosophical Core Concept

Dewey's philosophical core concept, "experience," finds its most comprehensive and detailed discussion in the two later works

*Experience and Nature* (LW 1) and *Art as Experience* (LW 10).[1] In *Experience and Nature*, which some have labeled Dewey's metaphysics, he elaborates on the close relationship between his idea of experience and his understanding of nature, a connection that is indicated not only by the title of the work, but also by Dewey's characterization of his own philosophical position and method as "empirical naturalism" or "naturalistic empiricism" at the very outset of the first chapter (LW 1:10).

It would be misleading, though, if the two characterizations of Dewey's position, naturalism and empiricism, were to be reduced to the conventional understanding of these terms in the tradition of Western philosophy. Dewey reconstructed both concepts and used them in a fundamentally new and extended way. So, "naturalism," for Dewey, does not refer to an understanding of nature as something essentially given, a fixed order of things, beings, or species. Following Darwin, Dewey's philosophical understanding of nature implies an open, dynamic, and contingent process in which identities and relationships emerge as the actualization of natural potentialities in the context of evolutionary interactions. Like all other natural affairs, human experience, too, emerges from natural interactions. This is why, for Dewey, "nature and experience are not enemies or alien"—as is so often suggested in the philosophical tradition. "There is in the character of human experience . . . a growing progressive self-disclosure of nature itself" (LW 1:5).

At the same time, Dewey's *empiricism* builds on a concept of experience that shows remarkable differences as compared to the classical understanding of that term, e.g., in John Locke and the tradition of British empiricism. Experience, for Dewey, is not restricted to the subjective experiencing of an objectively given reality principally independent from the process of experiencing itself and the one who has the experience. Nor is it, in the first place, a passive event, e.g., of receiving sense impressions. Rather, experience is characterized for Dewey by the two criteria of continuity and interaction (see LW 13:17ff.). The basic unit in his concept of experience is the act, "and the act in its full development as a connection between doing and undergoing" (LW 11:214) wherein meanings are actively constructed.

According to Dewey, experience is always embedded in cultural practices. He further distinguishes between "primary" and "secondary experience" (see LW 1:10ff.). "Primary experience" refers to the immediate qualitative unity of experiencing and experienced that constitutes an empirical whole—a total situation—*before* we begin to discriminate elements. Experience "recognizes in its primary integrity no division between act and material, subject and object, but contains them both in an unanalyzed totality" (LW 1:18). This totality, however, is partially broken up whenever we find ourselves in a so-called "problematic situation" where our so-far established habits of action and interpretation fail. We begin to reflect on the possible future consequences of actions within an ambiguous, contingent, and "open" situation and construct new meanings of behaviors, objects, and experiences. This is what Dewey calls "secondary experience": it designates the level of reflection, knowledge, and theory, from simple everyday solutions of problematic situations or conflicts to scientific and philosophical inquiries. However refined and sophisticated these secondary products of reflection may be, Dewey takes pains to remind us that they never completely cover the abundance and richness of meanings implicit in primary experience in all its heterogeneity, coarseness, and crudity. As to the relationship between the two levels, Dewey particularly stresses two things (see LW 1:39):

1. "Secondary experience" constitutes a process of construction that always answers a concrete problematic (or tensional) constellation in "primary experience" through selection based on interest; reflection and knowledge are therefore always context-related processes that can only be sufficiently understood within the cultural contexts of human experience.[2]

2. The secondary products of reflection must always be seen as hypothetical constructions to be tested in the realm of primary experience; they have to prove themselves in application; reflection and knowledge are therefore always of an ultimately experimental nature, be it in life-worldly everyday affairs, in science, or in philosophy.

Dewey's comprehensive criticisms of epistemology and his tackling of different models and traditions of Western philosophy draw heavily on these two ideas.[3] In *Experience and Nature* he articulates these criticisms from the perspective of a "naturalistic metaphysics" (LW 1:62) that deals with the "generic traits manifested by existences of all kinds" (LW 1:308). Metaphysics, in this sense, constitutes a kind of philosophical meta-criticism that provides "a ground-map of the province of criticism, establishing base lines to be employed in more intricate triangulations" (LW 1:309). In the view of Dewey's naturalistic approach, such "generic traits of existence" are characters to be found in every comprehensive experience and every universe of discourse—traits like "[q]ualitative individuality and constant relations, contingency and need, movement and arrest" (LW 1:308) as well as, generally speaking, the relative precariousness and the relative stability of values. According to Dewey, though, even these basic metaphysical assumptions must be understood as philosophical hypotheses that time and again have to be applied and related to new experiences, and thereby only gain meaning in the concrete life of human beings. "Barely to note and register that contingency is a trait of natural events has nothing to do with wisdom. To note, however, contingency in connection with a concrete situation of life is that fear of the Lord which is at least the beginning of wisdom" (LW 1:309). Even Dewey's metaphysics, therefore, is no "philosophy of the last word" but claims to be an integrated part of his comprehensive philosophical experimentalism.[4]

It should further be noted that in Chapter 5 of *Experience and Nature*—beginning with the gushing and succinct remark: "Of all affairs, communication is the most wonderful" (LW 1:132)—the reader will find Dewey's probably most pithy account of his theory of communication, which is so important for his philosophy, and especially for his later works. Dewey had already elaborated on that theme in Chapter 1 of *Democracy and Education* (MW 9) and thus had given a premonition of the central place the concept of communication was to acquire in his mature thought. In *Experience and Nature* he takes up these earlier considerations and discusses them on an immensely broadened scale by comprehensively working out the fundamentally communicative structure of human experience and analyzing that structure in its Pragmatic dimensions. Besides the instrumental phase of communicating meanings for the coordination of social interactions, he particularly exposes the qualitatively consummatory dimension of partaking in the construction of shared meanings. Communication, for Dewey, is at the same time means and end. Not only does it serve as a means for transferring ideas or information, but above all it is itself a process of "world-making," to use Nelson Goodman's phrase—the construction of a universe of shared meanings that brings about an enhancement of the immediate quality of experience for those who participate in it. For Dewey, every genuine communication releases creative as well as educative potentialities of human experience.

The following quote from the end of Chapter 1 of *Experience and Nature* may in many respects be read as a key motive, not only of this book, but of Dewey's Pragmatic philosophy altogether: "If what is written in these pages has no other result than creating and promoting a respect for concrete human experience and its potentialities, I shall be content" (LW 1:41).

Theory of Art

Dewey further developed his concept of experience especially in his book on art and aesthetics, *Art as Experience* (LW 10). It is primarily in the first three chapters of this book that one finds his most comprehensive account of the qualitative and aesthetic dimension of experience.[5] Dewey thinks that this dimension particularly manifests itself in the work of art, provided that "work of art" means more than just the expressive object—namely, the interaction of that object in the experience of either the artist or the recipient. The perception of a work of art involves creative and poietic potentials. Furthermore, *Art as Experience* can be seen as a further important contribution to Dewey's philosophic theory of communication, since he regards art as the most universal form of communication. He stresses political

implications as to the relation of art and democracy in a modern industrialized society and points out art's critical potentialities for the
advancement of democratic ways of life; for "[a]rt breaks through
barriers that divide human beings, which are impermeable in ordinary association" (LW 10:249).

Logic and Theory of Knowledge

Like Dewey's philosophical notion of experience, his logic and theory
of knowledge have been developed in several steps and over a number
of decades. I will mention only the most important works here. In
1903, a group of authors from the University of Chicago department
of philosophy published *Studies in Logical Theory*, under the lead of
Dewey, inaugurating what would eventually be known as the Chicago
School of functionalism and instrumentalism. Basic to their approach
was the view that the test of validity of an idea lies in its "functional
or instrumental use in effecting the transition from a relatively conflicting experience to a relatively integrated one" (MW 2:xvii). This
involves a very fundamental rejection of the correspondence theory
of truth and knowledge in all its traditional forms. "The truth of an
idea or theory," writes Dewey's student and colleague Sidney Hook
in his introduction about the position maintained in the *Studies*, "depends not on its agreement with an antecedently existing reality but
on the 'adequacy of [its] performance' in bringing into existence a
new state of affairs in which the situation that provoked thought is
reconstituted" (ibid.). Dewey further elaborated on this and other
ideas about truth and knowledge in a series of essays that were collectively published as *Essays in Experimental Logic* in 1916.[6] The book
*How We Think*, published in 1910 and again in a revised edition in
1933 (MW 6:177–356; LW 8:105–352), concisely summarizes his approach and focuses on implications for educational theory. In 1949,
in his ninetieth year, Dewey published the book *Knowing and the
Known* (LW 16:1–279), an extensive study coauthored with Arthur F.
Bentley, which was to become his last major work.

  Dewey's most comprehensive and thoroughgoing discussion of
logic and knowledge, though, is his book *Logic: The Theory of Inquiry*,

published in 1938 (LW 12). Today the book can be seen as the standard work on this part of his philosophy. As indicated by the subtitle, Dewey conceives his logic as a theory of inquiry. In Chapter 1 of the present volume, Larry Hickman has mentioned Dewey's five-step analysis of successful learning through inquiry. This model forms the background of the often-quoted definition of the term "inquiry" given in Dewey's *Logic*: "Inquiry is the controlled or directed transformation of an indeterminate situation into one that is so determinate in its constituent distinctions and relations as to convert the elements of the original situation into a unified whole" (LW 12:108; orig. in italics).

After what was said about Dewey's concept of "experience" it will not astonish the reader that this process, for Dewey, takes place on a twofold "existential matrix," namely, on a biological and cultural basis. Again, he thus emphasizes the continuity of experience and nature as well as the cultural contexts of knowledge. A result of the process of inquiry is the construction of true statements. In his *Logic*, Dewey further explores his Pragmatic notion of truth by introducing the term "warranted assertibility." Truth claims are seen as part of the temporal sequences of inquiry. They involve a *process* of construction that looks backward as well as forward.[7] On the one hand, the word "warranted" points to the past in that it relies on achievements of inquiry and proof already established. On the other hand, the word "assertibility" points to future inquiries and applications made possible by these achievements. These new inquiries might on principle warrant new assertions and thus lead to a revision of truth claims thus far established. This experimentalist notion of truth implies, among other things, a decided rejection of all transcendental claims to truth.

## Anthropology and Social Psychology

Dewey's anthropology and his conception of human nature are comprehensively and penetratingly explained in his 1922 book *Human Nature and Conduct* (MW 14). The book carries the subtitle "An Introduction to Social Psychology" and indeed represents an important result of Dewey's extensive psychological and social psychological works, which were in part influenced by the ideas of William James and George Herbert Mead. Among Dewey's other important writings in this field are, e.g., his 1887 book *Psychology* (EW 2), the pathbreaking 1896 essay already mentioned by Larry Hickman, "The Reflex Arc Concept in Psychology" (EW 5:96–109), and from the later works the 1930 essay "Conduct and Experience" (LW 5:218–35), to mention but a few. Dewey's approach to social psychology as laid down in *Human Nature and Conduct* builds on three crucial concepts, "habit," "impulse," and "intelligence." One central thesis of the book suggests that native impulses in man, although first in time, play a secondary role in human conduct compared to habits acquired and formed in the interactions with a cultural milieu. "In conduct the acquired is the primitive" (MW 14:65). Habits emerge from the interactions with significant others in the context of the customs and institutions of a sociocultural environment. They are of primary importance for human conduct because only through them do the otherwise aimless and ineffective impulsive activities of the human baby acquire social *meanings* and thereby gain structure and efficiency. Habits, then, are culturally informed ways of conduct. However, the use of the term "habit" should not be restricted to relatively passive habituations or routines, which, of course, play a certain role in human conduct. But even more important, for Dewey, are active habits that constitute dynamic forces of conduct that render a person capable of acting in the face of new and unexpected situations (see also MW 9:51ff.). He thinks that the demand to keep habits flexible and to extend and partially transform them time and again in a process of lifelong learning constitutes a crucial political and educational challenge of living in an industrialized society characterized by increasing dynamics and mobility. For him, this is a question of the social and cooperative intelligence of men and women to achieve constructive solutions of societal problems. These thoughts are taken up again in many of Dewey's political writings in his later works, where they are further extended and specified especially with regard to democratic communication.

## Ethics and Moral Philosophy

The most comprehensive presentation of Dewey's Pragmatist ethics and theory of morality is given in the 1908 textbook *Ethics* (MW 5), coauthored with James Hayden Tufts. The book was published again in a thoroughly revised edition in 1932 (LW 7). Between these two editions lie a number of important books, like *Democracy and Education* (MW 9), *Reconstruction in Philosophy* (MW 12:77–201), and *Human Nature and Conduct* (MW 14), in which Dewey, step by step, elaborates and develops his ethical positions.[8] Characteristic of Dewey's approach to ethics is his effort to find a middle position between absolutist-transcendentalist and relativist-subjectivist approaches. He rejects the attempt to establish a priori and universal norms and principles that precede concrete experience or are imposed, as it were, from outside. But he equally rejects positions that regard ethical norms as purely arbitrary determinations that eventually lack any normative force. For Dewey, moral reflection, like any reflection, begins in the context of primary experience, i.e., in the context of a specific, unique, and at first unanalyzed situation in which a moral problem appears and enforces a decision, e.g., between two mutually incompatible claims. This situational context must always be taken into account lest we neglect the vitality and diversity of moral life. However, we do not have to confront every moral situation completely unprepared and unequipped. From the abundance of concretely experienced moral problems there emerge moral principles and norms in a process that transcends generations. These principles and norms give us orientation. They play a *functional* role with regard to morality as a lived cultural practice. They are generalized moral ideas that draw their normative force not from themselves, but from their successful application in experience. They time and again have to prove themselves in new situations, where we always have to reckon with exceptions from the rule. This calls for a certain degree of moral flexibility as to the application, readjustment, and modification of inherited principles, "because life is a moving affair in which old moral truth ceases to apply" (MW 14:164).

In a word, moral philosophy, for Dewey, is a function of the moral life. If it strives to do justice to the diversity and changeability of human experience it must not regard morality as mere application of universal and eternal truths, but rather as a social and experimental practice that develops its own standards from within. Contrary to many other approaches, Dewey's ethical theory particularly stresses the affective, imaginative, and creative dimensions of lived human relationships.[9] It also draws attention to the genuine ambiguity and ambivalence of concrete moral situations, in which it is often impossible to attain a complete dissolution of conflicting claims. There will not always be one perfect solution to each moral situation:

> A moral philosophy which should frankly recognize the impossibility of reducing all the elements in moral situations to a single commensurable principle, which should recognize that each human being has to make the best adjustment he can among forces which are genuinely disparate, would throw light upon actual predicaments of conduct and help individuals in making a juster estimate of the force of each competing factor. All that would be lost would be the idea that theoretically there is in advance a single theoretically correct solution for every difficulty with which each and every individual is confronted. Personally I think the surrender of this idea would be a gain instead of a loss. In taking attention away from rigid rules and standards it would lead men to attend more fully to the concrete elements entering into the situations in which they have to act (LW 5:288).[10]

## Social Philosophy and Political Theory

At the heart of Dewey's social philosophy is his notion of democracy. He gives a systematic and comprehensive account of that notion in *Democracy and Education* (MW 9), and further develops it and broadens his perspective in successive political writings until the very end of his life. Dewey's democratic vision is characterized, among other things, by two central aspects. First, it implies the idea of a *participatory democracy*, which means that democracy is not just a form of government or a set of institutions, but denotes a way of life that relies on as comprehensive a participation as possible of all in the goods, values, and interests of society, on the same conditions and in all the areas of associated living.[11] Second, it involves the idea of a *pluralistic democracy*, which means that a diversity of different groups, communities, cultures, and societies does not represent a threat or a loss, but rather a gain for democracy, provided that the institutional prerequisites for as free and comprehensive an exchange as possible between the different forms of associated living are secured (see MW 9:87–106). In both respects, "democracy," for Dewey, means a meliorist project, not an account or description of societal reality. *"The end of democracy is a radical end. For it is an end that has not been adequately realized in any country at any time.* It is radical because it requires great change in existing social institutions, economic, legal and cultural" (LW 11:298f.; italics in orig.).[12]

In particular, the democratic vision contained in Dewey's social philosophy involves a keen criticism of the capitalistic system in the United States, which he considered one of the greatest hindrances to a more radical democratization. Especially after the Great Depression, this criticism gained in strength and definiteness, and Dewey's political writings as well as activities more and more approached the program of a "democratic socialism" as a third way between existing capitalism and fictitious communism.[13]

Several of Dewey's major political works in the 1920s and 1930s gained considerable influence in the public discussions of his time and, even today, may still be regarded as belonging to the most inspiring philosophical works about radical democracy in twentieth-century thought. In his 1927 *The Public and Its Problems* (LW 2:235–372), Dewey discusses the fundamental and still very important problem of how a democratic public capable of exercising an effective and sustainable influence on decisions of public import can be realized under the conditions of the "Great Society" of the industrial age. In *Individualism, Old and New* (LW 5:41–123), published in 1930, he addresses the necessity of a fundamental conceptual reconstruction of the traditional political notion of individualism. He explores the challenge of a similar conceptual reconstruction of the traditional notion of liberalism in his 1935 *Liberalism and Social Action* ( LW 11:1–65). In 1939, in *Freedom and Culture* (LW 13:63–188) he elaborates on the menace of totalitarianism for democracy, focusing his criticism not only on the foreign fascist and Stalinist systems of the time, but also on several anti-democratic tendencies within American society itself. Here we also find his most comprehensive discussion of Marxist political philosophy.

In addition to these major political writings, it is also worthwhile to pay attention to the multitude of smaller contributions in which Dewey time and again took a stand with regard to actual political issues in a rather journalistic way. For over fifty years, he wrote countless political commentaries, polemics, criticisms, analyses, and appeals as a well-known and influential public intellectual. Thanks to the critical edition of the *Collected Works*, these more fugitive works are today easily accessible for Dewey scholars. This is of particular importance because, in his major political writings, Dewey often avoided direct comments, recommendations, or suggestions to every-day political or institutional questions. If one looks into the abundance of his journalistic work,[14] however, one finds many examples of how his Pragmatic methods led him to very clear and detailed positions as to the day-to-day political issues of his time.


Theory of Education and School

In educational circles worldwide, Dewey is today recognized as one of the leading philosophers of education in twentieth-century thought. From the multitude of his writings on school and education I only select a few of the most important. In the little book *The School and Society* (MW 1:1–109), first published in 1899, Dewey provides an account of the pedagogical work in his Laboratory School, founded at the University of Chicago in 1896.[15] Presenting Dewey's first systematic draft of his theory of the school, the book would have a rapid and extensive international effect among educationalists of the time who were striving to reform and reconstruct the school. Dewey set out to rethink the relationship between school and society, in theory and practice, in the face of the fundamental and continuous social changes caused by the industrial revolution and the attendant urbanization in the second half of the nineteenth century. In his view, what was needed was to readjust the school to the life of the child and to avoid unnecessary waste of energy. Dewey's vision of the school as "miniature community" or "embryonic society" became famous. In the same context he uses the phrase "the child's habitat" (MW 1:12). At another place, writing about the needed changes in school and classroom practice, he argues for a shift of the center of gravity, a pedagogical revolution comparable to the Copernican shift in astronomy: "In this case the child becomes the sun about which the appliances of education revolve; he is the centre about which they are organized" (MW 1:23).

This is not a plea for a naive and one-sided *Pädagogik vom Kinde aus*; Dewey's interactive approach and his emphasis on the primacy of the interactions between learners and their (natural and sociocultural) environments should have prevented such a misinterpretation right from the start. This also applies to his understanding of the relationship between "The Child and the Curriculum," as expressed in his 1902 article (MW 2:271–91).

As Larry Hickman has rightly pointed out in his introductory remarks, learning, for Dewey, always begins in the middle of things. This is why the school, above all, must be open to life in order to be a place for learning. In the ideal school "the life of the child becomes the all-controlling aim . . . Learning?—certainly, but living primarily, and learning through and in relation to this living" (MW 1:24). The school must be opened to the life-worlds of the students and to the larger societal environment (see MW 1:39–56). As a place for learning it is organized after the model of the "laboratory" (in the large sense of that metaphor), which involves opportunities for learning through active experimentation, observation, construction, testing, discussion, and artistic expression in cooperation with other learners.

*Schools of To-Morrow* (MW 8:205–404), a book that Dewey co-authored with his daughter Evelyn, is a highly interesting work not only for the history of education, but also for current discussions about school and classroom reform. The Deweys present and portray a selected number of progressive schools in different parts of the United States, combining theoretical explanations written by John with accounts of school and classroom practice, observed mainly by Evelyn. Thus they nicely keep the balance between the theory and practice of educational reconstruction.

One year later, Dewey published his major work on educational philosophy, *Democracy and Education* (MW 9), in which he addresses the task of comprehensively and systematically working out the educational implications of the notion of democracy. He sets out to discuss the constructive aims and methods of public education from the perspective of his radical notion of democracy and to criticize those traditional theories of knowledge and ethics whose influence on education tends to hamper an adequate realization of the democratic ideal. He is concerned with the connection between the prosperity of democracy, the development of the experimental method in the sciences, the theory of evolution, and the industrial revolution, and wants to examine the educational consequences of these manifold processes of change (see MW 9:3). It accords with his philosophical notion of experience, and his concept of human nature explained above, that he conceives of education on the most general plane as a continual process of growth that has no end beyond itself (see MW 9:46–58). The most comprehensive aim of education, according to Dewey, can only be more education. "Since in reality there is nothing to which growth is relative save more growth, there is nothing to which education is subordinate save more education" (MW 9:56)—in the sense of a continual and lifelong reconstruction of experience (see MW 9:82ff.) in the interactions of learners within a world characterized by change and diversity. "The criterion of the value of school education is the extent in which it creates a desire for continued growth and supplies means for making the desire effective in fact" (MW 9:58).

For reasons of brevity, I can only hint at two further writings from Dewey's later works. First, the treatise on *The Sources of a Science of*

*Education* (LW 5:1–40) deals with questions about the nature of a science of education and the appropriate methods for inquiring into the subject matter of education. Among other things, Dewey calls for a more direct and immediate participation of "The Teacher as Investigator" in the educational research process. Second, the little book *Experience and Education* (LW 13:1–62), first published in 1938, further elaborates Dewey's educational thought on the background of his mature philosophical approach and his then considerably broadened theory of experience. He also replies to common misunderstandings and misinterpretations of his pedagogy in the context of the Progressive Education movement.

Theory of Religion

Finally, Dewey's theory of religion, or more precisely, the religious, should be mentioned. He exposed this theory most comprehensively in his little 1934 book *A Common Faith* (LW 9:1–58). There he distinguished between "religion" as a generic term for institutionalized religions of all kinds (often associated with ideas of the supernatural) and "the religious" as an empirical phenomenon, a quality of natural experience. He is especially interested in this religious dimension of experience insofar as it represents a component in the everyday life of common people. He draws a connection between the religious potentials of everyday experience and the values of democratic communities by indicating that the spiritual meaning of democracy can find expression in religious experience. His notion of democracy remains within the field of a consequently secular approach, although his use of the term "God" gave rise to many controversies and misunderstandings (see, e.g., Eldridge 1998, 126ff.).

*Some Notes on the Present Anglo-American Dewey Scholarship*

Although during his lifetime John Dewey was regarded as one of the leading American philosophers and ranked as an influential public intellectual, his work fell almost into oblivion in the decades after his death. The triumphant advance of analytical philosophy displaced interest in the classical tradition of Pragmatism in post–World War II America. But since the early 1980s there has been a broad renaissance of Pragmatism and, especially, a rediscovered interest in the philosophy of Dewey in the United States. One important influence in this connection came from Richard Rorty's 1979 book *Philosophy and the Mirror of Nature*. Rorty, himself a fallen angel from the analytical tradition and today widely regarded as one of the leading figures of so-called neo-Pragmatism, counts John Dewey together with Ludwig Wittgenstein and Martin Heidegger among the three most important philosophers of the twentieth century (see Rorty 1979, 368). Although some of his more specific interpretations of Dewey's philosophy have led to controversies among present-day Dewey scholars, his influence in promoting a broader interest in Dewey's philosophy in general is undisputed.

Meanwhile, there is an extraordinarily broad and multi-layered revival of Anglo-American Dewey scholarship, combined with an abundance of new publications, that is hard to survey for any single observer. The Society for the Advancement of American Philosophy (SAAP) plays an important role in organizing research exchanges. Dewey scholarship is one of the main focuses of the society's annual conferences and summer institutes.[16] The work of the Center for Dewey Studies, located at Southern Illinois University Carbondale (SIUC), provides indispensable resources for anybody interested in Dewey scholarship.[17] It is directed today by Larry Hickman, the co-editor and coauthor of this volume.[18] The critically acclaimed edition of the *Collected Works of John Dewey*, published by the Center under the direction of Hickman's predecessor Jo Ann Boydston, has set new standards and counts today as the basic reference text for Dewey scholars worldwide. The edition has been completely accessible in cloth or in paperback since 1991. It contains thirty-seven volumes, divided into three sections: "Early Works," "Middle Works," and "Later Works," plus one index volume. It is also accessible in electronic form. In addition to this complete edition, it seems worthwhile

to draw attention, especially to newcomers to the field of Dewey studies, to the excellent selection of some of Dewey's most important
writings contained in the two-volume edition *The Essential Dewey*,
edited by Larry Hickman and Thomas Alexander (Hickman and Alexander 1998).

Regarding the broad variety of subjects within the new Anglo-
American Dewey scholarship, I can only briefly indicate selected examples here. The standard in biographical work on Dewey's life and
career had for many years been set by George Dykhuizen (1973).
However, based on the broad field of new research materials provided
by the new Dewey scholarship in the last decades, there are now a
number of more specific and more extensive and detailed biographical studies. Robert B. Westbrook (1991) focuses his extensive biography on Dewey's relationship to American democracy, while Steven C.
Rockefeller (1991) pays specific attention to the import of his religious
background, and Alan Ryan (1995) to his liberal humanism. And the
research on Dewey's life is, by far, not finished yet. Huge amounts of
material (e.g., Dewey's correspondence) are still under examination,
leading to new publications, most recently Thomas Dalton (2002)
and Jay Martin (2002). For a good survey on the subject fields and
thrusts in present-day Pragmatism in the wake of Dewey, one may
consult the excellent anthologies edited by Jim Garrison (1995) and
Larry Hickman (1998). The contributions from a multitude of authors collected here cover many themes and provide the reader with
comprehensive reference material for further studies in fields like
Epistemological Foundations, Aesthetics and the Teaching of Art,
Popular Art and Education, Democracy and Education, Pragmatism
and Metaphysics, and issues of Coeducation and Science Education
in a time of lifelong learning (Garrison); and the Art of Life, the Pragmatic Concept of Community, Pragmatism and American Social Sciences, Philosophy as Education, Ethics and Morality, Religious
Experience, Theory of Inquiry, and Pragmatist Feminism (Hickman).
The latter field of research is further covered by an anthology of explicitly feminist interpretations of John Dewey, edited by Charlene

Haddock Seigfried (2002). The volume deals with historical perspectives on predecessors of Pragmatist feminism, such as Jane Addams, as well as current theoretical issues like the relation of democracy and education, subjectivity and the relation of objectivity and truth, and other issues of social and political philosophy. In a more recent publication edited by William Gavin (2003), a number of well-known Dewey scholars discuss issues of Pragmatic reconstruction in the face of changing cultural and philosophical contexts. Responding to the question of how much we, today, may (or, indeed, should) "pass Dewey by," the contributions of this volume differ considerably, ranging from attempts to build on his achievements to suggestions for radically reconstructing his approach.

From the abundance of monographs in the recent Anglo-American Dewey scholarship, I will only mention a brief selection without any claim to comprehensiveness. An influential study on the continuing relevance of Dewey's conception of philosophy is given by Ralph Sleeper (1986). With regard to Dewey's theory of art and aesthetics, Thomas Alexander's book (1987) has set standards in rethinking Dewey's concept of art within the broader context of his philosophical approach. More recent contributions in this field can be found in Philip Jackson (1998), with a special focus on educational implications, and Richard Shusterman (2000), who incorporates perspectives on contemporary popular culture (e.g., the culture of Rap). James Campbell (1992) reconstructs Pragmatist social philosophy in the context of the emerging Pragmatic concept of community in the work of Charles Sanders Peirce, William James, George Herbert Mead, and John Dewey. He also examines the relevance of classical Pragmatism's social thought for contemporary political theory and action. Michael Eldridge (1998) also provides a highly interesting study, in this connection, interpreting Dewey's approach as "cultural instrumentalism" and analyzing its bearings on the theory and practice of cultural and political processes of transformation. Charlene Haddock Seigfried can be regarded as the leading Pragmatist feminist. Her 1996 pathbreaking book examines the relationship between Pragmatism and feminism in historical and conceptual perspectives. Dewey's ethics is discussed by Jennifer Welchman (1995), his metaphysics

by Raymond Boisvert (1988), and, in a comprehensive discussion between John Stuhr, Ralph Sleeper, Raymond Boisvert, and Thomas Alexander, published in *Transactions of the Charles Sanders Peirce
Society* (1992). A study of Dewey's logic is given by Thomas Burke
(1994), and the implications of his instrumental theory of knowledge
and his cultural approach for a philosophy of technology are explored
by Larry Hickman (2001). The philosophical foundations of Dewey's
pedagogy have recently been discussed and further developed by Jim
Garrison (1997a). Harriet Cuffaro (1995) has published a study on the
theory and practice of early childhood education, while Stephen Fishman and Lucille McCarthy (1998) have provided an innovative approach to the challenge of classroom practice, both at the school and
university levels, based on Dewey's educational thought. Laurel Tanner (1997) reexamines Dewey's Chicago Laboratory School and draws
conclusions for the present. Among the classics of American Dewey
scholarship that still have a large impact on present research, the anthology edited by Paul Schilpp (1951) and Richard Bernstein's 1967
book with the plain title *John Dewey* should be mentioned. Schilpp's
excellent collection of critical assessments, written by some of the
most well-known contemporary philosophers of Dewey's lifetime and
completed by a lengthy rejoinder from Dewey, originally appeared
in 1939 on the occasion of his eightieth birthday. Bernstein's book,
according to the Dewey biographer Alan Ryan, helped more than any
other single publication to maintain Dewey's reputation as a philosopher in the decades after his death (see Ryan 1995, 23). Finally, the
reader's attention should be drawn to the bibliography *Works about
John Dewey, 1886–2006*, compiled and continuously updated by the
Dewey Center under the direction of Barbara Levine. This collection
is available in electronic format.[19]
    With regard to the broader context of the rediscovery and revival
of classical American Pragmatism as a whole and the attendant discussions about the relation between classical and present-day Pragmatism, the reader will find extensive, controversial, and very
instructive contributions in the anthologies edited by Lenore Langsdorf and Andrew Smith (1995) and Morris Dickstein (1998). The latter volume gives a good impression of the broad and multi-layered

spectrum of subjects characteristic of the current scholarship on (classical) Pragmatism in the Anglo-American discussion—reaching, in this case, from philosophy and knowledge criticism, through social theory and theory of law, into theories of culture and art. In all of these fields there is a rich exploration of the meaning of Pragmatism that includes even controversial exchanges about its very philosophical core concepts.

One important debate in this connection is carried out between two different camps in current Pragmatism. To simplify matters for reasons of brevity, one camp wishes to stick to the philosophical core concept, "experience," as expounded in the classical tradition, especially in James and Dewey, while the other wishes to exchange "language" for "experience" as a philosophical starting point in consequence of the so-called *linguistic turn* in twentieth century philosophy (see Kloppenberg 1998, 84ff.). As prominent protagonists, James Kloppenberg reckons Hilary Putnam and Richard Bernstein among the first group, and Richard Rorty and Stanley Fish among the second. Basically at issue in this debate is the question of how far we always frame our observations and descriptions of experiences already from within (and in the limits of) a particular language, vocabulary, or language game—thus speaking from a culturally specific position—and how far, on the other hand, we are able to get into experimental contact with a world beyond and independent of any specific language, a world of nature approached through culture. We will repeatedly come back to this and other related questions in the contributions that make up Part II of this volume, as well as in the comprehensive closing discussion in Part III.

# THREE

# CONSTRUCTIVISM: DIVERSITY OF APPROACHES AND CONNECTIONS WITH PRAGMATISM

Kersten Reich

I n this section I give a survey of basic constructivist assumptions and different constructivist approaches, then briefly elaborate on some connections between social constructivist approaches— especially the Cologne program of interactive constructivism—and John Dewey's Pragmatism.

## Constructivist Core Assumptions

Present-day approaches in the social sciences and humanities are more and more characterized by specialized discourses operating in particular scientific fields. "Local" networks operate to a surprising degree on their own terms, without even taking notice of similar or related work done in other networks. Contacts are lacking because of the increasing complexity and confusion of information in postmodern societies, which more and more entail specific research circles meeting at specific conferences or symposia and publishing their work in specific journals, without finding sufficient contact to other circles, even compatible ones. A survey of present-day constructivist approaches supplies evidence for this observation, as we will see. But, also, the relation between Pragmatism and constructivism, to my mind, largely testifies to a new failure of understanding—a failure that we wish to overcome with the present volume. We know, however, that even if we succeed, our attempt will eventually be hardly more than another contribution in a largely confused field. Nevertheless, it is an attempt to recover some clear views.

Throughout the twentieth century and up to the present day, constructivist theories have become increasingly more significant. Presently there is a diversity of approaches that have become influential, partly in the natural sciences, but especially in the humanities and social sciences. These approaches build on an interdisciplinary or transdisciplinary design. They have in common the attempt to elaborate and define a concept of viability that accounts for what scientific approaches, methods, and practical applications fit the currently crucial issues of inquiry, knowledge, and problem solving. And, if we discount for the moment some differences that I will discuss later, they have in common a threefold definition of science.

## 1. Constructions

Unlike metaphysical or realist approaches, constructivists do not look for copies or mirrorings of an outer reality in the human mind. Rather, they see humans as observers, participants, and agents[1] who actively generate and transform the patterns through which they construct the realities that fit them. Although in everyday practices these constructions often appear to be merely subjective, we must not forget the social contexts in which they are always embedded; thus there is no such thing as purely subjective constructions, but constructions and versions of realities are always mixtures emerging from transactions with already existing (cultural and other) realities. In science, we use discursive practices to generate these transactions and constructions; therefore our scientific constructions are not arbitrary or merely subjective, although they depend on the unique and concrete perspectives of the observers, participants, and agents involved. These constructors are embedded in the social and cultural conditions of their time. Only in this context and on this background can they claim, and try to realize, positions of autonomy and deliberation. As subjective agents they may possibly change the contexts of their time, but their dependence on these contexts also influences their possibilities. With the transition from modernity to late modernity or post-modernity (see Bauman 1993, 1997, 1998a, 1998b, 1999, 2000; Giddens 1991) and the attendant increase in degrees of freedom—as manifested in philosophical discourse, e.g., by the debates on deconstruction and poststructuralism—the constructivist assumption of the reality constructions of observers gains explicit acknowledgement. Constructivists, to be sure, suppose that observers have constructed their realities already in former times. But this constructive agency could easily go unnoticed because people mostly believed that they were just detecting elements of a divine order or some natural law. They were oblivious to the importance of their own contributions in those constructions. To the degree, however, that in more recent times radically diverse perspectives and versions of the world appeared in succession and juxtaposition, to the degree that even in science diversity could no longer be restricted by the temporary dominance of certain schools or traditions, the relativity of truth claims has more and more come to the fore. And with the acknowledgement of this relativity goes an increased consideration of both the constructive nature of those claims and the singularity of the events to which reference was made.[2] Thus it was a more or less necessary consequence that criticism of knowledge would eventually lead to a new approach—namely, constructivism.

Nelson Goodman (1978) describes the transition toward constructivism in the following way: The loss of the *one world* of classical metaphysical thought turns out to be a loss of the one, accurate, and comprehensive *version* of world. The sciences and humanities are seen as versions of world making. In my own terminology, this is to say that the sciences and humanities depend on observers, participants, and agents in cultural contexts who provide different versions of worlds through the observations and actions in which they participate in their respective roles in scientific discourses. But they have lost a last meta-observer as the ultimate source of legitimacy—be that a god or some allegedly final law projected into "outer reality." They are confronted by the predicament that there may be different accurate or right versions of the world coexisting at a given time or contending for each other's claims. There are no rational grounds for finding a common denominator for all of these versions, although within the respective approaches it is still possible to maintain conclusive logical argumentation and concise patterns of rationality. Therefore, Hilary Putnam (1992), in commenting on Goodman's work, insists on the necessity and legitimacy of formal assertions in science. But he agrees with Goodman that no such assertion or statement can claim to represent a reality independent of experience. For Putnam, too, there is not one single true description of reality.

This situation, however, may easily call forth the nightmare of postmodern arbitrariness for some, because from the perspective of constructions, philosophers and researchers can no longer make unambiguous truth claims with universal validity for everyone and in every context. But constructivists and Pragmatists alike do not plea for arbitrariness. They rather attempt to inquire into the viability of reality constructions and their practical consequences. This implies that they also look for instrumental and experimental ways of constructing realities, lest viability turns not into mere opinion, but leads to relevant, resourceful, and problem-solving constructions.

## 2. Methods

The arguments of Goodman and Putnam imply a preassumption that should be taken for granted in constructivist approaches, too, although it is sometimes neglected, especially in the writings of more subjectivist constructivists: Constructivists also use specific scientific methods of reasoning and make claims to validity, and they have to communicate about these methods and claims with others. In the contest between different scientific discourses critics sometimes blame constructivists for allegedly striving to replace scientific methods by arbitrariness. This reproach more or less applies to some proponents of constructivism. However, it must be rejected as misleading with regard to the approach as a whole. Constructivists, too, argue methodically for their claims to validity. The German approach of *Methodischer Konstruktivismus*, e.g., does this in a highly sophisticated way by implementing a logical analysis and reconstruction of scientific and technological procedures, including some of their so-far neglected cultural preconditions. While constructivists often talk about the diverse contexts and preconditions of science, their critics often counter this view by an exaggerated universalistic attitude toward science. Constructivists contest this attitude because they think that scientific universalism is not a methodically useful and viable approach in postmodernity. They suspect it of implying (and disguising) hegemonic claims to power that run against current pluralist tendencies and degrees of freedom in scientific discourses. This is not to say, on the other hand, that methodically warranted claims to truth simply depend on majority vote. Rather, the methodically warranted validity claims rely on descriptions of reality whose viability has to prove itself in the deliberations of interpretive communities (here majorities count) as well as in the success or failure of applications in certain fields (here constructions have to show their truth value in practices). Constructivism, like any other scientific approach, looks for methodical procedures, logical accuracy, and unambiguous analysis of preconditions and consequences, i.e., relative truth claims and empirical checks. Constructivists are especially open to experimental as well as instrumental applications, because only through such procedures can we find out how viable our perspectives are with regard to practical consequences, and whether we will be able to produce and transform experienced realities from our theoretical assumptions. However, constructivists are also cautious of exaggerated universalistic expectations toward scientific methods. No methodical quest for comprehensiveness of scientific reasoning, unambiguous-ness of claims to validity, or far-reaching or universal consensus can do away with the skeptical reminder that, until now, universalistic approaches time and again have failed, despite all their sophisticated methodical instruments. What remains as truth, for us, is what Hilary Putnam has called an "idealization of rational acceptability" that is temporarily valid within a specific discursive context. It rests on an idealization that attends all rationality. This view corresponds with fallibilism as maintained by John Dewey and presently advocated with particular clarity by Richard Rorty (2003). Constructivism, too, maintains that there is no pure and value-free rationality. For con-structivists, this implies that philosophers and scientists construct their methods as well as their objects through application of these methods. It further implies that criticism of methods and their atten-dant idealizations must be regarded as an indispensable part of their professional self-reflection. That is to say, they must learn to see and reflect themselves both as self-observers and as distant-observers, at one point working with the resources inherent to the methodological frames of their approaches, while at another point transcending that frame by critically assessing their approach from the outside view-point of alternative positions. Although this move, too, rests on an idealization of rationalities, the attendant reflection and account of multiple perspectives are a road to more transparency, open-minded-ness, and pluralism in philosophical and scientific discourses.

3. Practices

In the world of practices, routines, and institutions, constructions and methods are being delimited by interpretive communities ac-cording to needs, interests, power claims, definitions of failure and success, utility and futility, appropriateness and inappropriateness. The current practices of globalized capitalism involve strong tenden-cies of feasibility that especially support those endeavors that promise profit for those who invest in productions and services. The world of practices thus brings forth and supports a *mainstream* in science that may sometimes appear as the only way without alternatives. Yet there never is only *one* way in science, but a multitude of viable ways for different interests that also involve criticisms of current practices. Science must always be open to plurality and change. Although practices are not the all-decisive power that can suppress every construction and method outside the *mainstream*, the pressure of feasibilities and procedures accepted by majorities interconnects constructions and methods with practical requirements that one can hardly ignore. There is still freedom of construction, though, and the possibility of scientific outsiders whose work has innovative effects for the future. If we, for the moment, take cultural descriptions of our own current practices, we find ourselves confronted with often restless, unruly, and obstinate movements, no matter if we look from a modern or postmodern point of view. It has increasingly come to mind that what is at stake are limited viabilities for limited interests, needs, claims to power and profit that define validity, efficaciousness, and success in practice. This clearly runs counter to modern expectations that envisioned an ideal world of practice as the highest and complete consummation of reason toward which human life should develop in order to achieve a truly moral state. In both the twentieth and twenty-first centuries, practices have enforced skepticism about the great meta-narratives of modernity (Lyotard 1984)[3] that envisioned a happy state of reconciliation as the final rational self-realization of culture. In their place, we today witness processes of displacement, dislocation, and deviation from traditions and inherited values and norms, from the alleged certainties of logic and reason that now turn out to be contextual constructions and temporally valid methods of inquiry, reasoning, and warrant (Bauman 1993, 1997, 1998a, 1998b, 1999, 2000).

Summarizing the three aspects, we find that constructivist approaches are relevant for contemporary sciences, and especially the social sciences and humanities, because they provide the following advantages:

1. They do not underestimate the constructive side of human knowledge and are able to explain the mutual interrelation among constructions, reconstructions, and deconstructions. This makes

possible a very broad trans- and interdisciplinary approach to contemporary scientific discourses, taking account of discursive diversity, singularity of events, and the social and cultural contexts of constructions that are steadily being transformed through the use of constructions, methods, and practices. In consequence, constructivists in principle pay attention to the relativity of interpretations with regard to the respective interpretive system.

2. They do not restrict their methodological approach to narrow procedures of warranting truth claims, trying to exhaust all disturbing elements by a reduction in order to secure ultimate unambiguousness and validity in the frame of a scientific interpretive community. Rather, they explore methods in their interrelation with constructions and practices in cultural contexts. In this connection, they call attention to the ineradicable indeterminacy of knowledge that remains despite all methodical sophistication.[4]

3. They take the viabilities of human practices, routines, and institutions as the starting point for discussing the successes or failures of constructions and methods, their usefulness or harmfulness, beauty or ugliness, adequacy or inadequacy as seen by self- or distant-observers. The focus on practices helps to deconstruct and criticize strategies of safeguarding hegemonic discourses or ivory tower reveries that methodically attempt to immunize themselves against generous practical testing. Methodological constructivists, in the first place, try to inquire into the changes and occurrences in cultural practices that precede scientific discoveries and are tacitly implied in what is often taken as purely scientific developments (see Janich 1996; Hartmann and Janich 1996, 1998). But the interconnection applies also *vice versa*: Many cultural practices have become possible through constructions and methods in scientific and other discourses that have led to viable practical applications only after their invention.

This threefold perspective shows the strength of constructivism that consists in interrelating constructions, methods, and practices together with their respective implications in cultural contexts. The weakness, though, of constructivist approaches so far put forth most

often lies in overemphasizing one of the three phases at the expense
of the others:

1. If we overemphasize the aspect of constructions, we are readily
given to end in a rather subjectivist approach that neglects the cultural contexts of constructions. To underestimate the constructive
side, on the other hand, will render us oblivious to the constructive
powers necessary for the release and reflection of creative, spontane-
ous, and innovative processes.

2. If we overemphasize the aspect of methods, we can easily be led
to methodical rigidity that often not only blocks innovations but also
involves us once again in the old fallacies of naturalism and realism.
To neglect the methodological side, on the other hand, will plunge
our approaches into disasters of self-contradiction and weak
argumentation.

3. If we overemphasize the aspect of practices, we will readily end
in an uncritical sort of activism that accepts any view whatsoever as
viable as long as it fits the prevailing order. If we underestimate the
practical side, on the other hand, we may easily get lost in merely
theoretical speculations and fictitious contentions with practically irrelevant adversaries.

Contemporary constructivist approaches waver between these
poles of strength and weakness. However, discussions show that it is
possible to further develop the strength of constructivist arguments if
constructivism endeavors to discursively elaborate and justify its own
claims to validity and truth. From the perspective of the Cologne program of interactive constructivism, this endeavor must be regarded
as a basic requirement for constructivist thought.

### Constructivist Approaches in the Social Sciences and Humanities

If critics often blame constructivism for its alleged arbitrariness of
knowledge claims, this indictment very often rests on a superficial
and reductive account of constructivist tenets. It is true that some
proponents of so-called "radical constructivism" have occasionally

contributed to the rise of such simplifications by all too shortsightedly and without sufficient specification claiming that all reality is but "mere invention." Nevertheless, closer examination of even the more subjectivist positions of radical constructivism will show that they, too, provide criteria for delimiting arbitrariness.[5]

But constructivism cannot be reduced to one version, like radical constructivism, because the term as now established in the social sciences and humanities refers to a diversity of approaches. Especially in the English-speaking world, there is a strong advance of both cognitive and social constructivisms, the latter often emphasizing social interaction and intersubjectivity. According to Geelan (1997), e.g., we must distinguish among at least six versions of constructivism: radical constructivism (after von Glasersfeld or von Foerster), personal or psychological constructivist approaches (Kelly, Piaget), social constructivism (Solomon), social constructionism (Gergen), critical constructivism (Taylor), and contextual constructivism (Cobern). In addition to these English-speaking approaches,[6] (Fosnot 1996; Lambert 1995, 1996; Larochelle, et. al. 1998; Marlowe and Page 1998; Science and Education 1997; Steffe and Gale 1995; Tobin 1993; Siebert 1999) the German discussion has partly been characterized by a slow and profound transition from phenomenology to methodical or cultural constructivism (e.g., Gethmann 1991; Janich 1999). And then there are other cultural constructivist approaches like Jim Garrison's constructivist Pragmatism or the Cologne program of interactive constructivism that should be further added to the list.

To provide a more detailed survey, I will briefly outline some basic features and perspectives found in those versions of constructivism that, to my mind, are most important in current discussions. Essentially, we can distinguish among at least five influential constructivist movements. They are partly interconnected with each other as well as with other traditions (like Pragmatism).

Constructive Psychology: Piaget

Piaget's psychology bears a strong subjective orientation and is especially interested in the logical aspects of cognitive development in the individual. His approach has given rise to a largely cognitive account of constructive teaching and learning mainly focused on the individual learner. Social dimensions of learning are not completely neglected (Driver and Easley 1978; Driver and Oldham 1986; Fosnot 1993; Pines and West 1986), but they do not stand in the foreground. Among the advantages of the approach are Piaget's refined methods of research, which have inspired quite a number of applied perspectives in psychology and pedagogy. Critical perspectives on the importance of interaction in cultural contexts to the construction of knowledge are largely missing in Piaget's constructivism.

The biological theory that underpins Piaget's approach leads him to the assumption of certain universal principles in human cognition that can be detected with scientific objectivity. The implied naturalism of this claim is disputed by many constructivists today. The same applies to the brand of structuralism advocated by Piaget (Hartmann and Janich 1996; Reich 1998a). Social interactions and emotional aspects of learning do not get enough attention (see Furth 1990). Present research perspectives on social learning will have to transcend Piaget's approach toward a more thoroughgoing observation of cultural contexts.

Constructive and Materialistic Theory of Culture: Vygotsky

Vygotsky's theory of learning bears a stronger sociocultural orientation than Piaget's. In principle, knowledge is seen as socially constructed, although in Vygotsky, too, there is much emphasis on an objective account of the logics of development. A critical perspective on the production and validity of knowledge in the frame of scientific discourses is largely missing. Scientific knowledge is seen in a rather monolithic way. It is taken for granted as the basis for viable reality constructions of learners. Students shall be introduced to science. The logical analysis of developmental steps is supposed to help teachers and learners to find the appropriate points of access. The approach has been extended and introduced to the Anglo-American debate on learning by Bruner (1983, 1984, 1990, 1996; Bruner and Haste 1987).

Vygotsky's theory builds on a Marxist version of cultural theory that, on the one hand, bears a strong anti-metaphysical tendency and understands cultural constructions as expressions of human activities (especially manifested as productive forces). On the other hand, this interpretation supposes a kind of copy theory of knowledge and subordinates the diversity of human constructions to the dominance of *one* (objectivistic and materialistic) interpretation. Today the deconstructivist critique of this dominance, advocated, e.g., by post-Marxist proponents like Laclau and Mouffe (see Laclau and Mouffe 1985; Laclau 1990; Mouffe 1996, 1997, 2000), rejects the exaggerated objectivism and turns toward the field of plural cultures instead. They claim that there may be temporarily dominant "objectivities" in culture that for the time being are effective as hegemonic interpretations in the political sphere, but no culture or time is completely determined by detectable laws or totally transparent in the final analysis. Constructivism rather enforces the surrender of exaggerated claims to objectivism, especially when we turn to the field of cultures and cultural change.

## Subjective and Constructive Psychology: Kelly

Kelly's (1955) psychological theory of "personal constructs" represents a peculiar version of constructivism. Kelly radicalizes the subjective phase of reality constructions much more than even Piaget. Under critical examination, though, this subjectivism turns out to be the most problematic point of the approach. It one-sidedly emphasizes the innovative and creative role of the individual and exaggerates individual possibilities of learning, while at the same time neglecting social dependencies and involvements.

## Radical Constructivism: von Glasersfeld, von Foerster, and Others

Radical constructivism avoids the objectivism of the first two positions by putting more emphasis on the relativity of subjective knowledge. Knowing is analyzed and explained as a process of individual reality construction. There are quite a number of different brands of radical constructivism that have in common this strong subjectivist orientation. Especially in the work of the two pioneers of the approach, namely Heinz von Foerster[7] and Ernst von Glasersfeld,[8] we find a forceful and relentless emphasis on the relativity of knowledge. Although the philosophical debates on modernity / postmodernity characteristic of much late-twentieth-century criticism of knowledge do not find sufficient consideration in their writings, the specific views they advance on individual reality constructions allow them to draw conclusions that relativize knowledge claims. According to von Glasersfeld, individuals can only interact with each other through their subjective constructions of reality. They are seen as epistemological monads.

In the background of radical constructivism stands the reflection on changes in science, especially in the discourses on cybernetics, linguistics, and the psychology and biology of cognition. The works of Gregory Bateson (2000, 2002), Humberto Maturana (1978), Maturana and Varela (1988), and Piaget have been particularly important for the development of this approach (von Glasersfeld 1995). Sometimes this version of constructivism gives evidence of an implicit naturalism, in that its proponents refer to the objective findings of biology or brain research as proof for their claims. This tendency has become the object of much recent criticism. The same applies to the implicit monadology of the approach that all-too-much neglects social interactions, cultural contexts, and the distinctive features of the postmodern situation on whose behalf constructivism has gained practical relevancy (Hartmann and Janich 1996; Reich 1998a, 159ff.). Even the innovative findings in cybernetics and biology to which radical constructivists often refer, so critics say, must be seen in the context of these sociocultural changes.

## Social and Cultural Constructivist Approaches

Social constructivism has many faces. There are a considerable variety of social and cultural constructivist approaches that have come to the

fore in recent decades and have immensely broadened our understanding of constructions, methods, and practices in sociocultural
contexts. A classical position is that of Berger and Luckmann (1966).
Another useful approach is advanced by Knorr-Cetina (1981, 1999)
who analyzes the fabrication of knowledge from a social-constructivist
viewpoint. Many other approaches implicitly use constructivist arguments. The present discussion in the social sciences is characterized
by a number of social constructivist assumptions. This shows that
many social scientists share the recognition that their own constructions are among the very preconditions for their own discourses and
those that will follow. Consequently, the critical social deconstruction
and reconstruction of scientific constructs are now regarded as essential parts of the professional task. However, there is still dispute about
this point between constructivists and realists who think they are still
looking for "laws of nature" or some other form of external and independent reality to be copied in scientific knowledge.[9] Social constructivists clearly reject such assumptions and rely on the cultural
anchorage of constructivist theorizing itself. They also reject merely
subjective or personal perspectives on the processes of human construction, as well as exaggeratedly objectivist explanations, e.g., about
an alleged natural logic of development underlying these processes.

For the socioculturally oriented versions of constructivism, the
cultural transition from modernity to postmodernity is of great importance. They emphasize the radical plurality of interpretive communities and discourses that underlie the productions of knowledge
within postmodern societies. Even our propositions about nature and
natural processes, e.g., even our propositions about the human brain
that have become so important for some radical constructivists, are
always discursively constructed propositions from within the contexts
of culture. If we neglect these contexts, we may easily end up in a
naive and untenable naturalism. The sociocultural constructivists
criticize the more subjectivist brands of constructivism like Piaget or
the radical constructivists for underestimating cultural involvements
and intersubjectivity in the construction of knowledge. They think
that constructivism itself should better be regarded as an expression

of social and cultural developments than as a consequence of natural science (see Reich 1998a).

From the diversity of sociocultural constructivisms, I wish to select and highlight but five versions:

1. I have already mentioned the work done by German *methodical constructivism and culturalism* (e.g., Janich 1999). This approach specifically focuses on the methodical aspects that connect scientific constructions and cultural practices. It has so far been concentrated mainly on the analysis of scientific constructions in the way of methods and contents evolving out of cultural everyday practices (prototheories).

2. *Social constructionism* is by now a well-established approach, particularly in the field of social psychology. It has been developed in a number of publications (Gergen 1994, 1999; Burr 1995; Gergen et al. 1987–2005; Shotter 1994). The basic orientation of this approach is anti-realistic. Social constructionists see knowledge as an expression of culture and historical contexts, discuss language as a precondition of thought, conceive of language as a form of social action, and primarily refer to interaction and social practices.

3. *Pragmatist constructivism* builds on the many affinities and interconnections between Pragmatism and constructivism. The new scholarship on the work of the Pragmatist philosopher John Dewey has set new standards for productive and mutually fruitful interfaces between the two traditions. Implications of these theoretical exchanges are presently elaborated by philosophers such as Jim Garrison (1996, 1997a, 1997b, 1998a, 1998b), who also discusses consequences for the theory of education.

4. *Situated cognitive constructivism* represents the theoretical background of a great number of current research programs on cognitive aspects of teaching and learning. They regard the construction of realities as a process of situated learning (e.g., Lave 1988; Lave and Wenger 1991) or situated cognition (e.g., Clancey 1997). They discuss constructions in the context of learning environments in order to better understand the interplay between subjective agency and the undergoing effected by an experienced environment.

5. *Interactive constructivism* conceives of constructivism as a discourse that comprises constructions, methods, and practices[10] (Reich 1998a, 1998b, 2002, 2004a; Neubert 1998, 2001; Neubert and Reich 2000; Burckhart and Reich 2000; Reich and Wei 1997). It combines aspects of social constructionism with cultural theory and attempts to find new ways of approaching science and life-world. In particular, this version of constructivism puts emphasis on the dimension of sociocultural interactions as a precondition of communication and understanding. It extends the scope of perspectives by incorporating theories about the imaginative and the real in their interplay with symbolic representations in cultural experiences.

### Interconnections between Pragmatism and Interactive Constructivism

New schools of thought and philosophical approaches often show a tendency to reinvent and reinterpret the whole past of science and culture, especially those discourses that are somehow related to the problems with which the new approach preeminently deals. So it may not be surprising that explicit constructivism, too, discovers in its interpretations of the past an implicit or hidden constructivism in older and even bygone traditions. This does not only apply to direct forerunners of constructivism, e.g., in the history of philosophy, which frequently refers to figures like the eighteenth-century Italian thinker Giambattista Vico. But it potentially applies to each and every tradition of the past, because they all may be reinterpreted as constructions of different realities and seen in comparison, in their succession and juxtaposition, without a final and definite word about preference or refusal. It is a strength of constructivism that it provides such a broad and generous access to the history of thought; it does not have to exclude certain approaches because of discursive reservations (like constructions or claims that do not fit its own agenda). It cultivates an attitude of tolerance and open-mindedness and tries to understand why certain constructions and discourses have been developed in the history of culture, why they succeeded for their time, and what led to their eventual failure. And this view of the history of thought also applies to constructivism itself, because constructivism could only appear as a successful and convincing discourse of knowledge criticism at a time when universalist and absolutist approaches had become more and more doubtful.[11]

In the twentieth century, some philosophical and scientific traditions already implicitly showed such potential constructivist characteristics that they had contributed much to the emergence of explicitly constructivist approaches and entertained productive exchanges with them. I name but a few of the most important of these traditions before I turn in more detail to the close interconnection between constructivism and Pragmatism.

1. Phenomenology has influenced the emergence of constructivism to a large extent and still entertains important exchanges with constructivist concepts. Methodical constructivism in particular has been developed out of the phenomenological tradition. The social constructivism of Berger and Luckmann also stands in that tradition.

2. There are close ties between ethnomethodology (see, e.g., Goffman 1979, 1981; Lemert and Branaman 1997) and social constructivism.

3. Structuralism has helped to scientifically grasp and classify cultural constructions in highly differentiated patterns of symbolic order. The failure of attempts to establish universally valid structures has led to the rise of poststructuralism, which further contributed to the growth of constructivist thought. Authors such as Foucault or Bourdieu implicitly rely on many constructivist assumptions in their works and time and again inquire into the varied social, powerful, life-worldly constructions of truth claims and practices (as expressing different interpretive communities in sociohistorical change).

4. Derrida's deconstructivism provides a constructive principle of supplementation that opens an important space of criticism for constructivist thought. It helps to avoid a naive and positivist brand of constructivism that welcomes everything as viable that is culturally constructed. It articulates the critical deconstructivist potential that inheres in every cultural construction. This has led to many interesting perspectives, e.g., in the fields of literary, gender (Butler 1990,

1993, 1997), and postcolonial studies. Especially in the work of Ernesto Laclau and Chantal Mouffe (1985), the deconstruction of Marxism has opened new theoretical perspectives on radical democracy. They have had an important influence as to the political strategies of a New Left that do not collapse into postmodern arbitrariness. Symbolic systems and the discourses on which they build remain incomplete and unfinished. They cannot be seen as a sutured system, which would establish the closing of that universal seam that holds it all together. For Laclau and Mouffe discursive practices create common forms only through articulation. This constructive process prevents us from ever being able to reach a final solution or establish a final and best observer—whose discourse would inevitably relapse into the stagnation of a closed and final hegemony. This perspective helps us to better understand why constructivist thinking must be reflective and responsive to the cultural and social relationships that underlie its own discourses and practices. It must strive for radical democracy as the necessary underpinning of its own survival. Hegemonic discourses and practices are not an accident of history, but represent—as far as we can see—an inescapable and continual problem to which every approach must respond. This critical reminder applies to constructivism and deconstructivism as well as to any other approach. Among others, there have been discussions on these issues between deconstructivism and Pragmatism (see Mouffe 1996) that are highly relevant for constructivists, too.

5. Jürgen Habermas represents an approach in German thought that shares a postmetaphysical position with culturally reflected versions of constructivism. His philosophical focus on discourse theory is very important, although his conceptual split between communicative and strategic acting—following a central motive of enlightenment—is problematic for constructivists. This is primarily because it underestimates the cultural dependence of all ideal constructions of reason. Further, it neglects the importance of power relations in discourses. Nevertheless, Habermas's works can be very instructive for culturally oriented constructivists as a reminder of the importance of

political interests and the necessity to take life-worldly dependences of human reality constructions into account.

6. A lot of implicitly cultural-constructivist work has also been advanced in the Anglo-American discussion under the name of Cultural Studies. The name stands for a very comprehensive, multi-layered, and partly contradictory field of studies. Leading proponents of Cultural Studies build on theoretical grounds like poststructuralism, deconstructivism, and Foucault's power / knowledge analyses (see, e.g., Hall 1992, 1997; Hall, ed. 1997; Hall and du Gay 1996; Hall and Gieben 1992; Hall et al. 1992; Bhabha 1994; Giroux 1992, 1993, 1994; Giroux and McLaren 1994). They argue that humans construct their cultural realities in changing and often ambiguous symbolic practices, while at the same time living in contexts of symbolic order that condition and delimit their freedom of construction. Hence there is a tensional field between two poles: On the one hand, we have the quest for practical rationality and sociocultural regularities that allow for societal organization and delimit the structural frames for subjective ways of living and identities; while on the other hand, we have the need for re- / deconstructions in the context of changing cultural practices that exceed current established laws and regularities. This opens two important perspectives for constructivism: first, to take account of the preunderstandings involved in all cultural reconstruction and their implications in the way of discourses of knowledge, power, lived relationships, and unconscious or tabooed aspects of culture[12] (Reich 1998b; Neubert and Reich 2000); and, secondly, to take account of the constructive agencies of subjects that allow for individual creation and cooperative deliberation and lead to sociocultural change and new interpretations of lived realities. In particular, the volumes published by Stuart Hall and his colleagues at Open University in the 1990s (see Hall 1992; Hall, ed. 1997; Hall and du Gay 1996; Hall and Gieben 1992; Hall et al. 1992) clearly show a rich sociocultural constructivist approach.

Pragmatism, too, advances constructivist assumptions in many respects, even if in classical Pragmatism this still goes hand in hand with recurrent naturalistic claims. The philosophy of John Dewey is highly suggestive for constructivism (see Neubert 1998). The same applies to the neo-Pragmatism advocated, e.g., by Richard Rorty (1979, 1989, 1991, 2000, 2003),[13] whose work shows many affinities and commonalities with constructivist approaches, especially with the Cologne program of interactive constructivism.

However, if we were to take a closer look at the constructivist approaches listed above, we would find that so far hardly any of them have tried to tackle its relationship with Pragmatism at all. This lack of exchange is surprising, because trying to come to terms with the implicit connections between constructivism and Pragmatism could have been a great theoretical advantage. Jim Garrison's Pragmatist constructivism, as well as the Cologne program of interactive constructivism, tries to explore this possible gain and to make it explicit.

Of what sort, then, are the supposed affinities between Pragmatism and constructivism? What are the essential commonalities? From the abundance of answers given to these questions in the contributions collected in Part II of this volume—and condensed in the concluding discussion in Part III—I select but five arguments here.

Rejection of Metaphysics

Pragmatism turned its back on metaphysical thinking at a time when metaphysics was still regarded in the mainstream of philosophy as an indispensable and essential foundation. Even today Pragmatism still plays an important role in the critique of traditional world views. Although John Dewey misleadingly used the term metaphysics with regard to certain parts of his own Pragmatist approach, the content of what he had in mind stood in clear opposition to the traditional concept of metaphysics in the history of Western thought. In this sense, his approach was anti-metaphysical in at least the following assumptions: He rejected all absolutist claims to knowledge and all attempts to establish final reasoning without empirical or experimental support. This fundamental break with versions of Platonism or idealism said farewell to a speculative world of thought that avoided involvement in experience, present or past, through which theories can be tested in practical application and consequences in the world of action be critically discerned and assessed. But Pragmatism is also suspicious of materialist approaches, especially in the Marxist tradition, because they, too, at least partially place theoretical expectations *before* all experience, even if these theoretical constructions are often presented as already proven facts of human history. This is not to say that only those experienced affairs that are useful or "practical" in a narrow sense are relevant for Pragmatism. Characters like imagination, vision, and theoretical outlook are highly appreciated by Pragmatists like Dewey. But they prefer to take an anti-dualist position: Humans construct their life-realities by having experiences and responding to experienced problems in their life-worlds, from which they develop hypotheses, theoretical explanations, and imaginative visions. If these are not merely artificial, but real-life problems, the proposed solutions, together with the instruments, tools, procedures, and productive constructions of problem solving, must eventually be tested in practical application. They will have to prove that they really achieve what they intend. This may sometimes imply a "practice of theories" or "theoretical practice," but it must at no point be divorced from the field of life-worldly practices that forms the comprehensive sociocultural context of all theoretical problem solving. For to the degree that the gap between theory and practice grows, the very dualism tends to produce more and more illusions—of which the metaphysical illusions are but one particularly sophisticated version.

Dewey's notion of experience is an important precursor of the constructivist notion of viability: What we theoretically devise must fit the world of *experience* in which we act upon it. The wider the gap between design and reality and the more metaphysically elaborated the dualism between theory and practice, the less chances are that we will end up with scientific disciplines appropriate for practical, everyday life in the cultures of the industrial age in which we all have to live and survive. Present-day constructivists often insist that their interpretation of viability and of the fit between theory and practice necessarily implies an orientation toward resources and possible solutions. This interpretation is well anticipated by Dewey's concept of experience, his idea of instrumental and experimental practices, and his theory of learning through consequences in experience.

## Interactive and Pragmatic Claims Constructed in Discourse

Contrary to some European criticisms recurrent in the twentieth century, Pragmatism cannot be reduced to a mere philosophy of utility. It comprises a comprehensive concept of human life that does not commit the fallacy of construing humans as purely private beings (like in solipsist, monadological, or merely subjectivist theories of knowledge). At the same time, it avoids the fallacy of neglecting that there are practical interests, power claims, uniqueness of cultures, and economic and other demands at stake that condition the particular cultural requirements for societal and individual development. Humans as interactive beings and culture as a dynamic process alike have lost that innocence that only a pure theory or system of belief could secure for them. Especially in his later works, John Dewey's clear and critical view on the development of culture pointed out that culture must be understood as a powerful instrument. Even scientific thought and knowledge must be seen as constructed and situated in the context of culture. In Dewey, the philosophical discourse on culture and knowledge clearly recognizes interactions, or what the late Dewey himself would eventually call transactions.[14] In close acquaintance with the social philosophy of George Herbert Mead, whose work Dewey knew and appreciated, he always developed his theoretical discourse on experience and culture on the basis of human communication and considerations about community. The constructions of reality and versions of world-making that humans develop in succession and juxtaposition are, from Dewey's perspective, always culturally dependant. He considers them discursively from his philosophical outlook based on the appreciation of democracy as the most appropriate way of living, although he critically admits that democratic reality in most respects does not stand up to the democratic ideals. Dewey offers a very complex theory of culture whose examination seems worthwhile for all present-day cultural discourses, be it only to look for connecting points and contrasts. For constructivism, such interconnections promise very fruitful gains and opportunities to profit from the discursive breadth and richness of Dewey's cultural theory. In present-day discourses, many theoretical approaches tend toward high degrees of specialization and reduction of focus to selected parts or segments of an entire research field. Thereby the more comprehensive and generous view on the whole of the field gets lost. But Dewey's approach provides an impressive example for the usefulness of such a generous view.

The Necessity of Democracy

Democracy, for Dewey, implies openness toward others. It means pluralism and openness to development. It must provide for multiple and diverse ways of living. It is always in need of improvement, since it must further individual growth of all its members, i.e., especially the growth of those who have so far been handicapped or discriminated against. In this connection, again, Dewey's theory of culture addresses many problems that are still very relevant today. Constructivism, in particular, can find many important suggestions here, since the question of democracy is an essential question that concerns the very political preconditions of constructivism as a viable approach in postmodern multicultures. Already Dewey's two main criteria for democratic communities—namely "How numerous and varied are the interests which are consciously shared?" and "How full and free is the interplay with other forms of association?" (MW 9:89)—are of continual import for all democracies. They are especially relevant for constructivism, since constructivism, like Pragmatism, presupposes a clear stance as to the answers we give to those two questions: The more numerous and varied the consciously shared interests within a constructivist interpretive community, the more development and growth we may expect. And only if the exchange with other interpretive communities in a pluralist society is as free, complete, and diverse as possible, can constructivists and others further the chances of democratic reconstruction. For Pragmatism and constructivism alike, democracy means not only an external warrant of welfare and worthwhile living together, but represents an inherent precondition of the viability and prosperity of the philosophical approach itself.

## Experimentalism and Instrumentalism

The split between theory and practice has resulted in a dualism between knowledge and action. As Dewey insistently pointed out in his educational writings, this dualism is particularly detrimental with regard to learning. How do humans learn to think? This is an important question for Dewey that has especially important implications if we deal with the problems of truth, warrant of assertions, and validity claims. According to Dewey, these problems must be examined in the cultural context of thought acquired in education. Thought cannot be trained in a vacuum. It is best developed out of experienced activities in which we learn something about ourselves and our world. *Experience*, therefore, became the key concept in Dewey's theory of culture, education, and learning. Learning always begins in actual empirical situations in which we act more or less by trial and error to solve a relevant life-worldly problem. Learning requires continuity within experience. It is most successful when it is the response to a real-life problem within personal experience. But thinking is not the same as immediate experiencing. After a problem has been perceived and defined, its solution requires an instrumental as well as experimental attitude that combines readiness to respond and agency in execution.

The instrumental attitude, for Dewey, implies the functional deployment of tools and aims in the solution of problems. We can hardly find sustainable solutions through mere fantasy and speculation unless we deal with problems of a purely theoretical nature. Otherwise we need effective constructions that work in practical application—intentions, plans of execution, and tools and instruments for collecting data and defining facts. Dewey points to methods for controlling events, e.g., through recollection, observation, reading, and communication as essential powers of instrumental activity that may lead to suggestions, conclusions, explanations, and assertions. You can develop your own thinking only out of your own activities. The truth of your constructions lies in their practical effects and consequences. And, for Dewey, the best way to test theoretical explanations in practice is through experiments. I think that Dewey, by generalizing from the cultural experiences of his age, partly overestimates the nature of the "experimental method" developed in Western science. We today need to develop more multi-layered visions of "experimentalism," e.g., with regard to simulations and theoretical models. Nevertheless, the challenge for constructivism consists in further elaborating the basic constructive idea at the heart of Dewey's experimentalism—namely, that our constructions of reality are not arbitrary, but result from inquiry. And with regard to inquiry, we always have to take experimental conditions into account that lead to specific consequences in practice. Constructivism, like Pragmatism, does not plead for constructions for the sake of constructions, but looks for solutions to problems of human import based on the cultural resources at our disposal. In the face of the diversity of interests at stake in our societies we know that this also always implies questions of power.

Constructive Notion of Learning

Dewey's notion of education and learning aims at growth, which means, among other things, increase of possibilities, flourishing of diversity, life-long learning, and a comprehensive or holistic view on human life. Here, again, the connection with experience is decisive. It implies that we do not conceive of humans as mere spectators, but always as active participants in comprehensive situations. For Dewey, such educational growth can be secured best through inquiry and communication (conversation). Learners explore their environments (including theories) by experimentally inquiring into them and communicating about their findings. Although Dewey thinks that such

growth evolves out of *natural* activities and interactions, he also concedes that all truths and essences, all laws of nature and warranted
assertions, are but products constructed through inquiry. The crucial
turn inherent in his notion of learning—a turn that renders him a
major precursor of constructivist learning theories—consists of the
recognition that only through such inquiries and through their communicative interactions do learners generate the values they share, the
good communities they participate in, and the desirable growth they
experience. Even if Dewey here and there suggests rather naturalist
reasons for this necessity (see, e.g., LW 12:33f.; Garrison 1998b, 67), he
ends up with a straightforward constructivist view that is well up-to-
date and still very relevant for present-day constructivist research on
learning.

PART TWO

# PRAGMATISM AND
# CONSTRUCTIVISM AFTER DEWEY

# FOUR

# DIALOGUE BETWEEN PRAGMATISM AND CONSTRUCTIVISM IN HISTORICAL PERSPECTIVE

Kenneth W. Stikkers

The history of social constructivist thinking could be written in various ways. One might begin with the suggestions of the ancient Sophists: that knowledge claims are but functions of power. In the modern period constructivism begins with David Hume's assertion that the synthesis of "immediate, vivid, forceful, and distinct" sense impressions is accomplished through habit and custom. One might then examine Immanuel Kant's response to Hume and his attempt to account transcendentally for the lawfulness of the synthesis of perceptions. Next one might consider Hegel's efforts to historicize the Kantian categories of understanding, and one would likely identify Karl Marx and Friedrich Engels's *The German Ideology*, following Hegel, as the first text presenting anything resembling a coherent, systematic theory of social constructivism, grounded in Marx's assertion that knowledge claims are functions of economic structures and especially class interests. Surely one would want to note important contributions by Wilhelm Dilthey and Emile Durkheim and to include a major chapter on the sociology of knowledge, put forward by Wilhelm Jerusalem, Max Scheler, and Karl Mannheim and greatly influenced by Marx, Dilthey, and Durkheim, among others.

The aim of this chapter is to examine the important role played by American Pragmatism, especially Charles Sanders Peirce and William James, in the development of the sociology of knowledge and to see what lessons we might learn from such an historical investigation for social constructivist thought today. While our concern will be mainly with William James, let us begin, though, with some considerations of Charles Peirce.

Peirce already suggested, prior to Dilthey and Durkheim and without any apparent benefit from the insights of Marx's *German Ideology*, that the forms of human knowing are fundamentally the forms of social life, without reducing the latter, as did Marx, to the forms of *economic* life. What Peirce termed "the social impulse," viz., the desire to reconcile our personal beliefs with those of our neighbors, leads us to believe in "the independently Real." "Inevitably we find that others hold views different from ours, and sooner or later the strength of our tenacity [in clinging to habituated beliefs] is worn away. Unless we make ourselves hermits, we shall necessarily influence each other's opinion; so that the problem becomes how to fixate belief, not in the individual merely, but in the community" (Peirce 1986, 250). That others contradict us is a major source of what Peirce termed "irritation," which in turn is the impetus to inquiry. Inquiry is thus the quest for stable community, even more than it is a quest for disinterested knowledge, but communities look to the future: they seek to secure themselves not just for their present members but for innumerable generations to come. From this desire of a community to enjoy an indefinite future is borne, by Peirce's account, the idea of the "independently Real," which he defines as "that whose characters are independent of what anybody may think them to be" (271).

In another passage, Peirce offers his well-known definitions of "truth" and "reality" and his description of them as grounded in "the social impulse": "Different minds set out with most antagonistic views, but the progress of investigation carries them by a force out-side themselves to one and the same conclusion. This activity of thought by which we are carried, not where we wish, but to a fore-ordained goal, is like the operation of destiny. No modification of the point of view taken, no relation of other facts for study, no natural bent of mind even, can enable a man to escape the predestined opin-ion of truth and reality. The opinion which is fated to be ultimately agreed to by all who investigate is what we mean by the truth, and the object represented in this opinion is the real. That is the way I would explain reality" (274).

Such descriptions appear to identify independent reality, or "the independently Real," with objective reality, viz., what something sup-posedly is in the absence of any positioned, perceiving subject, a "God's eye view" or a "view from nowhere." But Peirce clearly indi-cates that such is not what he means. The first claim, that "the inde-pendently Real" is "that whose characters are independent of what anybody may think them to be," is qualified thusly: "reality is inde-pendent, not necessarily of [human] thought in general, but only of what you or I or any finite number of men may think about it." Moreover, "reality," viz., "the object of the opinion which is fated to be ultimately agreed to by all who investigate"—that object, that real-ity, Peirce claims, "depends on what that opinion is" (274). Thus, in-quiry, viz., the process whereby the social impulse leads inquirers to Truth, i.e., agreement, is not merely a process whereby the object of truth, viz., reality, gets reported and represented ever more accu-rately, but plays a vital role in the very constitution of the Real.

In light of the above important clarifications, then, Peirce's de-scription of truth as "the opinion which is *fated* to be ultimately agreed to by all who investigate," must be read as a psychological, or phenomenological, and not a metaphysical claim: the community of inquirers, animated by "the social impulse," experiences the agree-ment, the truth, that it seeks, and at which it might arrive, *as* fated. As Peirce says, "all the followers of science are animated by a cheerful hope that the processes of investigation, if only pushed enough, will give one certain solution to each question to which they apply it"

(273): our longing to secure an unlimited community for an indefinite future leads us to want *the* correct answer, a truth that serves not just me or any limited members of a community in the present, but all possible members for all time. Peirce summarizes the interrelationship of reality and community in this way: "The real, then, is that which, sooner or later, information and reasoning would finally result in, and which is therefore independent of the vagaries of me and you. Thus the very origin of the conception [of reality] involves the notion of a COMMUNITY, without definite limits, and capable of an indefinite increase of knowledge. . . . What anything real is, is what it may finally come to be known to be in the ideal state of complete information, so that reality depends on the ultimate decision [opinion?] of the community. . . . Reality [itself, not just truth] consists in the agreements that the whole community would eventually come to" (Peirce 1984, 239, 241, 252).

Thus we can see already in the Pragmatism of Peirce elements of a social constructivist metaphysics: "reality" is borne of the "social impulse" and is not merely represented but co-constituted through the "decisions," the opinions, the interpretations, of an evolving community.

Ironically, though, it was not Peirce or Dewey or Mead, but the Pragmatist with the least developed social theory, viz., William James, who played the greatest role in the development of the sociology of knowledge. James's influence on German thought was largely through the Austrian thinker Wilhelm Jerusalem. It is uncertain how James and Jerusalem came into contact with each other. Jerusalem was then a gymnasium teacher in Vienna and later became Professor of Philosophy at the university there. He stumbled onto James as an ally against transcendental philosophy and as a supporter of his belief that epistemology and logic are grounded in social psychology. They began a warm and sympathetic correspondence by 1900, in which James shared his evolving thoughts on Pragmatism and radical empiricism, and Jerusalem identified connections between these doctrines and developments in German-speaking Europe (Perry 1935, II: 580). In 1908 Jerusalem published a German translation of James's

*Pragmatism* (Jerusalem 1908), and in the "Vorwort" he praised James lavishly and declared himself a Pragmatist, but then mildly criticized James for ignoring the social conditions of human knowing, for ignoring how the forms of social life shape the empirical consequences of ideas in practical experience and the manner by which ideas are tested for their "truth." A year later (1909), upon receiving James's *A Pluralistic Universe*, Jerusalem wrote to James, again lavishing praise upon his newest volume but again criticizing him for failing to consider the relationship between cognitive structures by which we constitute a plurality of world realities and forms of social life. Jerusalem wrote (in English):

> What has struck me most is the compenetration and interpretation [interpenetration?] of our mental events (we say in German *"Erlebnisse"*) and [Bergson's] conception of "pure drives."
>
> To place myself inside the events has been the main purpose of my psychology of knowledge. Not only the sensational place of events but truly the process of thinking gets another aspect when considered from within.
>
> That Life exceeds Logic, as you formulate it, that is one of my fundamental convictions.
>
> I hope to send you in a few weeks, an article where the outlines of my future sociology of knowledge are given. I am very eager to hear what you think of this new way.[1]

The above is, I believe, the earliest appearance of the term "sociology of knowledge" in English, and the article Jerusalem promised to send was his essay "Soziologie des Erkenntnis," published in *Die Zukunft* (May) (Jerusalem 1909). What is significant here is that the impetus behind this seminal work in social constructivism was Jerusalem's desire to make James's Pragmatism and pluralism more complete: James, in Jerusalem's judgment, had offered an excellent psychological account of cognition, but it needed to be supplemented by an equally thoroughgoing sociology.

James died the following year, in 1910, and it is unclear if he ever received and read Jerusalem's article. Little attention was paid to it until Max Scheler recognized its significance and republished it as the lead essay in the first issue of the new journal he founded and edited, *Kölner Vierteljahrshefte für Sozialwissenschaften*, in 1921. Ongoing dialogue between Jerusalem and Scheler (Scheler 1963a, 27–35, 1963b, 327–30; Jerusalem 1921, 28–34), until the former's death in 1923, help to lay the foundation for the sociology of knowledge as a recognized discipline.

Scheler followed Jerusalem's article with his own, more extensive essay on the sociology of knowledge, "Probleme einer Soziologie des Wissens," which originally appeared as the introductory essay to the anthology *Versuche zu einer Soziologie des Wissens* (1924).[2] Two years later (1926) Scheler published his commentary on American Pragmatism, "Erkenntnis und Arbeit" (Scheler 1980, 191–382), and he claimed that the two articles ought to be read together as a "propaedeutic" to his metaphysics (12), the incomplete fragments for which were published posthumously only in 1979 as *Erkenntnislehre und Metaphysik* (Scheler 1979). But before discussing how Scheler saw Pragmatism and the sociology of knowledge together as the basis for his reconstruction of metaphysics, let us assess Scheler's familiarity with American Pragmatism: what were his main sources of information regarding it?

In "Erkenntnis und Arbeit" Scheler reported that, according to James, it was Peirce who first coined the term "Pragmatism" in his 1878 article "How to Make Our Ideas Clear" in *Popular Science Monthly*, and it is Pragmatism as presented in that article that Scheler takes as most representative of that doctrine and that he purports to discuss. That Scheler consistently misspells Peirce's name as "Pierce" led Herbert Spiegelberg to conclude that Scheler did not read Peirce firsthand but that his knowledge of him came largely from James's *Pragmatism* (Spiegelberg 1956, 183–84). Such a conclusion is too hasty—Scheler is notorious for errors of that sort. But the fact that Scheler, as we shall see, attributes to Peirce James's own understanding of Pragmatism, as presented in James's aforementioned work, including claims that Peirce explicitly rejected, make it likely that Spiegelberg's judgment is correct.

Scheler's references to very specific ideas in James's *Pragmatism* make it equally likely that he did indeed read that text firsthand, but it is unclear how carefully or completely. Indeed, Scheler's criticisms of Pragmatism in "Erkenntnis und Arbeit," especially that Pragmatism reduces all knowledge to that of practical effects and ignores religious knowledge of salvation, suggest that he did not read James's work very carefully and that he did not read at least its concluding chapter on "Pragmatism and Religion." Specific references to and quotations from English editions of James's *Varieties of Religious Experience* (Scheler 1972a, 23–24, 1954a, 286, 324fn.) and *A Pluralistic Universe* (Scheler 1972a, 24–25) clearly indicate Scheler's firsthand reading of those works, and occasional references to James's *Psychology* (James 1981; Scheler 1980, 337) and "The Moral Equivalent of War," suggest that Scheler's familiarity with these works may also have been direct. Other Pragmatists to whom Scheler passingly refers are John Dewey (Scheler 1980, 199, 458) and F. C. S. Schiller (Schiller 1912; Scheler 1980, 212, 219, 228, 455), James's British disciple, who preferred "humanism" for his brand of Pragmatism. However, my responses to some of Scheler's criticisms of Pragmatism question how carefully or completely he read any of Pragmatism's primary texts.

Scheler's principal source of information about Pragmatism apparently was Jerusalem, but he also derived much valuable information about it from his close acquaintance Emile Boutroux. Boutroux (1911) was the main disseminator of James's philosophy in France: he wrote, in French, in 1911, the first book-length commentary on James in any language,[3] which Scheler read in German translation (1912)[4] and to which he refers several times (Scheler 1980, 212fn, 224 fn). Boutroux and James discussed Pragmatism extensively in their correspondence, during a meeting in London, and while Boutroux was a visiting professor at Harvard University in 1910, the year of James's death (Perry 1935, II: 560–69).

We might mention also the possible influences of Rudolf Eucken and Hugo Muensterberg. Eucken, a neo-Kantian, directed Scheler's dissertation. James corresponded with him several times and cited him occasionally in his writings. Muensterberg in 1892, upon James's strong recommendation, assumed James's position at Harvard University as Professor of Psychology and Director of Psychological Research, after James moved to Philosophy, where he was to develop his theories of Pragmatism and radical empiricism. Muensterberg frequently returned to Germany and became a close acquaintance of Scheler. It is likely that Scheler learned something about Pragmatism, and about James in particular, through Eucken and Muensterberg, although there is no tangible evidence of this. It is worth noting, too, that James and Scheler corresponded with over fifty persons in common.

Seemingly, then, the only primary works of American Pragmatism that we can confidently say Scheler read firsthand were James's *Pragmatism*, in Jerusalem's German translation, and *Varieties of Religious Experience*; virtually all his information about Peirce seems to have come from the former work. The rest of his information about Pragmatism—almost exclusively James's—apparently came from Jerusalem, Boutroux, and other common acquaintances and from popular notions of that doctrine. Such limited sources of information help to explain Scheler's misrepresentation of Pragmatism, especially Peirce's.

Let us briefly delineate Scheler's main criticisms of Pragmatism. First, while Pragmatism does much in its functionalization of knowledge to overcome representationalism, it did not, in Scheler's judgment, go far enough. Pragmatism rejects traditional representational epistemologies, which conceive knowledge as a mental copy of some objective reality, but then introduces its own variation: knowledge as a correlation between thought and practical consequences, both actual and possible, empirically discerned. Second, Pragmatism misunderstands the relationship between knowledge and action by assuming that, because psychomotor processes accompany sense perception, the former is the necessary condition for the latter. Scheler would claim the relationship to be reciprocal. Third, this is Pragmatism's most serious error: it excludes knowledge of essences and salvation, reducing all knowledge to inductive knowledge of practical effects. We will return to this criticism later. And fourth, the fundamental principle of Pragmatist logic—viz., that a proposition is true if it functions to bring about consequences that are useful or life-enhancing—is false, because such a principle does not adequately explain the multiplicity of meanings generated by an empirically singular statement, i.e., does not adequately account for context.

Although there may be some validity in his criticisms of it, Scheler, on the whole, severely misunderstands American Pragmatism and reads it much too narrowly, and because his information on that philosophical school was quite limited and the primary texts he consulted too few, he projected onto it many false popular notions. Let me make just three points in this regard.

First, it is clear that Scheler was unfamiliar with the more fully developed theories of consciousness advanced by the American Pragmatists to complement their various Pragmatisms, especially James's "radical empiricism," and their rooting of such theories in Darwinian biology. Thus Scheler was altogether wrong in accusing Pragmatism of ignoring the vital roots of sensation and imagination, and he mistakenly read into Pragmatism much of traditional empiricism's reduction of experience to simple sensations and consequently accused it of reducing productive imagination merely to the reorganization of such sensations.

Second, throughout his discussion of it, Scheler explains Pragmatism in terms of "work" (*Arbeit*), apparently accepting a popular notion of Pragmatism as a doctrine holding that "whatever ideas work are true." Thus Scheler connects Pragmatism with both the "spirit of capitalism," as described by Max Weber, and Marxism: all three, he suggests, are guilty of forgetting knowledge of essences and of salvation, reducing all knowledge to that of practical effects. Only rarely did any of the American Pragmatists themselves connect knowledge with "work."

Third, Scheler repeatedly refers to the Pragmatist "theory of truth," even when speaking of Peirce. Peirce, however, did not include his own theory of truth within his Pragmatism. Rather, for Peirce, Pragmatism was strictly a method, without any metaphysical or epistemological commitments, and he criticized James for extending Pragmatism into a theory of truth. For Peirce, Pragmatism was a "method of ascertaining the meanings of hard words and of abstract concepts" by examining the sensible, practical effects of such words and concepts (Peirce 1972, 464). "Consider what effects, that might conceivably have practical bearings, we conceive the object of our conception to have. Then, our conception of these effects is the whole of our conception of the object" (402).[5]

In short, Scheler attributes to Peirce, whom he takes to be most representative of Pragmatism, a notion of that doctrine that Peirce explicitly rejected. These three points alone are sufficient to establish that Scheler's only familiarity with Peirce was secondhand, through James, but also indicate how badly Scheler misunderstood Pragmatism generally.

I recount Scheler's misreading of Pragmatism and his misguided criticisms of it, though, because his essay "Erkenntnis und Arbeit," as Hans Joas (1993, 81, 106) notes, was taken unfortunately as *the* authoritative source on American Pragmatism for much of German philosophy and sociology. For example, it was a main source for the early Frankfurt School, especially Horkheimer and Adorno, and it appears to be a source for Heidegger's caricature and criticism of Pragmatism. Moreover, Scheler's criticism of Pragmatism, as expressed in "Erkenntnis und Arbeit," is a major reason German thinkers who ought to have taken broader interest in Pragmatism, e.g., Habermas, did not do so.

Scheler's misreading and misguided criticisms of Pragmatism, however, should not overshadow his positive assessments and productive appropriations of it, especially James's. Perhaps because Scheler, in "Erkenntnis und Arbeit," presented his criticisms of Pragmatism first, many readers never bothered to read Scheler's very positive remarks regarding it later in that essay, and critical theory in Germany may have taken a very different direction if Scheler had placed his praise for American Pragmatism before his criticisms. In several places Scheler describes James as a "genius," and in a 1913 letter to Edmund Husserl, requesting a letter of recommendation,

Scheler asks Husserl to make special mention of his relationship to the Pragmatists, especially as allies against neo-Hegelianism.[6]

Positively—viz., within what Scheler calls the "relative truth of Pragmatism"—he credits Pragmatism with disclosing the fundamentally practical basis of knowledge: our relationship to the world is primarily practical, not theoretical, and knowledge is never merely the objective, disinterested collection of data but always expressive of definite interests of the organism. Natural science is thus practically conditioned: what it counts as knowledge is largely determined by prevailing values and interests, presently those of control and domination, what Scheler in his *Ressentiment* (1972b, 137) terms the "ethos of industrialism"—contrary to scientists' claims to value neutrality. Pragmatism rejects positive science's formal-mechanical models of nature because such models presuppose absolute notions of space, time, and motion—all of which are relative to the organism and its interests—as part of technology's effort to dominate nature.

Pragmatism's account of human knowing as a fundamentally practical relationship to the world thus offered, in Scheler's judgment, the first genuinely novel alternative to rationalist and traditional empiricist epistemologies. Knowledge lies, as James described, neither in the apprehension of ideas imagined to exist prior to our experience of the world (what James termed *"ideae ante res"*) nor in the abstracting of ideas from experience (*ideae post res*). Rather, knowledge is a function of our dynamic, creative interaction with the world: ideas do not merely report, mirror, or represent the world but emerge from our practical engagement in the world of things and function instrumentally to transform the world (*ideae cum rebus*) (James 1975, 104–06).[7] Pragmatism thus *functionalizes* knowledge: the meaning of an idea is its actual or possible practical uses for the organism, and hence relative to the organism's interests and preferences. This notion of the functionalization of knowledge Scheler incorporated into his epistemology and is central to his sociology of knowledge: knowledge, for him, is the functionalization of drive-rooted interests.

Indeed, what Scheler took as the central insight of Pragmatism, viz., the functionalization of essences, and its understanding of ideas and concepts as instruments by which organisms navigate their world, was invaluable to Scheler in at least three ways. First, from the time of his 1897 dissertation, Scheler had attempted to articulate a notion of "value" that escaped Platonism, i.e., that ascribed to "value" some ontological status that did not smack of the Platonic forms. In that work already he wrote: "As to the question, 'What is value?' I submit the following: insofar as the word 'is' in this question refers to existence (and not only to a mere copula), a value 'is' not at all. The concept of value does not allow any more of definition than the concept of being" (Scheler 1971, 98). And again in his *Formalismus in der Ethik* he insisted that values enjoy no ontological status independent from concrete acts of preferring: values "ride on the back" of such acts (Scheler 1954b, 216). Nonetheless, various writers identified Scheler with Platonism, most notably Martin Heidegger. Already in *Sein und Zeit*, Heidegger included Scheler in his generic criticism and rejection of value theory, and in his 1947 volume on Plato, Heidegger claims all notions of value to be derivative of the Platonic *"agathon."* Pragmatism helped Scheler to rescue his own theory of value from such criticisms: values—indeed, all "essences"—reside ontologically, come into being, are "functionalized," solely in concrete human acts. At the time of his death Scheler had begun rewriting his *Ethics*, and I am confident that the new edition would have borne the marks of Pragmatism's influence upon him.

Second, Pragmatism, together with the sociology of knowledge, provided, for Scheler, important correctives to phenomenological method. Much as Jerusalem thought that James's Pragmatism needed to be supplemented by a sociology of knowledge, so Scheler suggested that phenomenology needed to be so supplemented. Because, according to Pragmatism, consciousness is always that of a living organism already actively engaged in a world of practical affairs, what is "given," what is presented, in experience, the *"es gibt,"* must always be phenomenologically grasped in terms of how it is *taken* up into concrete practical acts: i.e., the essences that phenomenology aims to disclose must be grasped functionally. Moreover, "eidetic" structures of consciousness are embodied in concrete cultural practices and thus need to be described as the essential forms of social life. That is to say, there is, for Scheler, no universal form of life-world: rather the "life-world" is always that of a particular, historically situated social group. For similar reasons Heidegger and Gadamer would suggest, some years after Scheler, that phenomenology would need to give way to hermeneutics.

Third, to Scheler, Pragmatism, along with the sociology of knowledge, was vital for the reconstruction of metaphysics, which Scheler preferred to call "metabiology," because he believed that metaphysical concepts ought to express the world reality of a live creature rather than the forms of a dead mechanism. Pragmatism showed how metaphysical concepts functioned as the instruments of a living organism for the negotiation of its world and for dealing with the world's resistances to the organism's vital impulses. The sociology of knowledge, informed by Pragmatism, helps to reconstruct, and hence to restore, metaphysics in at least two ways. First, it demonstrates how metaphysical concepts are the forms of evolving cultural life. Pragmatism and sociology together rescued metaphysics from any form of absolutism, including the transcendental sort, which hailed from the neo-Kantian schools of the day, for whom Eucken was the leading spokesperson. Second, the sociology of knowledge provides the antidote to what Scheler took to be the greatest enemy of metaphysics: historicism, such as that put forward by various Marxists of his day; the relativism entailed in historicism rendered social critique and dialogue across cultures impossible. Scheler embraced Marx's key insights into the social nature of human cognition but rejected the reductionist tendencies in Marxist thought that made "history" a *Ding an sich*: i.e., he rejected theories that reduced reality to nothing other than social constructs. This second point is ironic because later sociologies of knowledge, such as those of Karl Mannheim, Peter Berger, and Thomas Luckmann, embraced relativist historicism, while Scheler saw the former as a strategy for overcoming the latter. The way to overcome relativist historicism, and hence to make cross-cultural dialogue possible, is, Scheler claimed, not to juxtapose it to some ahistorical absolutism, e.g., a transcendental one, but to historicize historicism itself. In this regard, Scheler claimed himself to be a more thoroughgoing Marxist than the Marxists of his day. One must examine how the historicist schools are themselves historically constituted. In the wake of Foucault, Scheler's call and challenge might mean that what is needed today is an archaeology of archaeological method and a genealogy of genealogical analyses. Scheler's approach to the sociology of knowledge, then, does not lead to cultural, historical relativism, thereby rendering cultural critique and cross-cultural dialogue impossible, but rather propels social groups to engage in self- and mutual criticism and to enter into dialogue, i.e., it propels them to move beyond their historical presuppositions.[8] As with Pragmatism, "objectivity" in judgment emerges intersubjectively as an outcome of inquiry and dialogue: it is no standpoint that one presumes to secure at the start. Pragmatism and the sociology of knowledge were central components in Scheler's vision of a "world-age of adjustment," wherein, he predicted, we would witness the coming together of the world's cultures to create a new cosmopolitanism, while simultaneously preserving much of their distinct identities. One thus finds in Scheler's sociology of knowledge, informed by American Pragmatism, already the seeds for so much of present-day constructivism, while avoiding the pitfalls of some of its directions.

The main point that the above account has attempted to establish is simply that one of the early schools of social constructivist theory, viz., the sociology of knowledge, emerged in close connection with American Pragmatism, especially through the figures of Wilhelm Jerusalem and Max Scheler. Let us now conclude by noting three routes by which the sociology of knowledge made its way into American philosophical and sociological circles, although never on a very large scale. The first in America to take interest in Scheler's sociology of knowledge were the Pragmatist sociologists at the University of Chicago—W. Thomas, Robert Park, Charles Cooley, George Herbert Mead, and especially Albion Small—apparently without realizing the Pragmatist influences behind it. Small wrote reviews for the *American*

*Journal of Sociology* of two works edited by Scheler, the inaugural issue of the *Kölner Vierteljahrshefte für Sozialwissenschaften,* containing Jerusalem's seminal essay, and *Versuche zu einer Soziologie des Wissens,* containing Scheler's own essay. Small found these works to be a breath of fresh air for American sociology, in contrast to the positivism that had come to dominate it by that time, viz., the 1920s. He wrote of the latter work:

> This book deserves to rank and to function among the principle orientation-monuments for all sociologists. It affords an outlook for the widest survey of the area of the adventure to which sociological pioneering is committed. . . . While it is true that sociology must deal with "pauperism, prostitution, and plumbing," it is all the more true that sociology must take part in explaining the highest, widest, and deepest reaches of the human mind. No previous methodological treatise has done as much to impress this fact as the volume before us. . . .
>
> Obviously the methodology thus contemplated is in direct antithesis with the prevailing sociological tendencies in the United States. Unless we are willing, however, to assume that wisdom begins and ends with us, here is a challenge which we cannot afford to decline. Perhaps the synthesis next in order is perception that all positive or "scientific" knowledge, as we call it, must eventually recognize its accountability to all the relativities that a valid epistemology discovers.
>
> At all events, this book opens up vistas of social relations compared with which our sociological searchings thus far have been parochial (Small 1925–26, 262–64, 1921, 92–94).

We quote this lengthy passage to demonstrate the Pragmatic sociologists' enthusiastic reception of the sociology of knowledge. When Scheler died suddenly of a heart attack in 1928, in his coat pocket were boat and train tickets to Chicago, apparently for him to lecture at the University of Chicago. It remains a mystery who had invited him.

A second route by which Scheler's sociology of knowledge made its way to America was through the American sociologist Howard Becker, who, while a student in Germany, was drawn to Scheler through his interest in the role of sympathy in social relations (Becker

1927–28, 637–42, 1931, 58–68) and attended Scheler's lectures, transcribing and then later translating them, only one of which was published. Also in Scheler's coat pocket at the time of his death was a notebook containing Becker's name and address in the United States (Wisconsin).[9] Following his return to America, Becker went on to a distinguished career as Professor of Sociology at the University of Wisconsin, and he included substantial chapters on Scheler and the sociology of knowledge in *Contemporary Social Theory* (Dahlke 1940, 64–89) and *Social Thought from Lore to Science* (Becker and Barnes 1952, 906–13; Becker and Dahlke 1942, 309–22), both widely used texts in American sociology for many years. Becker's most famous student, C. Wright Mills, took interest in the relationship between American Pragmatism and the sociology of knowledge, publishing several articles on it[10] and noting in his "Bibliographical Appendix" to *Contemporary Social Theory*, "Besides the French and German traditions . . . the literature of American Pragmatism is replete with unexploited suggestions for sociology of knowledge" (Mills 1940b, 892). Mills noted how Scheler was one of the few scholars who had picked up on these suggestions.

Thirdly, philosopher Paul Schilpp, in 1926 and 1927, published three articles on Scheler's sociology of knowledge in American philosophy journals (Schilpp 1926, 434–46, 1927a, 101–20, 1927b, 624–33). Like the Chicago Pragmatists, Schilpp used Scheler's sociology of knowledge to criticize mainstream American positivist sociology for its lack of a philosophy of culture. In 1928 Scheler accepted him as one of his first students at the University of Frankfurt, to which he was then still in the process of moving. Schilpp discovered only upon his arrival by boat in Germany that Scheler had just died, and he authored an obituary article on Scheler for *The Philosophical Review* (Schilpp 1929, 547–88). In 1938, after his return to America, Schilpp founded the distinguished Library of Living Philosophers, the subject of whose first volume was John Dewey. After several years at Northwestern University, Schilpp moved to this author's present institution, Southern Illinois University, Carbondale, bringing the Library with him. Here he worked until his death in 1993 and established a tradition of ongoing interest in Scheler's thought, in dialogue with American philosophy. Here at Southern Illinois University, Carbondale, which presently also houses the Center for Dewey Studies, thus continues the exciting and productive exchange between American Pragmatism and German phenomenology and social theory that was begun by William James, Wilhelm Jerusalem, Max Scheler, and others, now more than a hundred years ago.

# FIVE

# DEWEY'S CONSTRUCTIVISM: FROM THE REFLEX ARC CONCEPT TO SOCIAL CONSTRUCTIVISM

Jim Garrison

Thinking is preeminently an art; knowledge and propositions which are the products of thinking are works of art, as much so as statuary and symphonies (LW 1:283).

Dewey carefully distinguishes metaphysical existence from logical essences. This is an immensely important distinction for understanding Dewey's constructivism, because, while existence is given, essences are constructed, or, as I prefer to say, created. Dewey is a neo-Darwinian, and in a Darwinian universe every existence evolves; everything is in process; every individual "thing" is really an event. In Dewey's philosophy, existence or "nature is viewed as consisting of events rather than substances, it is characterized by *histories*" (LW 1:5–6). For him, natural events have no *antecedent* essences; instead, essences emerge as the constructed consequences of the processes of inquiry.

Logical essences or objects of knowledge are constructed. For Dewey, "Essence is never existence, and yet it is the essence, the distilled import of existence: the significant thing about it, its intellectual voucher" (LW 1:144). The subject matter of metaphysics is existence. The subject matter of inquiry and its logic is essence and identity. Evolving essences emerge as the contingent construction of culturally dependent inquiry.

So, one might ask, what connects existence to essence? Dewey's answer is straightforward: "There is a natural bridge that joins the gap between existence and essence; namely communication, language, discourse" (LW 1:133). Meanings emerge in human linguistic transactions while essences emerge in the construction of logical judgments during inquiry. Dewey insists, "Essence . . . is but a pronounced instance of meaning; to be partial, and to assign *a* meaning to a thing as *the* meaning is but to evince human subjection to bias" (LW 1:144).

Existence is like the event of natural grapes on the vine. Linguistic meanings are like the press that wrings juice from the grapes. Logical essences, the product of inquiry, are like distilled wine, the essence of the grape for our purposes. All meanings and essences, including the essence of human being, are the contingent products of constructive processes themselves subject to human need, desire, and purpose.

Dewey's reconstruction of Western metaphysics does for philosophy what Darwin did for biology. A species is the ultimate ontological subject of classical biology and classical metaphysics. The word "species" is also the Latin for the Greek word for essence—*eidos*. Dewey did for all essences what Darwin did for species. In "The Influence of Darwinism on Philosophy" (MW 4:3–14), Dewey concludes that for classical, and much of modern, philosophy, "The conception of ειδος, species, a fixed form and final cause, was the central principle of knowledge as well as of nature. Upon it rested the logic of science" (MW 4:6). Classical metaphysics, like classical biology, assumes that the telos of inquiry is knowledge of eternal, immutable essences. For Dewey, essences are the contingent logical constructions of inquiry, not antecedently existing necessary ontological givens.

Estimates are that 99 percent of all species that have ever existed are now extinct (Parker 1992). Dewey's neo-Darwinian insight is to realize that what holds for biological forms or essences also holds for linguistic meanings and logical forms. Dewey insists that "even the solid earth mountains, the emblems of constancy, appear and disappear like the clouds. . . . A thing may endure . . . and yet not be everlasting; it will crumble before the gnawing tooth of time, as it exceeds a certain measure. Every existence is an event" (LW 1:63). Human beings must construct enduringly useful meanings and essences from the flux of events, or soon become extinct. If we want to live well, we must create beauty together in an ethical and caring community.

For Dewey, individual events have no *antecedent* fixed meanings or essences; instead, they emerge as the constructed *consequence* of linguistic and logical transactions involving human beings and the rest of nature: "Empirical method finds and points to the operation of choice. . . . Thus it protects us from conversion of eventual functions into the antecedent existence: a conversion that may be said to be *the* philosophic fallacy" (LW 1:34; ital. in orig.).

We commit the philosophic fallacy whenever we assume that the contingent and constructed products of language or inquiry necessarily exist antecedent to the process that created them. Choices, including selective attention, selection of materials, and selection of operations to perform upon them are all part of creative inquiry.

### The Process of Functionally "Constituting" a Stimulus

Dewey's 1896 paper "The Reflex Arc Concept in Psychology" (EW 5:96–109), which sets forth the functionalism associated with the Chicago School of psychology, sociology, and philosophy, prefigures his constructivism. The standard version of the reflex arc concept assumes a passive agent that some "external" stimulus must prod to action. For Dewey, the live organism is always already active by virtue of being alive. Therefore, he thought, "we begin not with a sensory stimulus, but with a sensori-motor co-ordination" (EW 5:97–98). The real beginning is a functional coordination. It is a dynamic *equilibrium* or homeostasis, without which no organic creature can live. The active motor responses, including acts of attention, discrimination, and individuation, depart from a prior coordination of activity and function to restore coordination to the transaction.

The crucial realization is that a stimulus is the consequence of transactional processes involving the agent as a participant, and not an antecedent condition. Indeed, until the agent attends to, selects, and actively responds to aspects of its surroundings, nothing is a "stimulus" for that creature. Dewey insists that "it is the motor response or attention which constitutes that, which finally becomes the stimulus to another act" (EW 5:101–02). The agent's actions give form to an otherwise senseless flux of sensations and, thereby, "constitute" a stimulus.

Dewey reconstructs the reflex arc concept into an organic circle of functional coordination of the agent's transactions. Dewey concludes: "It is the co-ordination which unifies that which the reflex arc concept gives us only in disjointed fragments. It is the circuit within which fall distinctions of stimulus and response as functional phases" (EW 5:109). Stimulus and response are merely phases or subfunctions of a single functional unity of coordination. Dewey further states: "What we have is a circuit, not an arc or broken segment of a circle. This circuit is more truly termed organic than reflex, because the motor response determines the stimulus, just as truly as sensory stimulus determines movement. Indeed, the movement is only for the sake of determining the stimulus, of fixing what kind of a stimulus it is, of interpreting it" (EW 5:102).

The operations involved in the motor response "constitute," or construct, the stimulus that redirects and guides activity. What the stimulus is and what the response is emerge in the transaction. Neither is existentially given; both are constructed. Dewey boldly affirms, "The fact is that stimulus and response are not distinctions of existence, but teleological distinctions, that is, distinctions of function, or part played, with reference to reaching or maintaining an end" (EW 5:104). Stimulus and response are emergent subfunctions of a single functional coordination of the agent's transactions with other natural events.

*Logic, Rationality, and the Construction of Means, Ends,*
*and Essences from an Existentially Given Situation*

Having described language as a bridge between existence and essence, I wish to begin on the latter side by first looking at the logical construction of essences and truth. Dewey's instrumentalist rationality has a distinct character that is quite different from the ideals of pure rationality that dominate modern epistemology. Dewey writes, "Rationality is an affair of the relation of *means and consequences*, not of fixed first principles as ultimate premises or as contents of what the Neo-scholastics call *criteriology*" (LW 12:17). He eschews all efforts to find eternal, immutable, or supernal rational foundations. Dewey notes, "As a general term, 'instrumental' stands for the relation of *means-consequence*, as the basic category for interpretation of logical forms" (LW 12:22 fn.; ital. in. orig.). Natural events only gain meaning when used as means to bring about consequences. Once we have meanings we are ready to engage in rational inquiry and the construction of judgment; that is, the working out of means-consequence relations. The statement: "There is an angry eight-meters-tall gorilla crouching in the corner of this room about to charge" is meaningful, but, hopefully, inquiry will quickly judge it false.

Unlike modern champions of instrumentalism, means often constitute ends for Dewey, just as bricks, mortar, and artisanship constitute the building upon completion. The experienced builder may tell what kinds of materials and tools workers used on the job and can surely evaluate the quality of the artist who executed the work, as well as the architect's design. Dewey described the organic relations thus: "The connection of means-consequences is never one of bare succession in time. . . . There is a deposit at each stage and point entering cumulatively and constitutively into the outcome. A genuine instrumentality *for* is always an organ *of* an end" (LW 1:276; ital. in orig.). Just as with stimulus and response, means and ends are always organic subfunctions of a single functional coordination. They *emerge* together in the agent's effort to coordinate some indeterminate situation. Dewey insists on "the thoroughly reciprocal character of means and end in the practical judgment" (MW 8:37). Achieving functional coordination of some complex dysfunctional situation is a constructive process that resembles the constitution of a stimulus by the agent's responses.

Dewey speaks of intentional ideal "ends-in-view" that serve to guide inquiry at every stage of the process; such "ends" are means to their own realization; for example, blueprints for constructing a building. We may judge the value of present means by an ideal end-in-view, which functions to direct present action as a means to future consequences. Ends-in-view perform logical functions by providing tentative consequences for which the inquirer must seek means to obtain. Ends-in-view are constantly adjustable and usually evolve as the inquiry unfolds; only a bad builder refuses to modify her plans as she acquires contextual knowledge of materials, structure, design flaws, etc. At any point in the process of functionally coordinating means and consequences, we might decide that what we have thus far created is more valuable than our original end-in-view and decide to stop, satisfied.

We should not confuse the logically ideal end-in-view with the existential end actually obtained. While we may make an abstract and analytical logical distinction between means and ends, the final existential situation is simply whatever it is. Dewey insists that "the difference between means and end is analytic, formal, not material and chronologic" (LW 1:280). It is a distinction of the *inquirer's* language or logic to say what in some actual existential situation are means and what are ends. It expresses human intentionality including need, desire, interest, and purpose. As with stimulus and response, it is a teleological distinction, not a distinction of existence.

An end-in-view provides a tentative telos for our human intentional activity. In his *Theory of Creative Action*, Hans Joas (1996, 157) elaborates and expands on what he calls Dewey's "non-teleological interpretation of intentionally." Unlike the model of teleological intentionality, where the artist first develops an idea of the end in her mind and then moves in a straight line to construct it, in a nonteleological interpretation of intentionality the agent constantly plays with possibilities, rather than marching toward some predetermined, fixed, and final goal. There is an intrinsic hermeneutic play in Dewey's theory of logical functioning.

In an infinitely complex universe, the actual existential end achieved includes unintended consequences. Dewey's nonteleological theory of intentionality easily accounts for such consequences. They are simply those aspects of the existential situation obtained that we ignore because they do not appear relevant to our purposes. The structure of both Dewey's theory of creative means-consequence coordination and his theory of nonteleological intentionality resembles that of his reconstruction of the reflex arc concept into an organic circle of functional coordination.

Dewey finds that we construct essences (εἶδος), objects of knowledge, and truth in the formation of judgment. He insists: "[T]he object of knowledge is not something with which thinking sets out, but something with which it ends: something which the processes of inquiry and testing, that constitute thinking themselves produce. Thus the object of knowledge is practical in the sense that it depends upon a specific kind of practice for its existence—for its existence as an object of knowledge. . . . [O]bjects are not known till made in the course of the process of experimental thinking" (MW 10:368–69).

We construct objects of knowledge, forms, and such; they are products of the process of forming judgments. They emerge as a consequence of practical experimental processes much as the stimulus emerges as a consequence of active response. In both cases, the agent strives to functionally coordinate its transactions by constructing something that functions to resolve some indeterminate situation.

Let us back up and follow the constructive process by which agents create objects of knowledge from an initially confused situation. In what follows, I concentrate on Part II of Dewey's *Logic: The Theory of Inquiry* (LW 12) entitled, "The Structure of Inquiry and the Construction of Judgments." To fully understand the origin of inquiry, though, we must turn to Dewey's essay "Qualitative Thought" (LW 5:243–62).

Many consider "Qualitative Thought" the most important single paper of Dewey's later period. Dewey affirms, "The immediate existence of quality, and of dominant and pervasive quality, is the background, the point of departure, and the regulative principle of all

thinking" (LW 5:261). Every inquiry is situated; it involves an immediate anoetic sense of a given qualitative contextual whole. Dewey
states, "That which is 'given' in the strict sense of the word 'given,' is
the total field or situation" (LW 12:127). Dewey is very clear that all
inquiry begins with an "indeterminate situation" (LW 12:109 ff.). Regarding the existentially given situation, Dewey concludes: "This
larger and inclusive subject-matter is what is meant by the term
'situation'. . . . The situation as such is not and cannot be stated or
made explicit. It is taken for granted, 'understood,' or implicit in all
propositional symbolization. . . . Second, the situation controls the
terms of thought" (LW 5:247).

The situations in which we participate have us functionally in embodied feeling and action before we have them cognitively in thought.
Only later, after the processes of linguistic negotiation and reflective
inquiry, may we turn around and linguistically describe situations,
assign meanings, and determine essences.

We grasp the quality of an immediately given, anoetic existential
situation spontaneously. Dewey insists that "intuition precedes conception and goes deeper. . . . Intuition, in short, signifies the realization of a pervasive quality such that it regulates the determination of
relevant distinctions or of whatever, whether in the way of terms or
relations, becomes the accepted object of thought" (LW 5:249). The
very existence of a "problem," however, involves a process of
construction.

Dewey states that, initially, "The unsettled or indeterminate situation might have been called a *problematic* situation. This name would
have been, however, proleptic and anticipatory" (LW 12:111; ital. in
orig.). A long developmental process of linguistically describing the
situation occurs before an immediate intuition of an existential situation becomes a named problem. The immediately given situation
involves a convergence of existential events. Dewey writes: "The indeterminate situation comes into existence from existential causes, just
as does, say, the organic imbalance of hunger. There is nothing intellectual or cognitive in the existence of such situations, although they

are the necessary condition of cognitive operations or inquiry. In themselves they are precognitive" (LW 12:111).

Neglecting the intuitive background of a problem destroys the immediate, precognitive quality from which problems emerge. This leads us directly to the role of selective interests in setting the context of construction.

So, how does the indeterminate, anoetic, existential quality become conceptually discriminated? Dewey proclaims, " 'Parts' are discriminated, not intuited. But without the intuited enveloping quality, parts are external to one another and mechanically related" (LW 10:196). After intuiting the quality of a situation, emotionally influenced selective attention is the next step in constructing an object of knowledge. If we are to follow the logic of constructive inquiry, we must consider the role of interest. He indicates, "The directive source of selections is interest. . . . An artist is ruthless, when he selects, in following the logic of his interests. . . . The one limit that must not be overpassed is that some reference to the qualities and structures of things in the environment remain" (LW 10:100–101). Emotionally influenced selective interests are the first step from some given qualitative situation and objects. Interests select aspects of the complex whole; they yield something intermediary between qualitative events and eventual objects; such selections provide data for further inquiry.

A collection of data is the first product in the process of inquiry as we move from the qualitative whole to a specified object; it resembles grape juice in my analogy. Dewey wonders: "Just what did the new experimental method do to the qualitative objects of ordinary experience?" His answer is that it "substitutes data for objects" (LW 4:79; ital. in orig.). "By data is signified subject-matter for further interpretation; something to be thought about. Objects are finalities; they are complete, finished; they call for thought only in the way of definition, classification, logical arrangement. . . . But data signify 'material to serve'; they are indications, evidence, signs, clues to and of something to be reached; they are intermediate, not ultimate; means, not finalities" (LW 4:80; ital. in orig.).

Data are intermediary between a given quality and the objects we eventually construct. Selection according to embodied needs, desires, interests, and purposes start the process of creating essences, including the essence of human existence. Dewey concludes, "That which is 'given' in the strict sense of the word 'given' is the total field or situation," while data are "*taken* rather than given. This fact decides the logical status of *data*" (LW 12:127; ital. in orig.). The use of data is a subfunction in the emergent construction of judgment. Dewey insists, "To be a datum is to have a special function in control of the subject-matter of inquiry. It embodies a fixation of the problem in a way which indicates a possible solution. It also helps to provide evidence which tests the solution that is hypothetically entertained" (ibid.). Facts are artifacts constructed by specifiable and repeatable processes.

Once we intuitively grasp a situation, collect data, and make a preliminary statement of the problem, we may arrive at an idea (a hypothesis) for creatively transforming the situation and restoring functional coordination: "A *possible* relevant solution is then suggested by the determination of factual conditions [i.e., data; J.G.] which are secured by observation. The possible solution presents itself, therefore, as an *idea*, just as the terms of the problem (which are facts) are instituted by observation. Ideas are anticipated consequences (forecasts) of what will happen when certain operations are executed under and with respect to observed conditions" (LW 12:113; ital. in orig.).

Ideas are about the possible consequences that will occur if we perform certain *operations* upon the situation as determined by factual observation. Ideas begin as suggestions about how to ameliorate a situation. They function as means to resolving the problematic situation. Dewey states, "The suggestion becomes an idea when it is examined with reference to its functional fitness; its capacity as a means of resolving the given situation. The examination takes the form of [means-consequence; J.G.] reasoning" (LW 12:114). Dewey observes that because "ideas are of that which is not present in given existence, the meaning which they involve must be embodied in some symbol" (ibid.). Ideas have an abstract symbolic character that allows them to convey creative possibilities beyond actual existence.

Once we have a working hypothesis, we must recognize "the function of ideas in directing observation and ascertaining relevant facts" (ibid.). Dewey recognized the theory-laden character of "facts" long before that insight became popular in the philosophy of science. Indeed, Dewey insists that "perceptual and conceptual material are instituted in functional correlativity with each other. . . . Both are determinations in and by inquiry of the original problematic situation whose pervasive quality controls their institution and their contents. . . . As distinctions they represent logical divisions of labor" (LW 12:115). Dewey thought it important to recognize that both data and ideas are functions of the agent's efforts to transform some confused situation, which we can only grasp in terms of their functional "operational character." There is a functional difference between ideas and facts: "Observed facts in their office of locating and describing the problem are existential; ideational subject-matter is nonexistential" (LW 12:116). Supposedly, the great question of epistemology is how ideas and facts correspond. Dewey considers this an insoluble problem "save as it is recognized that both observed facts and entertained ideas are operational" (ibid.). Inquirers creatively construct facts and ideas via specifiable and repeatable operations that serve the purposes of inquiry.

Dewey indicates that "ideas are operational in that they instigate and direct further operations of observation; they are proposals and plans for acting upon existing conditions to bring new facts to light and to organize all the selected facts into a coherent whole" (LW 12:116). Data are operational in that they "are selected and described . . . for a purpose" (ibid.). If well chosen, they will "link up" with other facts; those that do not connect are "dropped and others are sought for" (LW 12:117). Dewey concludes, "Being functional, they are necessarily operational. Their function is to serve as evidence and their evidential quality is judged on the basis of their capacity to form an ordered whole in response to operations prescribed by the ideas they occasion and support" (ibid.). The relation between data and ideas is circular, but it is a virtuous, hermeneutic circle. Facts and ideas are actually subfunctions of the unified function of inquiry. "The operative force of both ideas and facts," Dewey affirms, "is thus practically recognized in the degree in which they are connected with *experiment*" (LW 12:117; ital. in orig.). The circular, functional, and operative relation between facts and ideas in an experiment resembles the relation between stimulus and response in an experience. Their construction is contingent upon the experimental operations performed much as stimuli are "constituted" as a consequence of an organism's responses.

Dewey proclaims, "*The subject-matter of logic is determined operationally*" (LW 12:22; ital. in orig.). Operations according to Dewey are of two types: "There are operations that are performed upon and with existential material—as in experimental observation. There are operations performed with and upon symbols. But even in the latter case, 'operation' is to be taken in as literal a sense as possible. . . . The former are performed upon existential conditions; the latter upon symbols. But the symbols [ideas; J.G.] in the latter case stand for possible final existential conditions while the conclusion, when it is stated in symbols, is a pre-condition of further operations that deal with existences" (ibid.).

Dewey prefers examples "from the operations of industrial arts," but insists, "the principle holds of operations of inquiry" (LW 12:23). To avoid confusion, we should take Dewey's constructivism literally. Reference for Dewey ultimately involves concrete, existential operations; it has nothing to do with how decontextualized inner representations in the mind refer to external reality. Abstract ideas and propositions allow us to imaginatively manipulate *possibilities*, but only concrete existential operations allow us to determine the *actual* consequences in any given situation.

Dewey understood inquiry as relying on operations that determine consequences capable of transforming a given situation. Dewey explains: "Existence in general must be such as to be *capable* of taking on logical form, and existences in particular must be capable of taking on *differential* logical forms. But the operations that constitute controlled inquiry are necessary in order to give actuality to these capacities or potentialities" (LW 12:387; ital. in orig.). What operations arrive at is "invariant in its logical sense" (ibid.). Specifiable and repeatable invariants are necessary for intelligent action, prediction, and control. Invariants are logical constructions instituted by methodological operations that actualize the potential of a given existential situation. Dewey is saying that an essence, a logical form, is whatever remains invariant under a specified set of operational transformations.

It is unlikely that Dewey was aware of Felix Klein's 1872 inauguration of the *Erlanger Programm*, which asserts that geometry is the investigation of those properties of figures that remain invariant when we subject the figures to groups of functional transformations. This program eventually expanded into the study of "abstract spaces" and became part of the representation of quantum mechanics. If we replace mathematical functions and geometrical entities with Deweyan logical functions and a qualitative situation, we may say that an object of knowledge, or essence, is whatever remains invariant over a specifiable set of operational transformations.

Logical forms such as the supposedly a priori laws of the excluded middle and the principle of noncontradiction are, for Dewey, a posteriori products of the constructive process of inquiry. Dewey states that "all logical forms . . . arise within the operation of inquiry and are concerned with the control of inquiry so that it may yield warranted assertion" (LW 12:11). Objects and logical forms emerge from a situation as an artifact of the artistic construction of judgment in inquiry. Dewey states: "As *undergoing* inquiry, the material has a different logical import from that which it has as the *outcome* of inquiry. In its first capacity and status, it will be called by the general name *subject-matter*. . . . The name *objects* will be reserved for subject-matter so far as it has been produced and ordered in settled form by means of inquiry; proleptically, objects are the *objectives* of inquiry" (LW 12:122; ital. in orig.).

Logical forms, objects of knowledge, ontology, or essences emerge in the course of inquiry when we carry out operations that transform

situations. Dewey's understanding of truth also depends on the operations of inquiry. In practice, for Dewey, "this is the meaning of
truth: processes of change so directed that they achieve an intended
consequence" (LW 1:128).

Creating objects of knowledge or truth is an art, the art of constructing warranted assertions. Dewey insists on this creative, artistic
dimension of inquiry: "Knowledge or science, as a work of art, like
any other work of art, confers upon things traits and potentialities
which did not *previously* belong to them. Objection from the side of
alleged realism to this statement springs from a confusion of tenses.
Knowledge is not a distortion or perversion which confers upon *its*
subject-matter traits which *do* not belong to it, but is an act which
confers upon non-cognitive [qualitative; J.G.] material traits which
*did* not belong to it" (LW 1:285; ital. in orig.).

In creatively transforming some confused qualitative existential
situation into a determinate and functionally coordinated context,
agents creatively actualize the potential of the situation.

### Constructing the Bridge from Existence to Essence: Meaning and Language

Dewey builds his theory of meaning out of means-consequence connections: "[T]hings gain meaning when they are used as *means to
bring about* [predict, or refer to; J.G.] *consequences* (or as means to
prevent the occurrence of undesired consequences), or as standing
for *consequences* for which we have to discover *means*. The relation of
means-consequence is the centre and heart of all understanding"
(LW 8:233; ital. in orig.). Meanings provide ready material for the art
of inquiry. The exercise of reason involves the appropriate copulation
of meanings. Unlike other forms of logic, though, in Dewey's theory
of creative inquiry, logical copulation gives birth to novel meanings.

For Dewey, "Meanings are rules for using and interpreting things;
interpretation being always an imputation of potentiality for some
consequence" (LW 1:147). Events acquire meaning when we impute

to them the potentiality of serving as means for bringing about, predicting, or referring to consequences. If, as a consequence of experimental inquiry, the imputed consequences, in fact, occur, then we have a warrant for imputing truth to the meaning.

I want to focus attention on Dewey's short essay "Knowledge and Speech Reaction" (MW 13:29–39) because it allows us to easily identify the connection between speech acts, the constitution of stimuli by responses, and the construction of knowledge objects by the operations of inquiry. Dewey asks, "When it is asserted that speech as thought is a reaction the question at once arises: What is its stimulus?" (MW 13:29). Dewey begins his answer with the following observation: "[S]eeing as a complete stimulus gives rise to the response of reaching and taking or withdrawing, not of speech. What has to be accounted for is the postponement of the complete overt reaction, and its conversion into an intermediate vocal reaction. There has to be some break in the seeing-reaching sequence, some obstacle" (MW 13:30).

Once the constitution of the stimulus is complete, the final response of reaching or withdrawing completes the emerging functional coordination. Without some obstacle to overt action the speech response is unnecessary. The qualitative situation of a nonnative speaker attending a dinner party at an international philosophy conference in Germany provides an example. There you might ask someone to hand you something within his reach but out of yours; for example, a platter of veal at a large dinner table. Perhaps because you cannot speak the native language, you might use a behavioral gesture, or operation, such as pointing, but the speech act "*das Kalbfleisch*" would serve you better. Also, note that in such circumstance you are using another person as a means to the consequence of obtaining an object. What you seek is a functional coordination wherein another person, yourself, and some object are subfunctions. This simple act involves all the characteristics of the social construction of the meaning.

In Dewey's reconstruction of the reflex arc concept, the insight that "the response is not merely *to* the stimulus; it is *into* it" becomes crucial here (EW 5:98; ital. in orig.). For Dewey, the same principle applies to the speech response: "Our problem is to name that distinctive feature of a speech reaction which confers upon it the quality of response, reply, answer; of supplying something lacking without it. . . . But a response in statement is intimately connected with that to which it answers. It is not merely to it or away from it, but is back *into* it: that is, it continues, develops, directs something defective without it" (MW 13:31; ital. in orig.).

Much as the response in the reflex circle helps constitute the stimulus, the speech response helps construct the meaningful object and perhaps, after inquiry, objects of knowledge. Determining a "speech reaction," for Dewey, involves achieving a unity, a functional coordination that includes naming a meaning on the way to knowing it: "[T]he response 'this is a knife' is produced by reactions of seeing and incipient reactions of reaching, touching, handling, which are up to the point of speech reaction fumbling, choked, and conflicting. The speech reaction unifies them into the attitude of unhesitating readiness to seize and cut [a final response; J.G.]. It integrates or coordinates behavior tendencies which without it are uncertain and more or less antagonistic" (MW 13:32).

The unifying speech response "this is a knife" is the product of a series of responsive operations that include behavioral acts, the operations of language, and the operations of logical inquiry that produce the final cognitive judgment regarding the object that is the objective of inquiry at the dinner table. In interpreting the qualitative situation as including an object called "a knife," you impute potential consequences. You might emit the behavioral speech response, "this is a knife," as a way to sum up the functional coordination between you and a native speaker at the dinner table, thereby grasping the meaning of a social transaction with a new colleague. When you can sum up diverse acts with a single symbolic name, you gain abstract cognitive control over the situation. If the interpretation you have constructed is true, subsequent responses, operations, or behaviors will instigate processes of change so directed that they achieve the intended consequence; e.g., something that cuts (*das Messer*) the veal you requested earlier. Perhaps, though, the putative knife is really just a qualitative reflection of light upon the plates and glasses; only a series of subsequent responses, an inquiry, allows you to say for sure.

Dewey warns, "It is easy to overlook the modifying, re-directive and integrative function of speech as a response" (MW 13:32). He insists: "Unless we acknowledge and emphasize this trait, the behavioristic theory falls an easy victim to the contention that language merely echoes or puts into verbal form an apprehension that is complete without it. . . . Either the speech reaction does something to what calls it out, modifying it and giving it a behavior characteristic which it otherwise does not have, or it is mere utterance of what already exists apart from it" (MW 13:32).

Note the use of the word "behavior"; Dewey, like his friend George Herbert Mead, is a social behaviorist, though later he would come to prefer words like "operation," action, or "conduct" to describe human activity, once "behavior" came to take on a more reductive connotation.

Just as ordinary responses constitute the stimulus in the reflex circle, the speech response helps construct the object by fixing an otherwise dispersed set of qualities as a fixed object. Dewey states that "the *object of judgment* is thus not the cause simply; it is the consequence, the modification effected in its cause by the speech reaction" (MW 13:33; ital. in orig.). We construct meanings through our acts, including speech acts, which help operationally fix a set of invariant means-consequence connections.

Having determined that agents first create meaning before adjudicating truth in the process of constructing a logical judgment, Dewey admits: "The analysis is still oversimplified. . . . A speech reaction . . . involves the auditor and his characteristic reaction to speech heard. Often and primarily the auditor is another organism whose behavior is required to complete the speech reaction, this behavior being the objective aimed at in the speech reaction" (MW 13:34–35).

Primarily, the speech response involves another organism. If you ask a colleague at a conference dinner to please pass you the platter of veal, you are using him as a means to the consequence aimed at in your speech reaction; he too acquires meaning in the transaction, and so do you.

The primordial origin of speech responses lies in the coordination of social transactions. Dewey declares: "Commands, optatives and subjunctives are the primary modes of speech reaction; the indicative or expositive mood is an amplification. For example, even a treatise by a mathematician or chemist is a guide to the undertaking of certain behavior reactions—a series of acts which when executed will result in seeing the things which the author has responded to with certain statements. It follows that the *object* of a speech reaction is the concordant responses which it sets up" (MW 13:34; ital. in orig.).

Commands and optatives are more basic than indicatives for Dewey. Primordially, any linguistic report, such as a research report, is a set of instructions as to how to perform specified and repeatable operations, such that anyone anywhere who carries them out will find they are means to bringing about the same consequences.

In linguistic activity, the qualities of events condense into meaningful objects and, perhaps, objects of knowledge. It is a miracle of creation next to which transubstantiation pales. Often and primarily, speech reactions are responses to other emergent sentient events responding to emergent objects; it is a three-term functional coordination of social transaction involving the co-construction of some object. When different agents respond to the same object in the same way, then a shared object has emerged. The object emerges when the various participants agree on how to respond to or interpret (i.e., impute the same consequences to) some aspect of a qualitative situation. For Dewey, meaning is primarily a social construction that renders some emergent object in common amid two or more emergent centers of action.

The following passage describes the emergence of *knowledge* objects as the product of social transactions: "The object of knowledge or speech is the ultimate *consent* of the coordinated responses of speaker and hearer; the object of *aff*irmation is the *con*firmation of co-adapted behavior. Its object is that future complex coordination of serial acts into a single behavior-system which would not exist without it" (MW 13:35; ital. in orig.).

A shared meaning emerges when an emergent "speaker" (A) and a "hearer" (B) can functionally coordinate their behavior, responses, or operations with regard to some emergent object. All three are subfunctions of a single qualitative context of action. A mother and a newborn infant provide a fine example of such emergent transactional coordination. *Not only does the object emerge in the transaction, but also the agents participating undergo such transformation that we might say in at least some small way, they too emerge simultaneously.*[1]

Let us turn to Dewey's (1925 / 1981) most detailed account of the emergence of meaning in Chapter 5 of *Experience and Nature*; there he proclaims: "Of all affairs, communication is the most wonderful . . . and that the fruit of communication should be participation, sharing, is a wonder by the side of which transubstantiation pales. When communication occurs, all natural events are subject to reconsideration and revision. . . . Events turn into objects, things with a meaning" (LW 1:132).

Communication transforms brute existential events into meaningful objects, including social objects; that is, other human beings. Dewey finds, "Failure to acknowledge the presence and operation of natural interaction in the form of communication creates the gulf between existence and essence, and that gulf is factitious and gratuitous" (LW 1:133). For him, "The interaction of human beings, namely, association, is not different in origin from other modes of interaction" (LW 1:138). Linguistic transactions emerge from other modes of natural interactions without breach of continuity.

Let us look at what I call "the flower game" in Dewey. It closely resembles the "slab game" near the start of Wittgenstein's (1953) *Philosophical Investigations*. I follow Dewey's description of the first few plays in the game. "A requests B to bring him something, to which A points, say a flower. There is an original mechanism by which B may react to A's movement in pointing. But natively such a reaction is to the movement, not to the *pointing*, not to the object pointed out. But B learns that the movement *is* a pointing; he responds to it not in itself, but as an index of something else. His response is transferred from A's direct movement to the *object* to which A points . . ." (LW 1:140; ital. in orig.).

We could substitute a platter of veal for the flower. Notice we are dealing with a three-term function involving A, B, and an object. The analysis becomes primordial when we think of A trying to teach B that some subset of qualities within a larger qualitative situation is a flower, or two people striving to overcome cultural differences.

Primordially, to grasp the meaning of another's response (pointing, or the speech act, "bring me the flower") toward a set of qualities (an emergent object) we must orient our responses to functionally coordinate with another's experience as well as our own: "The characteristic thing about B's understanding of A's movement and sounds is that he responds to the thing from the standpoint of A. He perceives the thing as it may function in A's experience, instead of just ego-centrically. Similarly, A in making the request conceives the thing not only in its direct relationship to himself, but as a thing capable of being grasped and handled by B. He sees the thing as it may function in B's experience. Such is the essence and import of communication, signs and meaning. Something is literally made common in at least two different centres of behavior. To understand is to anticipate together. . . . [It is] a transaction in which both participate" (LW 1:141).

What is crucial above is that something, some object, "is literally made common" in two or more centers of behavioral transaction. Dewey understands the *making* of objects as a social co-construction. The "object" (e.g., flower) is not "there" antecedent to the making of the meaning function; to think it is involves committing "*the* philosophic fallacy." The object is literally made from the qualitative material characterizing some social transaction; hence, the object is a socially constructed meaning. Negotiating the meaning of "objects" is the "objective" of dialogue just as knowledge of objects is the objective of inquiry and a stimulus the objective of basic responses.

Primordially, the potential persons A and B themselves are simply sets of qualities within a larger qualitative situation. Consider the plight of an infant. They must learn to identify a set of qualities within a larger qualitative situation as a caregiver. For example, an infant "A" must learn to identify its mother "B." For Dewey, "A" learns the meaning of its mother, along with its own identity as it learns the meaning of objects in the world. They *co-construct* each other as they construct the object. Further, if A and B succeed in functionally coordinating their transactions regarding some object, mother and child will both undergo transformation along with the larger situation of which they are participants. Reflective caregivers know they change in the course of their children's development. For example, the *identity* of the primary caregiver alters in the transaction of tending to a child, as does that of the child. Objects of shared reference, along with the social objects called persons, emerge simultaneously in the transactions that comprise a social situation.

Nowhere is Dewey's social behaviorism more evident than in his theory of meaning: "Take speech as behavioristically as you will, including the elimination of all private mental states, and it remains true that it is markedly distinguished from signaling acts of animals. Meaning is not indeed a psychic existence; it is primarily a property of behavior, and secondarily a property of objects. But the behavior of which it is a quality is a distinctive behavior; cooperative, that response to another's act involves contemporaneous response to a thing as entering into the other's behavior" (LW 1:141).

In his famous essay "Ontological Relativity," W. V. O. Quine quotes from this passage as expressing the kind of naturalism and "semantic behaviorism" he shares with Dewey.[2] Quine also notes that Dewey had already rejected the notion of a private language, while Wittgenstein still held his picture theory of meaning.

For Dewey, "Primarily meaning is intent and intent is not personal in a private and exclusive sense" (LW 1:142). In Dewey's example, an object emerges in a field of action when two or more agents co-construct and co-intend the same object in the process of coordinating their transactions. In functionally coordinating their transactions, agents creatively transform senseless existential events into shared meanings.

Secondarily, though, meaning is a property of objects. Existential events are brute existences. When, through social transaction, senseless existential events are taken and used as means to consequences, they acquire meaning: "[M]eaning is the acquisition of significance by things in their status in making possible and fulfilling shared cooperation. In the first place, it is the motion and sound of A which have meaning, or are signs. . . . But secondarily the *thing* pointed out by A to B gains meaning. It ceases to be just what it brutely is at the moment, and is responded to in its potentiality, as a means to remoter consequences" (LW 1:142; ital. in orig.).

Through language events become an object; a thing with meaning. When A and B functionally coordinate their transactions with regard to an object by arriving at a shared interpretation, the co-constructed object makes shared cooperation possible; that is why the object emerges simultaneously with the identification of the other and one's self as having a core identity. Without the function performed by the emergent object, the emergent transitory centers of action "A" and "B" (e.g., mother and child) could not achieve functional coordination.

Given socially constructed meanings, it is possible to carry out the construction of logical judgments. We should never forget, though, that inquiry relies on socially constructed meanings and, according to Dewey, we should always remember, "Inquiry is a mode of activity that is socially conditioned and that has cultural consequences" (LW 12:26–27). In many ways, inquiry is the quest for community more primordially than the quest for knowledge. We value knowledge most when it facilitates social coordination. Through language and logic we socially construct meaning and essences that not only allow us to maintain our tenuous existence, but connect to others while we derive joy from our acts of creation, which allow us to participate in the larger creation of which we are an intimate part.

## OBSERVERS, PARTICIPANTS, AND AGENTS IN DISCOURSES: A CONSIDERATION OF PRAGMATIST AND CONSTRUCTIVIST THEORIES OF THE OBSERVER

Kersten Reich

In his provocative afterword to the well-known (neo)Pragmatist volume *The Revival of Pragmatism*, entitled "Truth and Toilets: Pragmatism and the Practices of Life" (Dickstein 1998, 418ff.), Stanley Fish makes a remarkable comparison. The plumber who tours Europe and observes "the primitive state of showers and the absence of copper piping" (427) comes back talking about nothing else to his friends. If there is a philosopher among them, the philosopher will supposedly laugh at his friend the plumber, who takes a highly specialized perspective as exclusive—a perspective, at that, which seems to be irrelevant to the philosopher. Why then should we not equally laugh at the philosopher who tours Europe and comes back talking about category mistakes, truth claims, warranted assertibility, or poststructuralism? "The answer is that while we don't think that a focus on toilets is appropriate to any and all situations, we do think that a focus on philosophical puzzles can never be beside the point; but we think so only because we mistake a professional practice—and a professional conversation we may decline to join and be none the worse for it—for life itself" (ibid.).

This and similar relativizing propositions of Fish's, though, have not won the approval of those contemporary Pragmatists who, following the early twentieth-century Pragmatists, wish to establish a modernist discourse of inquiry by way of scientific communities who try to solve relevant problems through the experimental testing of hypotheses. Although even in classical Pragmatism this testing of hypotheses is always seen in the context of cultural transactions, there is a remainder of belief in universalism here, at least in that finding such problems and looking for solutions is claimed to be equally valid for all humans. This belief in turn supports an attitude on the part of philosophers to emphasize their importance for all humans, their problems, and solutions. Even now there are Pragmatists who hold this claim; according to James T. Kloppenberg (1998, 84), such prominent thinkers as Hilary Putnam and Richard J. Bernstein belong to this group. And I guess that Larry Hickman would also position himself among them. On the other side, we find Pragmatists like Fish and Richard Rorty, the latter one of the best-known philosophers of the present. The seriousness of his comprehensive philosophical work notwithstanding, Rorty persistently suggests that philosophy today has lost its universal claim; we can expand his argument and equally apply it to other disciplines in the field of the humanities. From this point of view, the decrease of general efficacy characteristic of many contemporary philosophical approaches evinces this loss. The "hypothetical Dewey" that Rorty repeatedly refers to in order to characterize his own position stands after and beyond the *linguistic turn*. He "would have said, we can construe 'thinking' as simply the use of sentences" (Rorty in Kloppenberg 1998, 93).

What do I want to say by these introductory remarks? If, in this volume, we argue about Pragmatism, constructivism, and the subtle philosophical criticisms both approaches often elicit (together, against, or beyond each other), there are first of all two central questions at stake: Do we still, as philosophers, claim to have universal answers that the world "out there" must not ignore lest humanity, to its own demonstrable detriment, lose secure truths? Or do we content ourselves with having only temporary answers—answers that nonetheless may be worth struggling for, since they can still warn us against possible detriments, even if we admit that an absolute security, by way of sufficiently universal warrant, is out of sight?

These questions point to a controversy in present-day Pragmatism that is already settled for constructivism, because constructivism on principle takes an anti-universalist stance. This general account, though, is still too indeterminate. I will have to make it more precise and examine some important implications. Possibly taking the reader by surprise, I wish to begin with a constructivist interpretation of the well-known fairy tale "Snow White and the Evil Stepmother," thereby introducing some basic concepts of interactive constructivism relevant for the discussion of universal claims. I start with a rather unconventional question—unconventional, that is, in connection with a discussion of the problems of universalist argumentation in the field of knowledge criticism: What circumstances could have possibly prevented the evil stepmother in "Snow White" from attempting to chase and kill her poor stepchild, and from eventually being sentenced to death for her cruel intensions?

This question may sound strange at first or even somewhat beside the point; I will try to show why it would have been better for the evil stepmother to consider her own doings and relationships from the perspective of a constructivist or Pragmatist criticism of knowledge. In particular, I will argue that it would have been better for her to distinguish carefully between what I will introduce as the roles of observers, participants, and agents. Although I choose to illustrate these roles by means of interpreting a fairy tale, they should not at all be understood as pre-scientific narration. They represent basic conceptual distinctions in the discourse theory of interactive constructivism (see Reich 1998b; Neubert and Reich 2000). From this perspective, "discourse," in the first place, refers to the symbolic order that underlies intentional processes of communication and understanding. Discourses fixate rules, allocations, and arrangements necessary for the establishment of reliable patterns of communication. These rules, al-locations, and arrangements, though, are not always as certain and final as the symbolic order seems to suggest. I hope my analysis of the three roles mentioned above will turn out to be fruitful and produc-tive, not only because it provides us with an illustration, but because it shows that the conceptual distinctions of discourse theory make sense in more than scientific language games.

Coming back to my introductory remarks, we may say that most language games in present-day life-worlds are nonscientific. In the following discussion, I will first examine an exemplary discourse on the nonscientific theme of "beauty." I will discuss this theme from the perspective of interactive constructivism and interpret it as a problem between universalist and anti-universalist approaches. Sec-ondly, I will explain the hereby applied constructivist concepts of "observer," "participant," and "agent" in more theoretical terms. Thirdly, I wish to examine by comparison if—and how far—these perspectives are already anticipated in the philosophy of John Dewey. I will ask about the place of universalism in Dewey, and about the differences between Pragmatism and constructivism that remain in spite of many commonalities and affinities between the two approaches.

### The Evil Stepmother in "Snow White" as Observer, Agent, and Participant

Let us begin with the facts of the fiction: After Snow White's birth her mother died. The king took a new wife who thought she was the most beautiful woman in the whole country. But who should confirm her belief that she was? Fortunately, she possessed a miraculous mirror so that she could ask for confirmation day by day: "Magic mirror on the wall, who is the fairest one of all?"

The queen was an acute observer. She stood before her mirror and looked at herself, but she knew that the mirror would always know more than she did. She could see herself as an observer and think for herself that she was the most beautiful, but objective evidence could only be found in the mirror's telling her so. As we see, the fairy tale asks a philosophical question: What warrant is there to support the truth claim of the statement that this queen is the most beautiful woman of all? There is the unquestionable final warrant that the mirror represents.

But the queen was not only an observer. Playing an important role at court, she was also an influential agent. In the eyes of a distant-observer—e.g., a stranger to the court who would have observed her—she might have appeared as a marvellous actress on the stage of the court who knew how to play her role as queen with perfection. The king could be content with her. At least the fairy tale tells us nothing to the contrary. And what we don't know, we must be silent on. Only to the subjects of the kingdom, so we may guess, her actions did not at all appear as a role that she played, but she undoubtedly *was* the queen and hence the most beautiful woman of all. And since the common man and woman anyway did not know of mirrors that provide final warrant for truth claims, we must suppose that there was not much epistemological doubt in anyone's mind.

So much for the facts of the fiction. Philosophically seen, they are unsatisfactory. Who defines the standards for measuring the beauty of a woman? In "Snow White," this is the business of the mirror. We may regard that mirror as a metaphor for the experience that we all sometimes appear as a picture that not only strangers, but we ourselves may critically look at. Such a mirror makes of us participants in a larger game: a game of comparison between our pictures, if only the mirror truly knows what beauty is.

But who or what is the mirror? In the fairy tale, the mirror stands for the final and best observer; the mirror equals God's eye before which humans cannot hide anything. Thus after Snow White has grown up, the mirror replies to the queen's question: "Famed is thy beauty, majesty. Behold, a lovely maid I see. Rags cannot hide her gentle grace. Alas, she is more fair than thee." The queen insists: "Alas for her, reveal her name." To which the mirror replies: "Lips red as the rose. Hair black as ebony. Skin white as snow."

This is the point where the dramatic development of the story begins, since the queen cannot bear this offending truth and takes mea-
sures to have Snow White killed. She fails, and Snow White escapes
to the seven dwarfs, who save her from all but one of the stepmother's
evil deeds to come. Finally she is rescued by a young man to whom
she will be happily married, while the evil queen in the end must bit-
terly repent her observations in the mirror: she has to dance in red-
hot iron shoes until she drops dead.

Could not the queen have prevented this cruel outcome? Where is
the discursive point at which a different interpretation could have
made possible the production of a different language game? You see,
sometimes it is not at all that good to ask philosophical questions,
because our positive answers could rob us of a marvellous tale—a tale
that, for reasons of rationality, we then could no longer avail ourselves of.

Nevertheless we *should* ask these questions, since the meaning of
such fairy tales implies a warning for us to beware of something. The
psychoanalyist Bruno Bettelheim (1980, 230ff.), e.g., interprets this
fairy tale as warning for us to beware of exaggerated narcissism (represented in the motive of the mirror). In the background stands the
whole drama of the Oedipus complex, a crisis of gender and identity
that leads (or seduces) us into the discourses of the unconscious. But
here we tell a different story that leads us back to constructivism and
Pragmatism.

Let us, then, risk a philosophical interpretation. The mirror sets
in advance the conditions of participation that largely determine the
queen's observations and acts: "You may see what you will, but you
cannot escape the truth of my judgment!" It is the light of truth that
the mirror reflects to us if only we honestly gaze. Therefore, the mirror cannot lie. The mirror makes of the queen and Snow White and
all the other women in the kingdom participants in a truth game
about beauty; it represents the indispensable pre-understanding
about such participation; it always knows with certainty who is the
most beautiful. On the other side, we have the subjective observation
of the queen before the mirror. She may see herself as beautiful; she

may think that she's the most beautiful of all. She may do so without dramatic consequences, as long as she does not ask for objective judgement and thus tries to transcend her subjective position as an observer. She is also free as an agent to act her role more or less elegantly, courteously, or provocatively. After all, she's the queen. And since she makes such a fuss about beauty in all affairs of her life, we may suppose that she permanently observes herself in her acts and deeds at court to make sure for herself that she really *is* beautiful. All of this is no tragedy and, as a rule, does not lead to cruel and premature death.

Thus we have identified the logical trap: basically, the only troublemaker is the mirror. The queen could have lived happily, and Snow White could have had a happy childhood, if only the mirror would not have set such rigid conditions of participation. So what could have helped the queen to prevent her cruel fate? Our three perspectives of *observer*, *agent*, and *participant* help us to make relevant distinctions:

1. As an observer, the queen looks at herself, her thoughts, and deeds. She is a self-observer who examines her own expectations, hopes, wishes, desires, but also her norms, values, and claims. To do so, she has to take the role of others and look at herself from outside. She has to behave at court in accord with certain rules. She has to reflect her own conduct with respect to set standards and adjust her behaviour to the rules of the court. After all, she is under the very acute observation of others. And as a distant-observer she observes these others, too. For example, it is from their reactions that she learns how good she behaves. Standing before the mirror, finally, she observes herself to see how beautiful she is. As a distant-observer, though, she can also imaginatively take the role of the mirror, comparing herself with all other beautiful women. She does so to assess from the perspective of an imagined distant-observer whether she is still the most beautiful of all. She could live happily in this role, as long as she relies on the moment and does not overcritically regard the mirror as an omniscient panoptical eye that pronounces stable

and objective truth. In and by itself, then, her role as an observer would do her no harm. She may look at others as well as herself; she may stop her actions for a moment to see what she does. As an observer, she should have known that the truth of her beauty is always her observed truth—and, as a rule, mirrors don't talk. And if they sometimes *do* talk inside of us and our observations, these are always signs of our time: the queen knows what counts as beautiful in her culture, what criteria are applied, which claims are set. But her view might be more tolerant than the word of the mirror—and her make-up might serve as a trick to turn her existing qualities into splendid appearance.

2. As an agent, the queen simply acts in accord with what she knows, how she habitually acts, how she feels, and what she has learned. From time to time she has to look at herself, maybe to readjust her conduct a little bit in this or that direction, maybe to prevent a breach of the complicated etiquette at court. The routines at court are exhausting, the moral rules and liberties are codified. Deviations will be recorded by protocol. Beauty inheres in any act: the marvellous dress, the precious jewelry, the luxurious ambience, the exquisite courtesy, this and more constitutes the frame of the spectacle, the furnishing of the role that the queen plays and acts on the stage of the life at court. In the degree to which the queen acts, she does not permanently have to observe herself in the mirror, although on stage she is under the unremitting observation of others. And while she acts she must look at herself from time to time lest she get lost to the world and possibly commit an offence against the ceremonial.

3. As a participant at court, even the queen's freedom is restricted. There are fixed conditions of participation that must not be offended. This participation is a process of communication that rests on preunderstandings that in advance define what observations can be made and what actions are allowed, welcomed, or forbidden. The essential thing, first of all, seems to be the king's benevolence. This benevolence is a primary condition of participation, and if her husband had been a cruel king, a somewhat different if no less cruel tale would have to be told. But in "Snow White," the queen falls victim not to

the king but to another authority of participation: the mirror. She gets involved in a truth game, and truth can be very cruel if you have certain definite expectations of it. If it had been possible for the queen to cancel her participation in this truth game (i.e., to give up her urgent desire to be the most beautiful of all), if—in the language of the fairy tale—she had not been that arrogant and high-spirited, all could have lived together happily. But participation in the discourse of the mirror seduces the queen to a cruel obsession with a rigid comparison of beauty. Through the objectifying eye of the mirror she defines her participation in high-spirited and ultimately impossible terms: nobody can in the long run succeed in being the most beautiful of all. Basically, everybody knows that, even without a mirror. Thus, in the fairy tale, the mirror represents an authority of knowledge criticism that transcends all observations and actions. May each and every observer at court say that the queen is the most beautiful woman of all, may each and every interaction at court demonstrate that she is— reflection on the general conditions of participation in the comparison of beauty will still suggest that such an assertion is futile and senseless. This is the generalized statement of the mirror that can be seen, then, as a metaphor for logical reasoning about the conditions of comparisons and comparabilities—i.e., as a discursive instrument.

Let us sum up by saying that the queen should have distinguished between her roles as observer, agent, and participant instead of one-sidedly following *one* fixed role (participation in the truth game of the mirror). However, the fairy tale's punch line that points to the futility and senselessness of a comparison of beauty—beyond the fleeting present of observations—is covered in the end by the very fact that henceforth, Snow White will occupy the place of the most beautiful of all. Should ultimately Snow White, too, fall victim to another beautiful woman? Or will she be able to use the three roles as observer, agent, and participant flexibly enough to allow now the one and then the other to stand in the foreground—without allowing participation in the truth game of beauty to become the one and only focus of her life? You see that philosophical questions can state and resolve relevant problems—even in the case of a fairy tale.

*Observers, Participants, and Agents in Constructivism*

From the perspective of postmodernism, we can tell that the mirror in the fairy tale lies. It has long since been broken into countless fragments. These fragments may in turn tell their respective owners that they are the most beautiful of all. But in the succession and juxtaposition of particular fragments of the mirror, comprehensive unity no longer can be found. Beauty appears more or less arbitrarily where it happens to be seen and recognized. Whereas metaphysics ventured to construct a final mirror by way of abstract reasoning that produced a unique, speculative, and intangible truth, the discursive situation of postmetaphysical thinking is considerably different. Pragmatism and constructivism ask for the terms of participation, implied as indispensable pre-understandings in the lived cultures we inhabit. They show that a universal, ultimately transcendental, final, or best truth valid for all humans—the truth of a mirror or another final authority—is no longer achievable. Our participation in truth is offended, and this offence has to do with our roles as observers, participants, and agents.

It may be helpful, here, to consider for a moment Michail Bakhtin's theory of carnival, which gives us some interesting suggestions for the use of these three perspectives. Following Bakhtin (1981, 1984), a crucial precondition for the transition from the Middle Ages to modernity has been the divorce between spectator and actor. It is true that this separation historically goes back to the theatre of antiquity. But now there is a teaching and educating motive that more and more becomes the crucial drive behind the separation between spectator ( = observer) and actor ( = agent). On the quasi-real stage of theatre as well as on the fictitious stage of belle-lettres there emerges a new attitude that establishes a lasting and pronounced distinction between the perspectives. And this attitude is characteristic for a new age.

This distinction of perspectives, I think, belongs to a new art of living. We can see medieval carnival as a harbinger of such diversity of perspectives. Carnival manifests and articulates a subversive culture of laughter in which all three roles may fall into one. Here I am simultaneously an observer (or spectator) of the others, an agent in my own disguised role, and a participant in a grotesque event that for the time being suspends conventional norms and hierarchies. Carnival simulates a world that might be—and is yet impossible because of the life-worldly norms and ranks that constitute normality. This is why the strict temporal limitation of the event is so important. In the present time of postmodernity, there is a tendency of expansion even to the point of a "carnival all the year round." This tendency, however, goes hand in hand with a transformation of carnival itself according to the practices and hierarchies of the mundane world, i.e., a betrayal of the original ideals of carnival that fall victim to its life-worldly "dissemination." Nevertheless, attention to the distinction of the three perspectives (Reich 1998a, 1998b; Neubert and Reich 2000), my basic thesis, becomes a crucial precondition for a sufficiently secure art of living (Schmid 2000, 2001a, 2001b) that balances individual striving for happiness with external standards and requirements.

It will not have escaped the reader that this chapter is characterized by a general tendency to pay attention to life-world. "Snow White" was not a casual choice. Carnival is not just one event in the life-world, e.g., of Cologne. It counts as a truth-founding ritual. Fairy tales like "Snow White" and events like carnival suggest a crucial problem of postmodern criticism of knowledge—the problem that, in our quest for scientific truth, we time and again come up against the limits of the field of observation that we ourselves mark out in order to keep our truth claims free from the distortions of life-world. This is why I have deliberately chosen the reverse way: arguing from the perspective of life-world, I will try to irritate and provoke the scientific truth game.

For constructivism, as I understand it, the constitution and maintenance of truth claims rest on two presuppositions. On the one hand, if we are to determine a claim to truth that transcends sheer subjective opinion or impression, we need an interpretive community. In some cases, though, this community may be rather small or specific. On the other hand, the conventional interpretation achieved by this community refers to an event that is seen in a sufficiently viable perspective. We need viability, in a word, to sustain truth. The claim here is that the viability of a statement about truth is tied to the event and other following events to which the statement applies. If, e.g., certain statements claimed as true by majority consent within an interpretive community repeatedly run counter to certain practical events that can be shown to be at odds with the theoretical statements, then the community will be wise to change its so-far-entertained concepts of truth. However, in most cases this change of research practices follows the way outlined by Thomas Kuhn (1976): only a different interpretive community will succeed in asserting itself against the prejudices of the former. It will temporarily displace the former's "version of world making" (Goodman 1978) by a competing view. But the newly constructed and established claims to truth will also have to stand the continual pressure of being subjected to processes of refutation, completion, and supplementation.

Why, then, do we time and again look for universalities? I will try to get to an answer by looking more closely at the roles of observers, participants, and agents as they function in scientific discourses—i.e. discourses of knowledge.[1] Table 6-1 sketches the course of my argumentation.

The methodological hopes of modern enlightenment theories consisted of attempts to attain and secure objectivity by precise observation founded on an accurate and sufficient theory of observation. This objectivity was thought to force all observers to recognize truth claims in behalf of ascertained facts. From the beginning, then, modern philosophy and science have attributed a pronounced and important role to observers, although their methodological discourses were at first mainly concerned with the peril that the subjectivity of particular observers might interfere with claims to objectivity.

Participation in scientific discourses was inspired by a desire and quest for universally valid knowledge claims, even if this unity was somehow to be found within the succession and juxtaposition of particular discourses. Science was not of necessity seen as a pluralistic endeavor, but plurality of approaches and viewpoints was considered

## TABLE 6-1

| Discourse of knowledge | Observer | Participant | Agent |
|---|---|---|---|
| Methodological aspirations of modernity | Observation Objectivism *Must be experienced by different observers to get common claims* | Unity Universalism *To be reached by participation and rational insight* (if only as contra-factual assumption) | Practices Procedures Applications *Are represented in theories* |
| Deconstructions in post-modernity | Subjectivism (in observation) Relativism Simulations *play an increasing role* but the ecstasy of simulations and virtual realities *produces the risk of "Gleichschaltung" through media* | Pluralism Social disembedding Risk society *Make participation difficult and diverse* but majority decisions, mainstream opinions and social networks *are still essential* | *Multiple ways and chances of acting Enforce the primacy of arbitrary action* but routines, institutions *appear as limiting conditions* |
| Validity claims at risk (from modernity to postmodernity) | Monoperspective versus multiperspective | Community of interpretation versus society of interpretive communities | Causality versus circularity |
| Universalism | Poses one-sided limits on the perspectives of observers but routines of observation are necessary in specific fields | Only in specific fields is it possible to construct clear methods and procedures of inquiry ( = Pragmatic "universalisms" for a given time), but there are generalizable ("universalizable") standards especially in technical and scientific fields through global acceptance | Poses one-sided restrictions on innovative and alternative ways of acting but specific common standards and procedures in specific fields of action remain |

an imperfect, distorted, or even abnormal state of affairs that called for amelioration by means of stricter insights into the necessary preconditions of participation in scientific truth finding. Such universalistic claims continue to have an effect until today, although they often appear in more modest and qualified versions than they used to do. There are, e.g., philosophers like Jürgen Habermas and Karl-Otto Apel who restrict philosophic claims to universality by their qualification that these claims be necessary only on a certain level of discourse theory—namely, insofar as the necessary conditions of rational, free, and equal communication between partakers in discourses are concerned. They concede, furthermore, that these claims for the time being are counterfactual and utopian, because in practical affairs hardly anyone keeps to them. It seems evident, then, that even from the viewpoint of modern critical philosophers like Habermas or Apel, observers and participants do not simply fall into one position. And this seems all the more true if we are further willing to concede that already the supposedly neutral philosophical metaclaims—which these philosophers attempt to universalize—are conditional on contexts of participation that influence observing and observation. Thus the question arises of whether the issues of participation have a more fundamental influence on the definition of observations than those theories assume. Is it possible for observers to sufficiently detach themselves from their contexts of participation so as to achieve a context-neutral—i.e. universal—viewpoint? Or are their possibilities to transcend context restricted to the invention of new theories (observations) about participation that get by without claims to universal validity? Constructivists clearly prefer the latter alternative. They argue that in postmodernity the proliferation of discourses and the dislocation of observer-positions have led to a situation where the participation in interpretive communities turns out to be profoundly—and irretrievably—pluralized.

There is another point to the matter. Many scientific theories completely neglect the role of the agent in favor of that of the observer and participant. Taking into account the role of agents, though, is to consider the meaning of concrete cultural practices, routines, and institutions as involving subjects with their particular activities, intentions, and agencies. This "taking into account" easily turns out to be a very difficult and complex task, provided that we do not confine ourselves to the observation of simple acts and routines, but also consider the creative, innovative, imaginative, and emotional potentialities of subjects. It is precisely the role of subjects as agents in cultural practices that most persistently eludes all attempts to be pictured in theory, at least if we are prepared to pay regard to the particularities of individual life-experience and do not merely subsume subjects under statistical rubrics. Pragmatism has been the first philosophical approach that wholeheartedly recognizes this impossibility, and constructivism further develops this recognition. Their common tenet is that practices cannot simply be pictured in theory. On the one hand, practices always involve the theoretical devising of positions of observation and participation that precedes concrete acts. On the other hand, there are always certain free spaces in between the preconditions and opportunities of acting that agents can make use of, thereby changing theoretical perspectives on practices as well as testing theory through practical application.

The methodological hopes of modernity have been shaken and relativized by the very developments of modern philosophy itself. Different theoretical traditions have contributed to these developments. Following Richard Rorty (1979), Heidegger, Wittgenstein, and Dewey, together with their followers, have contributed (among other traditions) to the improvement of modernity's understanding of existence, language, and culture. In the philosophical discourses of postmodernity, the implications of our three perspectives are further differentiated—provided that the qualifier "post" is not simply taken to indicate a final dictum *after the event*, but denotes a movement in time where some of the basic beliefs of modernity fall through its own claims (see especially Bauman 1993, 1997, 1998a, 1998b, 1999, 2000).

The role of the observer becomes ever more important, and there is an increasing tendency to recognize the import of the subjective positions of observers. This leads to an increased relativization of discourses, communities, interests, and power claims. Different "Versions of World-Making" (Goodman 1978) appear and exist next to one another, because they fit the different needs and viabilities of different interpretive communities. There is a growing amount and import of simulations. Experienced reality increasingly assumes an artificial, produced, and virtual character and appears as simulation of a hardly accessible (or not even existing) "outer reality" in the sense of nature as given at first hand. Hence observers more and more dismiss the epistemological model of a one-to-one transmission of experienced natural reality "out there" into inner states of consciousness or cognitive structures. At the same time, there is the danger of new ways of mental uniformity and *Gleichschaltung* lurking in these virtual reality constructions, largely provided by the electronic mass media. For here the subject matter of observation is already elaborated and ready-made to a degree that it barely calls for anything more than passive consumption.

The roles of participants change not only in life-world, but in scientific practices and discourses, too. The postmodern condition of vibrant pluralism and the postmodern search for freedom has to be taken into account. Although this pluralism is at times qualified by the claim that eventually there could or should be a unified or universal theory at some point of convergence in the future, more and more inquirers today acknowledge the concession that inquiry is not free from interests, power claims, dependencies on politics and economics, the pressures of quick feasibility, and other seemingly extrascientific motives. The release from traditions (Giddens 1991) implies that participations in many cases can no longer be founded on unequivocal and certain contexts of value contained in a clearly defined worldview. Furthermore, the shortsightedness of reductive causal explanations and solutions in science has in many ways contributed to the emergence of a "risk society" (Beck 1992) in which the material, ecological, and economical resources, as well as the health conditions of all participants of modernization and globalization, are lastingly put at risk. Nevertheless, we still console ourselves—even in science—with the majority solutions of a *mainstream* and with the social networks that help us to delimit plurality through dominant interests, released through the fixation of certain values and norms. However, participation in social practices makes it more and more evident that the very unifying and universalistic ideals of science crumble. As I will show later on, classical Pragmatism has already contributed to this process of decay. Constructivism makes it more radical. But neither Pragmatism nor constructivism strives for claims to an arbitrariness of the criteria of knowledge criticism.

As to the role of agents, questions of agency are becoming ever more complex and multilayered in present-day life-worlds. There is an abundance of opportunities to act and attain goals in different ways and with quite different resources and repertoires of acting. Calls for flexibility, dynamism, and mobility indicate roles of agents that suggest freedom of choice, on the one hand, while representing a compulsion to choose, on the other hand. This compulsion furthermore tends to untie the networks of solidarity that have been fought for and established not so long ago. While routines and institutions still provide some counter-balance, the responsibility for delimiting the ecstasy of possibilities increasingly falls back upon the individual agents who have to learn to determine their observations and participations for themselves, to assess their powers and to deploy their resources properly. To choose a trade or profession, e.g., in former times, as a rule involved that one's role as agent, at least in this respect, was largely determined for a lifetime. Today these roles are much more taken, and the chances of success are often hardly accessible in the long run. There is also no longer any intrinsic value in "picturing" practices in theory or applying theories to practice, unless a (mostly material) success is involved.

Let me briefly come back to "Snow White." Looking into the mirror, the stepmother has premodern as well as modern expectations of her problem and possible answers. As an observer, she puts her trust in the one-dimensional objectivity that the mirror offers as an answer. She puts her trust in this assertion, because she takes it to be universally valid. To her mind, assertions about beauty are not dispersed definitions of interpretive communities, of which the mirror could possibly represent but one. She interprets the answer she is given in a strictly causal way, i.e., she is unable to think of beauty as a *process of ascribing or imputing*, because she believes that there *must* be a final word about beauty. She is unable to see that this *must* is but a *shall*—one possibility among many.

Were the stepmother to live in postmodernity, though, she would probably be skeptical even of the psychoanalyst who offers her a narcissistic interpretation of the mirror metaphor. Maybe she would kindly say that this explanation *could* be true and accept it, as long as she finds it to be helpful. But she has already learned to look in multiple perspectives and to recognize that her role as an observer has gained importance in new ways: "Do not only focus your eyes on what others tell you who are powerful, outstanding, or influential, but also on what they say against each other and what this might mean for you!" As a participant she knows that there are different interpretive communities, and that one may now take part in one and then in another. For example, she is a convinced environmentalist who votes for the Green Party; nevertheless, she loves to drive her car or travel by plane when she goes on holiday. The fact that she lives in a society of interpretive communities makes it possible for her to bear these and similar contradictions between different participations more or less successfully. And she has long since learned that in comprehensive human communication, causal attributions are seldom very promising. Although they are helpful in limited technical procedures, they are not at all helpful with regard to touching issues like beauty.

My recourse to the fairy tale indicates difficulties connected with validity claims in postmodernity. Maybe some will object, insisting that these difficulties were already effective in modernity, but my response is that there was no comprehensive awareness of them. If we neglect the difficulties and their effects today, however, we will get involved in serious contradictions.

I wish to indicate such difficulties with regard to scientific claims to universality. We speak of a universal claim if we have a statement that stems from a final and best observer. Usually this observer-position itself is being universalized, such that the truth of the statement can be agreed to by all humans, as it were, who observe or are able to observe. Let us take an easy example: The statement "$1+1=2$" is a true statement. It is true here, there, and anywhere, and we cannot simply abolish or dismiss it by way of an arbitrary majority decision, provided that we do not want to dismiss the idea of truth altogether. We could add countless other examples from the natural sciences or from mathematics. But we have to observe here that all imaginable interpretive communities who get involved in problems like these are already enclosed in a comprehensive frame of understanding in societies. The field of mathematical understanding comprises certain logical conventions. Dissent about certain alternatives is possible only on the basis of these conventions. If you surrender these basic understandings, you surrender the possibility of mathematical truth findings that can be agreed upon only on the basis of specified rules.

If we look at the diversity of sciences, though, we find approaches that are organized through completely different paradigms and rules that lead to very different versions of realities. Thus we have to introduce criteria for deciding when our confidence in the reliability of truth constructions is globally or universally warranted—and when it is not. But such criteria can only emerge from the very practices of particular interpretive communities themselves. Only if a particular interpretive community decides that its rules and paradigms are valid for all others—i.e., if this interpretive community defines a comprehensive frame of understanding in societies—are universal claims to truth possible. However, we must critically add that these claims could not imply that further developments in the frame of these conventions are impossible. New research may even entail an overall revolution of rules and paradigms hitherto taken for warranted. For these rules and paradigms are at best temporarily valid as a precondition of participation in such interpretive communities. They may be enlarged or modified through new and changed observations or actions.

Hence, as to the realm of possible observations, we should on principle reject universalistic definitions, because they delimit the possibilities of multiple perspectives that are our great need if we want
something new or innovative to be observed. We also have to learn
that science is not at all as clearly marked off from life-world as hitherto often supposed. The universalistic solutions and claims maintained in present interpretive communities are reducible to certain
disciplines characterized by highly sophisticated logical languages and
mathematical conventions, technical procedures, and means-end relations (Hartmann and Janich 1996, 1998; Janich 1996, 2001).[2] Larry
Hickman refers to examples from these fields, in the first place, when
he insists on compulsory standardizations in Chapter 7 of this volume. Seen from a constructivist viewpoint, though, this is but one
part of the role of observer. Here scientific education makes sure that
routines are sufficiently established and mere arbitrariness is ruled
out. But the agency of subjective observers in science is not identical
with admittance for arbitrary fantasies and nonsense. A certain
coherence with foregoing rules and findings must of course be de-
manded of every scientific observer. Yet—as Hickman clearly recognizes—new combinations, experiments, and experiences (in the
Deweyan sense) involve and presuppose an open-mindedness on the
part of observers that allows for the possibility of seeing things in new
perspectives, observing new problems, and inventing new and unexpected solutions. The touchstone of this open-mindedness is the degree to which Pragmatism and constructivism are actually better
prepared for (and more successful in) tolerating, recognizing, and
furthering lateral thinkers and troublemakers. Without such visionar-
ies, observers of other possibilities, we soon get caught in the stagnation of our once-successful and then less and less closely scrutinized
paradigms.

There are indeed procedures in some sciences that can be reconstructed for the participants through very clear and unambiguous descriptions, e.g., in the techno-sciences and the natural sciences.
Reliable work procedures help us to achieve predicted results. Although, as it seems to me, Dewey was mostly an adversary of universalisms, he saw universalizable tendencies in the techno-sciences.

These are procedures of means-end relations, in the first place, that can be reconstructed quite unambiguously. We could also say that in the field of the techno-sciences, a specific culture has already succeeded to prevail—namely, the culture of Western industrialized societies. A specific hegemony has already been established. Identity is achieved because, in this case, there are no different relevant interpretive communities, but only the language and the rules of a comprehensive frame of understanding (in industrialized societies), dominated by the West. Larry Hickman's specific focus in Chapter 7 of this volume has largely been on these issues. But even here we find certain limits and indeterminacies—problems that the qualitative evaluation of any management of industrial productions must concede. Or think of Chinese medicine, which shows another constructive method after the triumphant advances of Western medicine. Or think of atomic energy and the quarrels about its dangers or safeness. Confronted with complex questions like these (questions of techniques and technologies, too), the more narrow consensual approaches almost always fail.

Furthermore, it is always important to reflect the role of the agent in addition to the more or less well-defined roles of participants and observers. There are, of course, reliable routines, well-tried procedures, habitually ordered activities in many acts that humans perform. But there are also leaps, time and again, even in the field of techniques and technologies. Such leaps show continuity with older achievements as well as revolutionary advances, such that older technologies have to be partly abandoned. Every claimed universalism is but a temporary option, preferable for Pragmatic reasons. Often there is a colonialist claim inherent in it, tending to make other cultures accept this and not something else that has been successful somewhere else. This is why even a modest Pragmatic universalism may in some respects support or produce hegemonic structures. Constructivism attaches great value to the critique of such hegemonies. Its anti-universalism is grounded in the assumption that we should always critically reconstruct and scrutinize the presuppositions that we paradigmatically introduce into a scientific discourse. It aims to make transparent the participant roles implied in our understandings and recognitions. This may be incomparably less problematic in the case of mathematical equations than in the definition of the best way to decrease unemployment, to handle immigration, or to provide appropriate ways of education.

There is yet another argument against universalism. Once a universalistic claim is made and established, its proponents tend to become blind as to their omissions. The universalistic claim has to be valid for all cases and all times. In science, though, such completeness is not only improbable *in the long run*, but it altogether constitutes a handicap to innovative agency in all more complex matters. Universalisms often have too strong a tendency to formal and abstract models that focus on a few basic figures of mostly linguistic presuppositions of reasoning. But they seldom really succeed in grasping concrete issues sufficiently. The precision of statements is often adversely affected by this failure. Would it not, then, be more viable for science to abandon the claim for universality and the "last word"? This is not at all to abandon the temporary construction of truths; in some specific fields such constructions may and shall be valid for very long times.

I get back to "Snow White" one last time. We will hardly be able to formulate the truth of beauty as universality. Nevertheless, it is possible to reconstruct and deconstruct what images (of self and others) render certain beauties beautiful. It is a question of constructions in certain interpretive communities. And even today the fairy tale disseminates the illusion of absolute beauty. The postmodern observer knows, though, that she observes but one version amongst countless others. The participant recognizes the futility of relying on the verbal statements of a mirror (and in this respect certain magazines may be bad company, too). The agent constructs her changing, unstable, and ambivalent definitions of beauty, provided she has the opportunity to practically try out her visions of what is beautiful and what is not. And don't think that beauty is the only affair where this is the case. Quite to the contrary, the number of concepts and expectations of a complex nature is not decreasing, but considerably increasing in our time.

## John Dewey on "Observation" and "Participation"

After having so far developed a constructivist perspective, I want to turn to John Dewey, now, and ask how far the distinctions made in the above can be found in his works. Given the overall importance of agency in Pragmatist philosophy, I wish to focus especially on his perspectives on the relation between observation and participation, in order to relate his theory of knowledge, culture, and communities of inquiry to the Cologne program of interactive constructivism.

First, I want to turn to a closer consideration of Dewey's concept of truth. In the little 1910 essay "A Short Catechism Concerning Truth" (MW 6:3–11), Dewey presents an imagined dialogue between a Pragmatist teacher and a pupil who makes objections and questions the Pragmatist of truth. In one of his objections the pupil poses what we might call the transcendentalist objection to Pragmatism. He says that he has been informed that the Pragmatists understand truth as an "*experienced* relation, instead of a relation between experience and what transcends it" (MW 6:4). The teacher's reply includes that it is crucial for Pragmatism to deny traditional ideas of transcendence. For Dewey, there is no transcending of experience, in the sense that we can find truth, e.g., in "Things in Themselves" or any other substance or essence independent from the cultural realm of experience. To identify truth with pure transcendence in the traditional metaphysical sense would lead us into the fallacies of speculative thought or "intellectualism" that Dewey radically rejects.

A little later he warns us against a second misconception with regard to truth. The pupil here states what might be called the traditional realist objection to Pragmatism. He insists that one take into consideration that the Pragmatist notion of truth contravenes common sense, because it claims that the "correspondence that constitutes truth does not exist till *after* ideas have worked, while common sense perceives and knows that it is the antecedent agreement of the ideas with reality that enables them to work" (MW 6:6). This realistic objection is very much founded in scientific common sense to the present day. It could also be labeled a copy theory of truth: Would it not be inevitable to say that our ideas are copies of an outer reality? The pupil gives an example of commonsense thinking: Columbus discovered America in 1492. This is an antecedent reality followed by ideas. If the reality itself depended on the future ideas we conceive about it, then we would land in "the most fantastic of philosophies" (ibid.).

The teacher replies that we must take care not to confuse two different aspects—event and truth. There are many events that humans observe, but the events themselves do not represent truths. "The existence of the Carboniferous age, the discovery of America by Columbus are not truths; they are events" (ibid.). As a constructivist, I agree that the observation, interpretation, assessment, and evaluation of events depend on the perspectives we take. But this alone tells us nothing about the truth of events. Truth is first constituted if we make truth claims warranted by effects and functions of events, by consequences observed in inquiry. What is true for us, then, always implies an interpretive community. Truth needs "warranted assertibility," as Dewey later says in his *Logic* (LW 12), which always means an interpretation of events, undertaken by a community of inquirers, that makes claims to validity. It is essential for the Pragmatist (and constructivist) notion of truth, then, that making truth claims is a *procedure*: "the Pragmatist claims his theory to be true in the Pragmatic sense of truth: it works, it clears up difficulties, removes obscurities, puts individuals into more experimental, less dogmatic, and less arbitrarily skeptical relations to life; aligns philosophic with scientific method; does away with self-made problems of epistemology; clarifies and reorganizes logical theory, etc. He is quite content to have the truth of his theory consist in its working in these various ways, and to leave to the intellectualist the proud possession of a static, unanalyzable, unverifiable, unworking property" (MW 6:9).

Referring to William James's *The Meaning of Truth*, Dewey's notion of truth takes for granted that there is a reality independent of consciousness, which, however, we as humans cannot grasp. There-fore, all attempts at knowing this reality beyond our experience are useless. To be true in the Pragmatic sense, a statement must be consis-tent with regard to the knowledge, the pre-understandings, and the beliefs of a subject as participant in interpretive communities. These beliefs have to prove themselves continuously in the severe test and evaluation of experience (comp. Kloppenberg 1998, 86). And this definition shows a great affinity to interactive constructivism. The Cologne program insists in this connection that there is a world inde-pendent of our consciousness and beyond our knowledge (e.g., not-yet-discovered realities). Whenever we experience a lack of under-standing in our reality constructions, we call this the appearance of *the real*—not as a copy of reality in our minds, but as a limiting con-dition of our previous realities. The appearances of the real in this sense motivate us to make new discoveries and move beyond our so-far established "versions of world making" (Goodman 1978). This concept of the real has similarities with Dewey's notion of "problem-atic situations," because it indicates a starting point for the necessary search for solutions in the sense of symbolic and imaginative con-structions of reality. In both approaches this refers to versions of world making in different fields of human experience like science, philosophy, art, politics, and education.[3]

If we propose such an open, pluralistic, and dynamic notion of truth, however, it could be possible that some interpretive communi-ties claim their religious beliefs, for instance, as truths because they have agreed upon these beliefs and have viable arguments that sustain these claims in their own chosen perspective. Surprisingly from a Eu-ropean perspective, in contemporary American society it is even pos-sible for creationists to assert that God as designer has created the world and that the evolutionary theory therefore is false and should not be taught in schools. In the scientific sense, this proposition must of course be dismissed as false. But the difficulty with an open and dynamic notion of truth, like that maintained by Pragmatism and constructivism—as far as yet discussed—could be that it does not provide clear enough limitations to allow for the exclusion of truth

claims made by communities that deny or distort the validity of scientific experimentation. How do Pragmatists and constructivists
react to those positions? What possibilities for knowledge criticism
remain for excluding arbitrariness and the hegemonic claims of specific groups that try to impose their beliefs and prejudices upon all
others?

First of all, we have to concede that Pragmatism and constructivism are themselves "weak theories" with regard to expectations of
universalization. But they are "strong theories" with regard to an inquiring, open, diverse, experimental, and antidogmatic stance. The
essential criterion for generalizing truth claims is, according to constructivism and Pragmatism, the existence of a society of pluralist interpretive communities. If one of these communities claimed to have
the one and only access to truth for all, that claim would of necessity
deny our pluralist criterion. In Dewey's words, this criterion implies
"numerous and varied . . . interests which are consciously shared"
within a democratically organized community, as well as its "full and
free intercourse with other forms of association" (MW 9:89). Nevertheless, he concedes the possibility of generalized or even universalized truth claims valid for the majority of cultures, provided that the
context of human experience itself is generalizable or universalizable
to that extent. For example, we can say that in modern science and
scientific education we have established standards that render evolutionary theory an indispensable component of knowledge. In religious belief, this standard may be questioned; there may be religious
truth claims that contest the relevance of scientific knowledge for
their beliefs. But both perspectives have to consider that their respective truth claims are only valid in the context of their experiences and
discourses. Following Dewey, warranted assertibility in evolutionary
theory is principally not an appropriate claim within a religious discourse. From the perspective of interactive constructivism, I might
add that truth claims must be viable, and this very viability implies
that we avoid confusing contexts. In science, evolutionary theory
alone counts as scientific knowledge; in religious beliefs, the absolute
reference point may be seen in God's creation, and even those who

regard this as an exaggerated absolutism must respect and recognize this position *as a possibility of religious belief.* But they do not have to accept the furthergoing claim that confuses religious beliefs with matters of science. In the context of a pluralistic society, it is not possible (in the sense of viability) to enforce a common sense between both perspectives, because we then would have to choose one side only and deny the other. To avoid this trap, the scientific standards of a modern and postmodern society separate both fields, even if this separation for some may lead to contradictions in their personal life. If children, e.g., were not allowed to acquire scientific education, say the basics of evolutionary theory, on behalf of respect for religious feelings and opinions, their participation in the achievements and developments of science would be restricted in an illegitimate way. But these achievements and developments represent an essential part of our culture and a necessary cultural resource. From the perspective of "Old Europe," the age-old battle between religion and science seems to have resulted in a clearer separation than in the U.S.

Constructivism, like Dewey, principally rejects dogmatic restrictions of knowledge by external power because these restrictions obstruct scientific inquiries by observers, participants, and agents. Interactive constructivism sees Dewey as a strong ally against traditional metaphysical beliefs and a naive realism. Nevertheless, Dewey also seems to embrace an early-twentieth-century kind of optimism informed by aspirations of modernity. His Pragmatism bets hope on finding less arbitrary and skeptical relations to life-world. This optimism—or meliorism, in Deweyan terms—is implied throughout his writings and has consequences for his theory of observation. I shall give a brief outlook on Dewey's concept of observation.

First, I wish to recall James's Pragmatism paradigm of observation: "Hands off: neither the whole of truth nor the whole of good is revealed to any single observer" (James 1958, 188f; Kloppenberg 1998, 103). This position presupposes tolerance based on the agreement that all observers will be allowed to have their specific view and say as far as they are not themselves intolerant against the views and says of other observers. This is an essential commonality between Pragmatism and constructivism.

In "Are Naturalists Materialists?" (LW 15:109ff.) Dewey, in critical response to Sheldon, discusses the question of how far scientific observations must be built on empirical evidence warranted by the confirmation of others (see LW 15:119ff.). If scientific methods demand experiments and observations confirmed by others, then it seems to be important to have access to the consciousness of others. But the crux of a narrow empiricism, according to Dewey, lies in the false conclusion that "the private and hidden" room of subjectivity—e.g., feelings like pain, love, beauty—is therefore ruled out of public court, as claimed by Sheldon. The argument runs like this: An individual pain, e.g., cannot provide sufficient access for other observers. Therefore, it cannot be observed objectively and verified publicly. Dewey writes:

> For let us grant, at least for the sake of the argument, that $A$'s mental states can not be observed by his fellow men. Let us even accept the much stronger claim that statements like "$B$ can not experience $A$'s feelings" are *analytically* true, so that it is *logically impossible* for $B$ to experience $A$'s feelings. Does it follow that $B$ can not publicly verify that $A$ does experience some feeling, of pain, for example? That it does not follow will be evident from applying Mr. Sheldon's argument to the supposition that a subatomic interchange of energies is taking place in accordance with the specifications of modern physical theory. No one will claim that such subatomic events are literally observable, at least by human investigators. Nevertheless, though those events are not observable, propositions about them are certainly confirmable or verifiable—and in fact publicly verifiable by observations on the behaviors of macroscopic objects. Evidently, therefore, there may be states and events which are not observable, even though propositions about them are publicly verifiable (LW 15:120).

Dewey here insists on the connection, often neglected by empiricism, between observing affairs and communicating about their being true. Insofar as they always presuppose more than one neutral observer, truth claims always imply interpretation and communication, i.e., the frame of an interpretive community. In the process of interpretation and agreement they are publicly warranted as probable or improbable. To present our truth claims publicly, especially in science, we always have to interpret our observations intersubjectively and interactively with others.

On the other hand, (post)modern societies often show a tendency to delegate observations, especially the fields of technology, to expert elites in order to increase efficiency. Dewey insists that these observations must be integrated deeply into education to achieve a broad interpretation of scientific possibilities. The practice of education, according to him, must allow for participation of learners in every field of scientific and socially relevant observation from the very beginning. If we succeed in promoting the experimental approach to learning as a viable way for all learners, this would increase innovative power in all areas of human living. And it seems especially necessary for democratic development.

Dewey has an acute sense for the necessity of communication across diverse interests and between diverse communities of inquiry. And he also observes that such interpretation succeeds best on the basis of face-to-face communications that allow for an open, honest, and thoroughgoing exchange. But his philosophy of communication sometimes tends toward harmony and an imagined *Great Community*. Although Dewey's democratic approach does not neglect dissent, conflicts, and struggles for power, he sometimes seems to underestimate the predicament of dissenting interests in modern societies. So at least goes one often-stated critique that reads his approach as too harmonic and apologetic of Western modernity. Although this critique, to my mind, is one-sided and partly overexaggerated, it has resulted in many misconceptions and prejudices against Dewey's work in the German reception. This damage is unfortunate, because criticism of *this one tendency* in Dewey led many to underestimate the productive potentials of his work.

There are, indeed, many passages in his work in which he emphasizes the recognition of difference as a change for the flourishing of democracy in plurality, diversity, and communication across differences. Time and again he elaborates on the interrelationship of observation and participation in cultures. Present-day Pragmatists, following this tradition, rightly ask radical constructivism, e.g., why its proponents only focus on an observer theory and neglect a theory of participation. The problem of such neglecting has already been accurately criticized by Dewey. Richard J. Bernstein, e.g., shows in *Beyond Objectivism and Relativism* (1983) that Dewey, when discussing issues of communication and understanding, always draws attention to education and growth in community. In the terminology of interactive constructivism, Dewey's idea of education as a social function implies that participation in setting the frames of understanding is a key for observation in everyday affairs as well as in science. Dewey's very idea of experience involves that we always take this interrelationship of observation and participation into account. For him, experience always includes possibilities that have not yet been explored or constructed, i.e., alternatives in all fields of communication and science. But the realization of such alternatives can only be secured by democratic participation and dialogues across different interests and communities in cultures. Bernstein thus rethinks Dewey's approach with regard to current questions of methodology, and it is surprising how relevant for our days Dewey's works appear.

To understand participation in cultures, following Dewey, we have to reconsider the relationship between democracy and community (Bernstein 1998, 147ff.). If Peirce focused mainly on a "community of inquirers" and Royce on a "community of interpreters," then Dewey broadens the concept of community by his idea that democracy must be radical, in the sense that all involved by the consequences of decisions must have the chance to participate directly, as far as possible, in the processes of decision making. For all members of society to partake democratically and actively in decisions and be recognized in their very own interests, however, turned out (and still turns out) to be difficult in political realization. Dewey was disappointed, time and again, by the real political, social, and especially economical conditions in America. His response was not so much a profound critical analysis of capitalism—as developed in the Marxist tradition—or a systematic inquiry into social injustices, although he was aware of many social ills of his time. His most productive reaction to this situation was to develop an approach of cultural criticism and transformation that allowed for positive solutions.

Principally, Dewey's response to the crises of democracy is always more democracy. This basic intention is focused on participation. Democratic participation as an ideal is in the foreground of Dewey's thinking. It stands for a primacy of politics comparable to some current articulations of post-Marxism in the New Left (Laclau 1990; Laclau and Mouffe 1985; Mouffe 1996, 1997, 2000). But he partly idealizes communities as organic wholes that can be misunderstood as underestimating the complexity, ambivalence, and contradictoriness of structural conflicts. On the other hand, he offers an approach oriented toward solutions that productively respond to conflicts by negotiating difference and developing plurality. Dewey thinks that democratic negotiation and deliberation give us the chance to transform dissenting interests into consent on solutions—at least as far as the respective problematic solution allows. Characterized by critical, open, and tolerant communication, his approach offers many affinities between Pragmatism and constructivism. One may even say that today constructivism, in this connection, develops concepts of systemic communication, therapy, supervision, and other contexts of communicating on relationships that stand in the wake of Dewey's philosophy.

In interactive constructivism, as I have argued above, a systematic theory on participation must be accompanied by an equally systematic theory on the role of observers and agents. And here it seems to me that Dewey, while developing perspectives on agency, especially in his educational theory, underestimates the importance of a comprehensive theory of observers, although he has a lot to say about observation. But from the view of interactive constructivism, his treatment of human observers is often too narrowly bound to specific interpretive communities and the role as participant in these.

When talking about observation, Dewey mostly has in mind two crucial cultural contexts—education and inquiry. His idea of observation implies participation in these contexts.[4] The rich and complex understanding of observation that Dewey develops on this basis can, e.g., be read from the following passage in *Experience and Nature*. First, he explores the habitual contexts involved in observation: "objects of knowledge are not given to us defined, classified, and labeled, ready for labels and pigeon-holes. We bring to the simplest observation a complex apparatus of habits, of accepted meanings and techniques. Otherwise observation is the blankest of stares, and the natural object is a tale told by an idiot, full only of sound and fury" (LW 1:170). Second, he discusses the importance of imagination in and for observation especially of social issues. He tells us that in the "case of social objects and patterns, institutions and arrangements" there is a crucial contrast between "an existence which is actual, and a belief, desire and aspiration for something which is better but non-existent" (ibid.).

In both fields Dewey shows that observation is part of a comprehensive and complex intellectual operation that "involves (1) observation of surrounding conditions; (2) knowledge of what has happened in similar situations in the past, a knowledge obtained partly by recollection, and partly from the information, advice, and warning of those who have had a wider experience; and (3) judgment which puts together what is observed and what is recalled to see what they signify" (LW 13:44; LW 12:136ff.). He rejects any idea of observation that takes facts and events as entities isolated from context and independent from any frames of interpretation (see LW 6:3ff.). The meaning of an observation is part of its scientific import (see, e.g., MW 12:161). There is, for Dewey, a natural desire behind our observations in different fields of life. This desire is indispensable for human activities, for the solution of theoretical and practical problems, and for scientific work (see LW 8:316ff.). Education and schooling have to take this necessary desire into account and need to support and further it (see LW 8:319ff.). Constructivists find many affinities in these positions.

In his *Logic: The Theory of Inquiry*, Dewey takes the anti-universalistic stance that scientific progress has devastated the idea of eternal and immutable essences, objects as "fixed stars," truth claims valid for now and all times alike. This, he says, leads to a problematic situation: "If the logical subject cannot be identified either with an object or sense-datum directly given to judgment for qualification through prediction, nor yet with an ontological "substance," what is meant by being an object substantial *in any sense* that makes capable of serving as a subject?" (LW 12:130)

Dewey's answer to this question first insists on the observation that all issues of scientific research are characterized by singularity, i.e., a set of unique events. There is no universal and complete account of such events. But there are, from the view of a Pragmatist theory of inquiry, two essential keys for the possibility of rendering something an object of scientific research, at all: (1) The problem of inquiry must be defined and stated in a way that allows for a possible solution; and (2) This way must be such that the finding of new data by observation is directed through provisional hypotheses that allow for the construction of a coherent and whole situation. The eventual object of inquiry must show logical consistency and unity of elements. "For it is union of connected distinctions so held together that it may be acted upon or with as a whole; and it is capable of incorporating into itself other predicted qualifications until it becomes, as such, a unity of inter-connected distinctions, or 'properties'" (LW 12:131).

What Dewey here calls "properties" of scientific research based on warranted constructions in inquiry are not ontological essences. But inquiry, for Dewey, seems to allow for a logical position that enables us to make quasi-universalistic claims, e.g., with regard to specific scientific findings and technological applications like the melting of tin.[5] From a constructivist perspective, his theory of inquiry does not sufficiently reflect the role of observers in cultural contexts. Even if Dewey is at times acutely aware of the importance of context—compare his essays "The Inclusive Philosophic Idea" (LW 3:41ff.) and "Context and Thought" (LW 6:3ff.)—he does not always draw the consequences of this idea to the last point. How do observers decide which object in natural or social sciences can count as universal without falling back on immutable essences like "fixed stars" or any other apparently eternal views?

We don't have to go as far as Rorty, here, who declares that all scientific propositions are language games, which assigns to literature the same status with regard to the consequences and import of truth claims as to philosophy and other sciences. In all sciences, we find specific language games that fit the requirements of specific discourses. These discursive particularities must be taken into account in criticizing truth claims. But even in the natural sciences, I suggest, quasi-universalistic claims are not necessary and, indeed, are often obstructive. There is, in every scientific discourse, the need to acquire a common language, to follow established methods and practices; i.e., every scientific discourse rests on conventions shared by a community of inquirers / interpreters. It is not necessary, however, to claim that these conventions are universally valid. This claim could even be dangerous for science in that it may seduce us to adhere to conventions that delimit scientific innovations. Although Dewey repeatedly cautions us against this danger (see, e.g., MW 12:262ff.), he remains ambivalent with regard to its anti-universalistic implications. From a constructivist view on science, we time and again have to secure the viability of our truth claims and put conventions at risk. But any form of universalism tends to assert a best or final observer position that allows us to define a comprehensive list of adequate conventions. This is the obstructive aspect of universalization, because such definition always risks hindering the articulation of new perspectives and could promote dogmatism. Dewey clearly has a premonition of this problem when he speaks of "relative—that is *relational*—universality" (ibid.), but it would seem wiser to me to jettison the philosophical claim to universality altogether. For it is better to assign the reconstruction of conventions to the plural practices of science and to diverse communities of inquirers than to superimpose the conventional games by particularly powerful communities of interpretation. Constructivism clearly favors this way. In the context of his time and the scientific optimism of American progressivism, Dewey neglects the problem of power in science. Here it would be interesting to reconstruct some parts of his philosophy with the help of Foucault.

According to Rorty, this problem even concerns Dewey's use of the term "experience," which is itself always part of specific language games that often produce ambiguous connotations. Indeed, the late Dewey himself would eventually decide to drop the term and replace it by "culture," because he found that his specific use of it had led to misunderstandings (LW 1:330ff.). The term is difficult to handle because it combines two perspectives in one: the existential activities of human subjects and the contents and communications in and about these activities. This holistic view, as useful as it is in overcoming traditional philosophical dualism, might too easily swallow up different observer positions and interests. There is a related problem here, as with Heidegger's concept of *Dasein* ("being-there") that equally posed complicated tasks for hermeneutic interpretation. What for Heidegger is the permanent quest for orientation in "Being-in-the-World"—a world that is differentiated in complex configuations—is significantly implied in Dewey's idea of experience, too. It is the search for a coherent and comprehensive whole from which we can productively and successfully observe differences, without ever being able to completely grasp and fixate this wholeness altogether. Positively, with regard to the three roles distinguished in this essay, Dewey's concept of "experience" largely focuses on the roles of agents and participants and shows their constructive potentials, especially as opposed to traditional copy theories of experiencing. In one of his last writings, *Knowing and the Known*, coauthored with Arthur Bentley, Dewey argues the following: "We introduce no knower to confront what is known as if in a different, or superior, realm of being or action; nor any known or knowable, as of a different realm to stand over against the knower" (LW 16:111). And even more precise: "We tolerate no 'entities' or 'realities' of any kind, intruding as if from behind or beyond the knowing-known events, with power to interfere, whether to distort or to correct" (ibid.). And in conclusion: "We tolerate no finalities of meaning parading as 'ultimate' truth or 'absolute' knowledge" (LW 16:112).

The participants of knowing-known events are thereby recognized as competent to be open-minded for what happens: They are not seen as depending on superior powers or authorities to tell them what shall or must happen. As Thomas S. Kuhn in his "Structure of Scientific Revolutions" suggests, however, this is an ideal construction that underestimates the role of different interests and the ambivalence of paradigm shifts. Rorty has learned a lot from Kuhn in becoming careful about the ambiguity of participant roles in inquiry. In my view, a constructivist observer theory can be helpful in furthering critical reflection of this ambiguity and to partly withdraw the Pragmatic idealization. In Dewey, inquiry is focused on the practice of inquiring: "Any statement that is or can be made about a knower, self, mind, or subject—or about a known thing, an object, or a cosmos—must, so far as we are concerned, be made on the basis, and in terms, of aspects of event which inquiry, as itself a cosmic event, finds taking place" (ibid.).

But in Dewey, the theory of inquiry presupposes an idealization of community that does not sufficiently make explicit the powers, interests, and contradictions implied in all scientific discourse. From the perspective of interactive constructivism, it is not enough for a theory of inquiry to favor discourses of knowledge alone, but we also have to take into account discursive aspects of power, lived relationships, and also, partly, the unconscious. In the Cologne program these perspectives on discourses have been differentiated in controversy with different modern and postmodern discourse theories (comp. Reich 1998b). The reconstruction of discourses, even in science, always implies the critical reflection of preconditions of observing, participating, and acting. In this connection, postmodern theories of deconstruction are a fruitful way to extend our attempts at self-criticism, in culture and in science, that Dewey in his time so forcefully called for.

There have been many relativizations of scientific truth claims since Dewey's death. Therefore it seems helpful to me to have a hypothetical Dewey as a discussion partner, as Richard Rorty suggests. This hypothetical Dewey would be someone who speaks in his sense and from his perspective. He argues about issues on which we don't have authentic words from Dewey himself. This would be an imag- ined Dewey, but the imagination follows the perspectives found in his work. This suggestion seems to me to be in accord with the spirit of Dewey's philosophy, for he was not a thinker of stagnation or a philosopher of last words. Instead, he reinvented himself many times over his long philosophical career, because he was well aware that every era has to rethink and reinvent its versions of the world over again. Thus Dewey can give an orientation for constructivism through his work. All sciences construct different versions of world, having different effects, within different interpretive communities. These versions of the world may find rather narrow or broad scales of recognition. We need them as orientations. In that we are in the same position as the evil stepmother in "Snow White," who, if she lived today, would count as mad for trusting her mirror's voice. In- deed, it would be even worse today: In complex affairs of life she could not even trust her own thoughts and words, because these are subverted faster than she would have hoped for. Any inquiry, espe- cially in the social sciences, is very much in the same situation today. We live in an anti-universalistic age, but maybe this very situation calls for new universalizations on the part of specific communities to find consolation. Interactive constructivism suggests that we read and reconstruct Dewey in an anti-universalistic way. Universalism—so my hypothetical Dewey—is not in his perspective, because it would attract precisely those voices from the past that Dewey himself re- jected and wished to pass by as not viable anymore.

# SEVEN

# PRAGMATISM, CONSTRUCTIVISM, AND THE PHILOSOPHY OF TECHNOLOGY
Larry A. Hickman

Despite the overall attractiveness and the many benefits of the Cologne program of interactive constructivism, I suggest that its practitioners may have shifted too far in the direction of a neo-Pragmatist postmodernism. I take the Cologne program to advance a variety of cognitive relativism and argue that Dewey's classical Pragmatism undercuts the claims of cognitive relativism. In Dewey's view, certain judgments within the techno-sciences and the social sciences are universalizable: they are globally reliable regardless of individual and cultural variability.

My general aim is to suggest that there remains a good bit more life left in the program of classical American Pragmatism than has been attributed to it by the program of interactive constructivism as I understand it. More specifically, I have the impression that if we were to draw a line between two points, with the neo-Pragmatism of Rorty at one pole and the classical Pragmatism of Dewey at the other, the Cologne program may have positioned itself just a bit too far in the direction of Rorty's postmodernism. So let me see if I can make a convincing case for what I regard as a salutary shift toward the pole of classical Pragmatism.

As a point of departure, I will examine some of the claims advanced in Professor Neubert's excellent essay "Pragmatism and Constructivism in Contemporary Philosophical Discourse."

One of the things that I find most interesting about this essay is its assertion that "there is no claim to true knowledge that *per se* warrants the consent of all observers and thus evades the possibility of relativization" (page 3 in paper as originally presented). This claim, we are told, turns on certain postmodernist insights regarding the "inherent paradoxes of the absolute and the relative in the field of truth claims" (Neubert 2001, 3).[1]

As I read this assertion, I find that it falls within the category of claims generally known as "cognitive relativism." For purposes of triangulation, I'll cite a similar statement of that position from a 1996 essay published in the journal *Philosophical Forum* that seems to make more or less the same claim in slightly different terms.

"The kind of relativism I wish to defend here," writes this author, "is a very general form of cognitive relativism which takes as its object judgments in general. . . . It is based on two theses: (1) The truth value of all judgments is relative to some particular standpoint (otherwise variously referred to as a theoretical framework, conceptual scheme, perspective, or point of view). (2) No standpoint is uniquely or supremely privileged over all others" (Westacott 1996, 131).[2]

In order to keep matters as simple as possible in what follows, I will just refer to Professor Neubert's view as "cognitive relativism," with the full understanding that he may wish to object to this label.

Of course his text can be read in a number of ways, depending on what is meant by "*per se,*" what is meant by "consent," what is meant by "relativization," and, perhaps most importantly, what is meant by "warrant." If it is intended to assert that human knowing, including the type of knowing that has been termed "techno-scientific," is context-sensitive in some sense or other, then any observer not prepared to consent to its truth would probably be dismissed as impertinent at best, or irrational at worst.[3] The speed of light, for example, is relative to the medium through which *it* travels. (I will leave aside the issue of whether *it* refers to waves, particles, or "wavicles.") The melting point of pure tin at 232 degrees Celsius, like the amount of time it takes to bake a cake, is clearly relative to the altitude above sea level at which the performance takes place.

Moreover, if the text means to claim that knowing tends to be fallible and corrigible, then it also warrants our consent, even though that warrant requires some qualification. William James's expression of fallibilism is clear enough on this point: "there can be no final truth in ethics any more than in physics, until the last man has had his experience and said his say" (McDermott 1967, 611). This is, of course, just a general restatement of what C. S. Peirce had said, more precisely, about truth involving a kind of convergence toward an ideal limit.

We now know, for example, that the earth is more or less spherical, and that it revolves about the minor star we call the Sun. Since 1962 we have known the value of *pi* to 5,000 decimal places, and the latest information that I have (which is by now probably already out of date) is that its value has since been calculated to over 6.4 billion places. There was a time, however, when none of these judgments—the empirical truths of the spherical shape of the Earth and its rotation about the Sun, or the more abstract truth of the value of *pi* to 6.4 billion places (a type of truth that William James once termed "necessary" or "a priori") had yet been constructed. There were people who had not yet had their experience or their say.

But what James wrote in his next sentence is also germane to our issue: "In the one case as in the other, however, the hypotheses which we now make while waiting, and the acts to which they prompt us, are among the indispensable conditions which determine what that 'say' shall be" (McDermott 1967, 611). I thus take James to be suggesting that not all methods are created equal, that there are in fact standpoints—perspectives, if you will—that are superior to others if one is interested in attaining truth.

I am quite happy, even eager, to use the term "constructed" in this context. On one side, the judgments I just mentioned are *per se* neither just subjectively nor culturally arbitrary. On the other side, as judgments, they were not just waiting somewhere, prior to inquiry, ready to be discovered like a banana on a tree or a fossil on a hillside.[4] They had to be constructed from what Dewey in 1916 had already termed the raw materials and intermediate stock parts of experience, including experienced data, previous judgments, and rules of inference.

But now, in their role as judgments, they can be asserted with warrant and with confidence in any part of the Earth, whether one is in Kansas City, or Cologne, or Kandahar. Moreover, asserted as intermediate judgments that support other, final judgments (relative to a sequence of inquiry) or affirmed in the form of propositions (again, relative to a sequence of inquiry), they are able to support a wide range of further judgments. Their presence enriches the world. As judgments, *per se*, it is difficult indeed to imagine a situation in which they might ever need to be revised. As fallibilists, we can say that such a revision is possible, but highly improbable.

If the situation I have just described is an accurate one, then it leads me to wonder about the central claim of cognitive relativism, namely, that all judgments are dependent on the perspectives of particular observers or groups of observers. I freely admit that there are two special senses in which this claim can be sustained. One of these senses points us to the history of the judgments: they have been constructed over time by particular observers and groups of observers. The other sense points us to expectations about the future: these judgments are open to interpretive application (and perhaps even revision) by particular observers and groups of observers. Like everyone else, those who constructed these judgments and those who will interpret and enlarge their meanings have been and will continue to be bound by their own perspectives. None of them was or ever will be omniscient.

During this period in their history, however, these judgments are objectively true. What this means is that they continue to stand the pragmatic test of experimental deployment. They have undergone and are ready to undergo further rigorous peer review. The conditions that led to securing them as judgments are repeatable.[5] They continue to be used in ways that have validated them as judgments. They are ready to get up and go to work every morning as reliable employees of common sense and techno-scientific inquiry, no matter where or to whom they are sent.

Shall we then characterize such judgments as absolute, or as relative? For reasons that I have just indicated, I am not sure that talk of the absolute or relative truth of judgments gets us very far. In the strict sense of "absolute," of course, nothing is absolute. And in the strict sense of relative, everything is relative. So I am led to wonder whether such talk does not in fact sometimes lead us down the wrong path.

Perhaps it might be better to deploy Dewey's term "warranted assertibility," a concept that he developed in his 1938 *Logic: The Theory of Inquiry* and further explicated in a 1941 reply to Bertrand Russell as a *definition* of truth, or what he termed "knowing in the honorific sense" (LW 14:168). Following Dewey's definition, the truth of these judgments is Janus-faced.

Their *warrant* points backward to a *terminus a quo*, to propositions affirmed and inferential rules formulated and deployed: they point backward to evidence already marshaled and constructive work already done.

Their *assertibility* points to the future: such judgments point forward to a *terminus ad quem*. We can *bank* on them as providing the basis and support for things that we need to do, including further experimentation. They can serve as intermediate judgments for other judgments that are, with respect to a particular sequence of inquiry, final. And they can also be affirmed in the role of propositions in future sequences of inquiry.

So much for the past and the future. What about the present? At the present, their warranted assertibility denotes that they are stable and reliable as platforms for future actions. They have satisfactorily terminated a sequence of inquiry, and there has not been sufficient disequilibration with respect to their employment that they have been put into doubt. To use William James's felicitous metaphor, their status is that of the perch that terminates the flight of cognitive activity and at the same time serves as a resting place prior to the next cognitive flutter. It is in this sense that judgments are stable; they serve as indicators that a state of equilibrium has been attained. A problematic situation has been resolved and has thus become balanced, harmonious, and free of doubt.

Their reliability is not subjective, nor is it culturally contingent. These judgments *do* work. And they do *work*. Moreover, they *are able* to work, even where and when they are not accepted as warranted. As such, judgments of this sort are neither absolute (without relation to other data and other judgments), nor are they relative in any but the most trivial of senses, namely the sense in which there is nothing that we can conceive or of which we can speak that is not related to something else.

Put somewhat differently, the interesting question for cognitive relativism, or so it appears, is not whether judgments are absolute or relative, but whether or not they are reliable, either locally or in the global sense that I term *universalizable*. Looking backward, I hope that we can agree that they have been constructed, and we can probably even agree that the conditions that have facilitated their construction have pertained or even been unique to one particular culture and not another. Robert Kaplan, for example, has done a wonderful job of tracing the constructive work that went into the construction of the concept *zero*, beginning with the Indian notion of an unfilled container and continuing with the modifications that the concept underwent as it moved west (Kaplan 2000). Each culture in its turn contributed something unique to the construction of the number (if it *is* a number) *zero*. We constructivists, of course, are not comfortable with the views of old scientific realists such as the Vienna Circle or new ones such as Alan Sokal.

But among us constructivists who agree on so much else, there nevertheless seems to be a crucial line of fissure. Some forms of constructivism, influenced by so-called postmodernist writers, have questioned—even to the point of denial—one of the central claims of Dewey's version of constructivism. This is the claim that there is truth—or warranted assertibility—that transcends observational variability. Dewey argued, for example, that what he called the "denotative method," the method developed and deployed with the most spectacular results in the techno-sciences, is both superior to other means of knowledge-getting and globally reliable—universalizable—across individual and cultural perspectives. Unless I am mistaken, the Cologne school of interactive constructivism has under the influence of postmodern writers abandoned, or at least substantially weakened, this central claim of classical Pragmatism.

Looking forward, then, as the Pragmatists insist on doing, to the fruits of our ideas, what can we say of the *import*—the usefulness—of judgments such as the ones I have discussed? Are these judgments of the type that are *globally reliable*, that is, *universalizable* across the entire range of perspectives, whether those are the perspectives of individual observers or groups of observers?

Of course I am not asking the question of whether such judgments have been or ever will be universally *accepted* as reliable, that is, *universalized*. There can be little doubt that at this very moment there is someone somewhere who professes a flat earth theory, or that there is someone somewhere—perhaps the same someone—who holds some variant of pre-Copernican cosmology or pre-Darwinian population biology. Anyone who understands the rich religious and cultural diversity of the popular culture of the United States will doubtless know that there are Christian fundamentalists who believe that the fossils of the Burgess Shale were put there by one of their minor deities in order to mislead gullible evolutionists. Further, given the marvelous variation and plasticity of human belief systems, it doesn't take much of a stretch to imagine that someone might hold that current calculations of the value of *pi* are faulty. (In 1897, for example, the Indiana House of Representatives passed Bill #246, which defined the value of *pi* as 3.0! Happily for Indiana, its Senate refused to follow suit.)[6]

I hope, therefore, that I will just be allowed to stipulate as empirically obvious that not every judgment that the techno-sciences have warranted as assertible has yet been, or is even likely ever to be, deemed reliable by everyone.

But according to the classical Pragmatists there are nevertheless judgments—and more importantly there are methods—that *are* universalizable across perspectives. Speaking generally, for example, Dewey claimed universalizability for the *methods* of the techno-sciences. In 1921, during his stay in China, he wrote that "the idea is gaining ground that the real supremacy of the West is based, not on anything specifically western, to be borrowed and imitated, but on something universal, a method of investigation and of the testing of knowledge, which the West hit upon and used a few centuries in advance of the Orient" (MW 13:110). These methods had not at that point (and still have not) been universaliz*ed*, but they were then (and still are) universaliz*able*. Of course Dewey did not mean to say that the development of the methods of the techno-sciences has come to an end, that is, that such methods are now fixed and finished and that they will evolve no further. Universalizability in this sense has no quarrel with fallibilism. But, as C. S. Peirce reminded us, universalizability *does* have a quarrel with non-experimental means of fixing belief. All of its alternatives—including tenacity, authority, and a priori reasoning—have historically proven to be defective.

For reasons that I have just indicated, then, I must admit that I have difficulty giving a positive construction to the idea that "there is no claim to true knowledge that *per se* warrants the consent of all observers and thus evades the possibility of relativization."

It might be objected that there will be cultural differences in the manner in which the value of *pi*, for example, or the melting point of pure tin at one standard atmosphere, or heliocentrism, is *employed*, and therefore that the *relevance* of these judgments is relative to the interests and projects of a particular culture. This is a point that I am happy to admit. That different cultures express and utilize techno-scientific judgments in different ways is hardly a debatable matter. As Dewey reminded us, such judgments are tools for further action. And as Melvin Kranzberg reminded us, tools are neither positive, nor negative, nor neutral.

Even in such cases, however, if such projects are to come to a fruitful end, there are effects to be taken into account, lessons to be learned, feedback to be measured, and perhaps even more importantly, *peer review* to be endured. I freely admit that effects taken into account, lessons learned, feedback measured, and reviews written by one's peers may indeed all be influenced by the perspectives of observers and groups of observers. As Dewey argued however, if the methods of the techno-sciences are faithfully employed, then the results of such observations will be additive or even multiplicative, and not primarily subtractive, with respect to the fund and reach of techno-scientific knowledge. In a community of techno-scientific peers, everyone keeps an eye on everyone else for error. Some members of the community even make their careers detecting the errors of their colleagues.

Will there be paradigm shifts? Of course: Dewey anticipated Thomas Kuhn in describing that particular historical phenomenon. That there have been paradigm shifts in the techno-sciences in no way undercuts the position I have outlined. If anything, such events have strengthened that position. It is clear that the methods of the techno-sciences have evolved as a consequence of such shifts. Novel—even radically novel—judgments have become assertible with warrant. New platforms for further experimentation have been constructed. Novel results have become universalizable. What has been determined to be good and valuable as means to the management of the human environment has come to enjoy wider circulation. As Dewey put the matter, "universalization means socialization, the extension of the area and range of those who share in a good" (MW 12:198). I hope that I may be allowed to assert that the warranted assertibility of judgments such as those that express the value of *pi*, heliocentrism, and the melting point of tin under one standard atmosphere constitutes *goods*.

Though some postmodernist writers have derided his view as an old fashioned, un-reconstructed version of Enlightenment rationality, it is clear that Dewey thought that such experimental activities are among the means of "disclosing the realities of nature." As he put it, "nature and experience are not enemies or alien. Experience is not a veil that shuts man off from nature; it is a means of penetrating continually further into the heart of nature. There is in the character of human experience no index-hand pointing to agnostic conclusions, but rather a growing progressive self-disclosure of nature itself. The failures of philosophy have come from lack of confidence in the directive powers that inhere in experience, if men have but the wit and courage to follow them" (LW 1:5).

What I am suggesting is that the fact that we live in a built-up or constructed world does not warrant the claim of perspectival variability with respect to the warranted assertibility of hard-won judgments such as the value of *pi*, or the melting point of pure tin at one standard atmospheric pressure, or heliocentrism, except perhaps in the sense that such judgments *have been* constructed and that they *will be* open to perspectival variability during their application to further research and innovation. These are the "realities of nature" that Dewey termed its "traits," and they are rooted in other, more immediate realities of nature that he termed its "qualities."[7]

Moreover, and perhaps even more important, the *means* and *methods* by which the truth of these judgments has been constructed are also among the realities of nature. To deny them that status would involve a form of idealism that veils nature because it treats construction as if it were all foreground—an idealism that knows only the activities of linguistic and other mental activities and is unable to penetrate beyond discourse and textuality. In such a view, the immediate experiencing of nature, of nature as nature, would be entirely swallowed up within nature as culture; experiment would be empty because cut off from its roots in immediate experience and its fruits in the modification of existential events.

Dewey put this matter clearly enough late in his career as part of a discussion of what he called his "denotative method":

> The experiential or denotative method tells us that we must go behind the refinements and elaborations of reflective experience to the gross and compulsory things of our doings, enjoyments and sufferings—to the things that force us to labor, that satisfy needs,

that surprise us with beauty, that compel obedience under penalty. A common divisor is a convenience, and a greatest common divisor has the greatest degree of convenience. But there is no reason for supposing that its intrinsic "reality" or truth is greater than that of the numbers it divides. The objects of intellectual experience are the greatest common divisor of the things of other modes; they have that remarkable value, but to convert them into exclusive reality is the sure road to arbitrary divisions and insoluble problems (LW 1:375–76).

Now it might be objected that the assertion of cognitive relativism—that "there is no claim to true knowledge that *per se* warrants the consent of all observers and thus evades the possibility of relativization"—that this assertion has to do with matters that involve the social sciences, but not the techno-sciences. That would constitute an interesting turn in the argument, but one that would generate some very woolly problems of its own. This is because it would have the effect of splitting the humanities and social sciences off from the techno-sciences as fundamentally different types of knowing.

I have argued elsewhere (Hickman 2000, 501–13) that this is the very move that has created serious problems for the program of Jürgen Habermas. Since the 1970s Habermas appears to have held fast to a separation of the strategic action of the techno-sciences (which he claims to be concerned with facts) from the communicative and emancipatory action of the humanities and social sciences (which he claims to be concerned with meanings or values). From the viewpoint of classical Pragmatism, this is a fact-value split that is both unwarranted and counterproductive.[8]

I think I am on fairly good ground when I say, with Dewey, that even within the social sciences there are judgments that are sufficiently reliable to be universalizable in the sense in which I have employed the term. There are numerous value claims that fit that description, because they have been derived in precisely the same ways that judgments within the techno-sciences conventionally termed "factual" have been derived. In other words, they have been constructed in a rigorous manner, taking into account existentially supporting or compelling factors. And they have undergone peer review. Dewey seemed never to tire of arguing that problematic situations that involve valuation are subject to the same types of deliberative methods employed in the techno-sciences. When what is valued is called into question, inquiry is called for in order to ascertain whether what is valu*ed* can in fact be proven to be valu*able*. In Dewey's view, such tests are no less objective and universalizable than those utilized to determine whether what has been eat*en* is in fact ed*ible*.

It might be objected at this point that what is edible is determined on a case-by-case basis with respect to individual organisms, and is therefore relative to the particular perspective of an observer or observers. Even if we discount the situation in which someone persists in eating things that are not edible for him or her (and there seem to be quite a lot of people who do this), it is a happy fact that different cultures have different cuisines. If there were ever a case that could be elicited to support radical perspectivism, or radical relativism, surely this must be one.

But this situation is not quite as simple as it might seem. Two further points have a bearing on the matter. First, the observable fact that some people have specific food intolerances does not undercut the warrant for generalizations such as, for example, "mangoes are edible by (food for) human beings." This judgment is built up of numerous cases, and it is true that it is subject to certain exceptions. Taken in one of its senses, however, the objection that some people cannot tolerate (are allergic to) mangoes is rendered irrelevant. (Since we are talking about food, I will call this objection what it is: it is a red herring.) It is at least locally reliable in the sense that mangoes will continue to be approved for sale by the appropriate authorities and will continue to appear on the shelves of supermarkets.

That some individuals have mango intolerance does not, therefore, militate against the usefulness of this generalization, this judgment that mangoes are food for human beings. It is simply not a judgment that is relative to the perspective of an observer, except in the senses that it is based on the past experiences of individual observers and that there may also be individual observers who will employ that judgment in variable ways as the basis of further experimentation. In other words, even though it allows for certain exceptions, it is nevertheless *locally reliable* in the sense that it provides a reasonable, limited basis for further action.

Second, with respect to individual human beings who constitute exceptions, the fact remains that there are *globally* reliable methods for finding out what is edible and what is not edible. The judgment that "John can't eat mangoes," if true, must itself be the result of one or more reliable experimental tests—tests that would work (would be repeatable) for other people in Kansas City, Cologne, or Kandahar. These tests are not just reliable generalizations from existential material, but state conjunctions of traits that have been observed and confirmed without an exception being found. These are the tests that an allergist undertakes, and they involve traits that allow inference that is globally reliable.

To put this point a bit differently, generalization is not the same as global reliability (universalizability), but the two types of propositions work together—they are, as Dewey puts it, "conjugate."

In addition to locally reliable generalizations of the type "mangoes are edible by humans," then, there is a second sort of generalization, exemplified by the type of judgments that allergists make, and perhaps more perspicuously by the generic proposition "all samples of pure tin are members of the class of objects that melt at 232 degrees Celsius at one standard atmosphere." This proposition is further removed from specific existential material than the proposition about mangoes, which is to say that it is more refined—more abstract—and therefore capable of wider application with respect to the control of existential materials. Its predicate refers to a class that is less existentially involved than the class referred to in the previous example, since it contains two idealized (constructed) conditions, namely, a standard measure of atmospheric pressure and an abstract measurement of heat. It is sufficiently abstract, in fact, that it might even be stated in a form usually identified as a universal proposition,[9] namely,

"If a sample of pure tin is heated at 232 degrees Celsius at one standard atmosphere, then it will melt" (or something similar). Someone might write that sentence down in a chemistry textbook, for example, without fear of contradiction. As such, the judgment is universalizable. It is a globally reliable guide for action, as I have suggested. Moreover, it is reliable whether one is in Kansas City, Cologne, or Kandahar. (If they are melting tin in Kandahar at this very moment, then regardless of their political or religious or other cultural persuasions, they will need to attend to this point.) This judgment is a very good instrument for controlling future inferences.[10]

What I have termed global reliability or universalizability thus has to do with propositions that are limited in the sense that they have been abstracted from particular existential affairs, but also such that they are applicable to existential affairs in ways that allow us to control future inferences. Discussing such cases, Dewey writes of "the fact that sciences are largely occupied with determination of singulars, and that generalizations do not merely grow out of determination of singulars but that they constantly function in further interpretation of singulars" (LW 12:434).

Some propositions, of course, are maximally abstract and therefore have the widest application. In the case of the equation "$2 + 2 = 4$," for example, *all* existential material has disappeared.[11] It functions as a universal proposition. But even, or better put, *especially*, in its status as a universal proposition abstracted from all existential affairs, this judgment is able to serve as a powerful tool for constructing further inferences with respect to existential materials.

Between these two extremes, namely, between low-level generalizations heavily dependent on the existential material from which they have been constructed (such as "mangoes are edible by human beings), and universal mathematical propositions devoid of existential content from which they have been constructed (such as "$2 + 2 = 4$"), there are at least two further types of propositions. There are propositions that state physical laws of the sort "pure tin melts at 232 degrees Celsius at one atmospheric pressure" (which formulates the interrelation of the existential object "pure tin" and the abstract conditions "one standard atmosphere"[12] and "application of heat to 232 degrees Celsius"), and there are physical laws such as the law of gravity, which formulates the interrelation of the abstract character's mass, distance, and "attraction." In other words, the further from existential matter, the more abstract a judgment is, the more it is likely to be *globally reliable* as a guide for further inference, and thus for further application to existential affairs in the form of a tool for experimentation.

In other words, techno-scientific experimentation exhibits a recapitulation of the historical development of inquiry: there is a move beyond the type of empirical observation that is satisfied with the selection and organization of cases, to a type of experimental action that institutes tools, both concrete and abstract, in order to control outcomes. The key difference between the types of propositions I have been discussing is not primarily their logical form. It is their power to control inference with respect to the resolution of existentially problematic materials.

In Dewey's view, this characterization of less and more abstract judgments is warranted not only with respect to inquiry in the techno-sciences, but with respect to inquiry in the social sciences. What this means is that the relation between inquiry in the techno-sciences and inquiry in the social sciences is more than simply analogical. The most general of the ends-in-view of these disciplines are the same. Inquiry into the value of *pi*, for example, may have numerous benefits, including the aesthetic satisfaction that accompanies exploration of games and other formalized systems. It may also be used to support evidence of a high level of personal proficiency with computing languages. Beyond that, however, more generally, such inquiry increases knowledge of things *as they are* because it allows for the expansion of techno-scientific research into the realities of nature, and therefore promotes the growth of human intelligence. The same is true with respect to inquiry into fields more directly or more broadly concerned with valuation.

It is in this sense that the value judgment that "women should not be excluded from available educational and employment opportunities" is reliable. It is in fact universaliz*able* in the sense in which I have constructed the term as *globally* reliable. It is not just locally reliable in the sense of the generalization that mangoes are edible by humans, but globally reliable across individual and cultural variations.[13] Whenever and wherever there is an increase in educational and employment opportunities for women (absent other factors that counteract the benefits of such opportunities), development follows without exception.

Of course someone might want to advance the cognitive relativist claim, namely, that since "there *is no claim to true knowledge* that *per se* warrants the consent of all observers and thus evades the possibility of relativization," then this particular judgment fails to warrant the consent of all observers. In other words, someone might want to argue that it is not reliable, or that it is reliable only locally, that is, that it is a pretty good generalization of the type "mangoes are edible by human beings" but that it is not globally reliable (universalizable) across individual or cultural perspectives as is the judgment about the melting point of pure tin at one standard atmosphere. The implicit argument here, I take it, is one that has been advanced by certain postmodernist writers. Since there is no "God's-eye view," no "master narrative," then such judgments can at best be asserted within narratives that are invariably and irrevocably local: they may not be assertible within other narratives such as, say, the political / cultural narrative in force in parts of Afghanistan until recently.

In fact, anyone who is informed about the activities of the party of Islamic fundamentalists in power in certain parts of Afghanistan until recently knows full well that this is a value judgment that is far from having been universalized. But the same might be said of the judgment that the Earth is more or less spherical and the judgment that pure tin melts at 232 degrees Celsius at one atmospheric pressure.

As for the past, the judgment that "women should not be excluded from available educational and employment opportunities" has clearly been constructed over time. It is a judgment that has been warranted by means of the generation and application of various data, by setting up repeatable experiments and taking account of their results, by peer review, and by attention to the details of its application in practice. Studies that correlate gross domestic product with educational level of women in developing countries, for example, have collected, refined, and presented hard data in its support. Nobel Laureate Amartya Sen has cited such data in his book *Development as Freedom* (1999).

As for the future, this judgment regarding educational and employment opportunities for women is assertible as an intermediate judgment in the construction of judgments that are final or ultimate within a particular sequence of inquiry, in just the same sense that in · a court of law some judgments are intermediate and instrumental to other judgments that are termed final or ultimate. For example, it can be used to support another judgment such as "meritocratic social systems are better than their alternatives."[14] It is affirmable as a premise within future sequences of inquiry, such as one in which someone might attempt to determine the relative health and sustainability of a particular society.

Since it is more than an empirical generalization, it is a judgment that is *almost* as well established in terms of supporting evidence and experimental results as the judgment that pure tin melts at 232 degrees Celsius at one standard atmospheric pressure. (The "almost" qualifier in this context just calls attention to the fact that the social sciences are more complex than the physical sciences, in the sense that, as a rule, they must take account of more complex variables.) "If you have a sample of pure tin then it will melt, provided that you subject it to one standard atmosphere and heat it to 232 degrees Celsius." Further, "if a society provides educational and employment opportunities for women, then that society will enjoy increasing social benefits (provided that there are no factors that counteract the benefits of such opportunities)." Both of these are generic propositions: both have to do with ways in which existential materials can be regulated. Both are universalizable in the sense that they are globally reliable across individual and cultural variants. Both serve to direct future inquiry.

As judgments, they have been constructed within contexts of perspectival variability, and they are also doubtless open to various types of interpretations that reflect perspectival variability. But at this time, however, as reliable platforms for action, they are stable across individual and cultural perspectives. This, I believe, is what Dewey had in mind when he wrote about the perspectival character of knowledge; what he meant when he wrote about stable platforms for action; and what he meant when he wrote about warranted assertibility.

Try as I might, I can come to no other conclusion than that it would be difficult, if not impossible, to imagine a situation in which consent from these judgments could be withheld in a manner that is itself warranted. As stated, I am hard put to understand how the warranted assertibility of these judgments might be relative to a particular observer or set of observers. If, in some extreme case, it is objected that the "value" judgment about education and employment for women assumes certain conditions that might have been otherwise, then the same might be said of "factual" techno-scientific judgments such as "pure tin melts at 232 degrees Celsius at one standard atmospheric pressure." It is possible to imagine alternative worlds that include very little of what holds in this one. Speaking of *this* world, however, the Pragmatists are clear enough. In *this* world, the truth of a judgment is found in the measure to which it satisfies the conditions of an objective problematic situation. The truth of an idea is its warranted assertibility, or how well it works to settle doubt, that is, to control existential affairs.

As I have already indicated, I am concerned that some of the doctrines commonly known as postmodern have had an infelicitous influence on certain strands of neo-Pragmatism. My claim is that some of the ideas of the classical Pragmatists, which have been diluted or abandoned by some neo-Pragmatists, are better and more serviceable than what has been brought in to replace them.

This is not to deny that postmodernism appears to have adopted several of the positions worked out by the Pragmatists in the late nineteenth and early twentieth centuries, such as anti-foundationalism, perspectivism (of the type I have discussed), anti-transcendentalism, fallibilism, and contextualism. (Unfortunately, lack of time and space dictates that I draw attention to these shorthand "ism" terms without providing much in the way of explanation.) But postmodernist thinkers have not, as near as I can tell, adopted one of the central ideas of classical Pragmatism, namely the view that inquiry is experimental and that it can provide reliability that is not just local but global, or universalizable. Inquiry begins with concrete existential doubt, and involves the formulation and testing of hypotheses against the data that provoked the initial doubt. Once doubt has been settled, a firm and reliable platform for action persists until it is successfully challenged. It is this experimentalism that seems to be missing from the texts of postmodernism as I know them. This is an experimentalism that relies on an underlying commonality of human experience as having evolved within nature, and the continuity of experience and nature as exhibited in the denotative activities of human inquiry.

As Dewey put the matter, "Nothing so fatal to science can be imagined as elimination of experimentation, and experimentation is a form of doing and making. Application of conceptions and hypotheses to existential matters through the medium of doing and making is an intrinsic constituent of scientific method. No hard and fast line can be drawn between such forms of 'practical' activity and those which apply their conclusions to humane social ends without involving disastrous consequences to science in its narrower sense" (LW 12:434–35).

If this commitment to experimentalism is just assumed by or encapsulated within postmodernist theories of narrativity and discourse, then I have not yet seen evidence to that effect and so hope to be supplied with appropriate citations. As I said, I believe it to be missing in the work of critical theorist Jürgen Habermas, and I think it is lacking in the work of neo-Pragmatist Richard Rorty as well. I am also afraid that it may have been supplanted by what appears to be a plank of cognitive relativism in the platform of interactive constructivism.

# EIGHT

# PRAGMATISM, CONSTRUCTIVISM, AND THE THEORY OF CULTURE

Stefan Neubert

Pragmatism and constructivism share a common interest in cultural theory. Classical Pragmatists like John Dewey and George Herbert Mead held their philosophies to be contributions to the theory and criticism of culture. In the case of Dewey it is well known that "culture" increasingly became the dominant focus of much of his thinking in his later period, so much, indeed, that by the end of his life he was ready even to exchange his favorite philosophical candidate, "experience," with the term "culture" as it was then established in its anthropological sense (see LW 1:361–62). Present-day Pragmatists prove their continuing interest in culture by focusing their work on themes like technology, art, education, democracy, or community—topics that in the tradition of Pragmatist thought are deeply embedded in the overarching concern for culture. Present-day constructivists, on the other hand, have witnessed in the last decades what some have called a "cultural turn" in constructivist discourses.

It is by now a well-established conviction among most of its expo-
nents that constructivism cannot be radical or methodologically consistent without broadly taking into consideration the cultural
contexts always implied in the human production or construction of
realities.

Given these shared interests, then, what specific contributions and
suggestions can Pragmatism and constructivism offer each other with
regard to cultural theory? What points of coincidence and what lines
of divergence do their respective views of culture amount to? What
can they contribute to and learn from each other with respect to the
theory of culture? In this chapter, I will try to give some answers to
these questions from the perspective of Cologne interactive constructivism (Reich 1998a, 1998b, 2000a; Neubert and Reich 2000; Neubert
1998). I will largely confine my discussion to the relationship between
constructivism and Deweyan Pragmatism, indicating here and there
some implications for the contemporary neo-Pragmatist program of
rereading Dewey through postmodern eyes.

## Cultural Theory in the Deweyan Tradition

I want to confine myself in the first part of this chapter to highlighting three major perspectives on cultural theory to be found in Dewey's thought (Neubert 1998). Each of these perspectives has been
developed most comprehensively and extensively in his middle and
especially in his later works, although in many ways they draw upon
sources that go back to the very early and formative periods of his
thinking (see Westbrook 1991). In general, I agree with Jim Garrison
on his claim that "Dewey was a 'social constructivist' decades before
the phrase became fashionable" (Garrison 1997a, 39), and I think this
claim in particular holds true for Dewey's views on culture. The perspectives I want to sketch are in my view still highly relevant for
present-day constructivist theories of culture, even if I suggest that
they should in part be critically reviewed and reconstructed in the
light of more recent theoretical developments.

## Culture and Experience

Important for Dewey's theory of culture is first of all his philosophical core concept, "experience." Experience in the Deweyan sense is characterized by continuity and interaction. It is an active-passive continuum of human sense production whose basic unit is the act, "and the act in its full development as a connection between doing and undergoing, which, when the connection is perceived, supplies meaning to the act" (LW 11:214). In its most comprehensive sense, experience means life-experience, the sum of a "life-career of individualized activities" (LW 5:224) and learning processes that each in their turn have contributed to the quality of subsequent experiences. In its most immediate sense, primary experience constitutes our very being-in-the-world or being-in-situations as an unresolved wholeness. " 'Experience' ( . . . ) recognizes in its primary integrity no division between act and material, subject and object, but contains them both in an unanalyzed totality" (LW 1:18). When reflected upon, the materials of primary experience are discriminated and turned into objects of secondary experience, i.e., objects of thought. That happens whenever we are involved in a troubled, problematic, or tensional situation that demands inquiry into its constitutive elements in order to resolve the problem or tension at hand. Dewey makes clear that for him this is a process of construction (see LW 1:16) that implies a circular logic of reflection: the secondary and refined objects of thought are constructed out of the "gross, macroscopic, crude subject-matters in primary experience" (LW 1:15) to which they have to be returned and applied for test and verification. All knowing, for Dewey, is involved in this circle between primary and secondary experience.

Most important, in my view, for the Deweyan theory of culture are two crucial points in this concept of experience: (1) Primary experience, although immediate in quality, is never simply unmediated or void of meanings. Quite on the contrary, since human beings grow up and live in life-worldly contexts long before they begin to think about their lives and contexts, their experience is always already filled and imbued with an implicit abundance of cultural meanings stored

up by tradition and passed on by education and all forms of associated living. Life-experience, says Dewey, is "already overlaid and saturated with the products of the reflection of past generations and bygone ages. It is filled with interpretations, classifications, due to sophisticated thought, which have become incorporated into what
seems to be fresh naive empirical material. It would take more wisdom than is possessed by the wisest historic scholar to track all of
these absorbed borrowings to their original sources" (LW 1:40). (2)
Reflective or secondary experience, i.e., the symbolic systems and orders of knowledge, is never exhaustive as to the materials and possible
meanings to be found in "crude, macroscopic" primary experience.
"What is really 'in' experience," Dewey writes, "extends much further
than that which at any time is *known*" (LW 1:27; ital. in orig.). Dewey
takes pains to pay due attention to the unrevealed, the dark and twilight, the obscure and vague limits of knowledge that symbolic systems of science and philosophy so readily tend to explain away. This
is of course a philosophical criticism that, in the first place, contests
one-sided forms of rationalism or "intellectualism," as Dewey calls it
(see LW 1:28). But it says a good deal by implication about his view
of culture as an open and pluralistic universe with multilayered horizons of meaning, where hermeneutic skills and scientific scrutiny can
at best partially penetrate into the semantic abundance of life-experience as it is lived in the concrete. Experience in this sense means lived
cultures, and there are always remains of ambiguity, vagueness, uncertainty, and novelty whenever we inquire into cultural meanings.

## Culture and Habit

Dewey's theory of habit further elaborates on the embeddedness of
action and meaning in cultural contexts. His account of human conduct is always sensitive to the life-worldly situatedness of human
practices. The analysis that Dewey gives, e.g., in his 1923 book *Human
Nature and Conduct* (MW 14), elaborates on the subtle interplay
among what he calls habits, impulses, and intelligence. Most important here is the fact that, although Dewey's philosophy made strong

claims to naturalism, his account of human behavior never indulged in simple forms of biologism. Indeed, Dewey was very suspicious of any attempt to fix human nature once and for all in terms of drive or instinct theories, on the grounds that these theories all too readily tend to naturalize—and thus to petrify—what in the end are only contingent and changeable interpretations of a given culture (see, e.g., MW 14:76–87). For him, what are primary in human conduct are not impulses or native activities, but habits formed in the intercourse with others that participate in a cultural milieu. "Impulses," he writes, "although first in time are never primary in fact; they are secondary and dependent," because "the *meaning* of native activities is not native; it is acquired. It depends upon interaction with a matured social medium" (MW 14:66). The formation of habits in the individual appropriates meanings from customs contained in the cultural practices, routines, and institutions that precede his existence as an individual. Appropriation, though, does not mean passive accommodation to what already exists. Only in extreme cases of petrified routines does habit imply the more or less mechanical copy of a social model. What interests Dewey most are the productive and constructive powers of habits wherever conduct is individualized and ready to respond and readjust to changing and unforeseeable situations. This is a highly dynamic process, which Dewey describes with a keen "phenomenological sense" (see Kestenbaum 1977, Alexander 1987) for the perceptual, emotional, cognitive, and imaginative phases of human experience. Furthermore, it is a process that depends on a constant readiness to combine powers of "Construction and Criticism" (see LW 5:125–43)—or what we interactive constructivists call powers of re-/deconstruction, for to respond creatively and constructively to changing conditions one has to reinquire at least partially into "the equipment of beliefs, religious, political, artistic, economic, that has come to him in all sorts of indirect and uncriticized ways, and to inquire how much of it is validated and verified in present need, opportunity, and application" (LW 5:142). Thus constructivism, in Dewey's sense, must always involve cultural criticism, too. "Creative activity is

our great need," he writes, "but criticism, self-criticism, is the road
to its release" (LW 5:143).

## Culture and Communication

Dewey's philosophy of communication further deepens his views on
culture. His is a genuinely social-constructivist understanding of the
production of shared meanings through processes of symbolic interaction (see Garrison 1997b, Alexander 1987).[1] Equally important for
me is his acute sense of the importance of the imaginative in communication. This sense distinguishes his theory of communication from
more recent approaches that conceive of communication as being
largely a cybernetic process of information transmission within systems of human interaction (see, e.g., Watzlawick et. al. 1967). Not
only in his theory of art, but also in his general account of communication—e.g., to be found in Chapter 5 of his "Experience and Nature"
(LW 1)—Dewey is quite aware of the imaginative desire that drives
humans to seek fulfillment and consummation by participating in the
shared meanings of a life-world. His descriptions of the impulsive,
emotional, volitional, and aesthetic phases of this desire that under-
pin even the most sophisticated forms of symbolic reasoning yield a
rich and multilayered picture of the role of imagination in culture.
The Pragmatist theory of the self as emerging in processes of social
cooperation through the imaginative act of "taking the role of the
other" has certainly been developed in more detail by his companion
George Herbert Mead. Nevertheless it is at the very heart of Dewey's
philosophical account of subjectivity, too. And not only Hans Joas
has noticed that Dewey's and Mead's approach to "practical intersubjectivity" sheds particular light on the creative and constructive side
of human action (see Joas 1989, 1996).

Dewey's account of communication is of course closely connected
to his political thought. He is today widely considered one of the
most important fathers of the discourse of radical democracy in
twentieth-century thought. His democratic ideal of a life of full and
unconstrained communication has been accompanied by penetrating

criticisms of the anti-democratic tendencies in social, political, economic, and educational practices that he witnessed in his time. And although some commentators think today that his democratic vision of a search for the Great Community expresses a holistic trait that sometimes tends to underestimate "the 'hard facts' of power and domination in social life" (Fraser 1998, 158–59), there is certainly up to the present day a strong and productive tradition of social criticism that stems from early Pragmatism. For example, Larry Hickman's version of Deweyan "productive Pragmatism," to my mind, aligns itself with the best achievements of this tradition (see Hickman 2001).[2]

## The Constructivist Theory of Culture

### OBSERVERS, PARTICIPANTS, AND AGENTS

In my view, constructivist theories of culture can profit a lot from perspectives of Deweyan Pragmatism like the ones I have just sketched. There are many affinities and similarities between the two approaches. Nevertheless, as I have argued elsewhere (see Neubert 2001), there is also one crucial conceptual shift involved in the step from classical Pragmatism to contemporary constructivism: the shift from "experience" to "the observer." As Deweyan philosophy begins and ends with "experience," so constructivist argumentation always takes its start from and comes back to "the observer."[3] From the perspective of interactive constructivism, though, observers are not detached spectators, in the first place, but should be seen as cultural participants and agents, too (see Neubert and Reich 2001):[4] they partake in cultural practices, routines, and institutions before they are able to observe and produce descriptions of the specific observations they make. Furthermore, as to observers / participants / agents in culture, we distinguish between self-observer positions and distant-observer positions. The self-observer observes himself and others from the inside of the practices and interactions in which he, for the time being, finds himself immediately involved. The distant-observer observes others in their practices and interactions from the outside. For every self-observer the presence of (potential) distant-observers implies a constant element of strangification, a constant challenge to relativize his own observation by trying to grasp the alien view. In postmodernity, philosophical discourses on difference and otherness increasingly emphasize the importance of such relativization as a necessary component of pluralist culture. I will come back to this issue later. At the moment, I want to introduce three further perspectives of interactive constructivism that in my view are particularly viable and relevant theoretical aids for a constructivist understanding of observing, acting, and participating in culture: the registers of the symbolic, the imaginative, and the real. These registers have been very influential in the cultural theories of Lacanian poststructuralism. Interactive constructivism draws on these resources, but reinterprets them from a considerably broadened view, which abandons the narrower ontological implications of Lacanian psychoanalysis (see Reich 1998a).

## The Symbolic, the Imaginative, and the Real in Culture

### SYMBOLIC REPRESENTATIONS

Recent approaches to cultural theory conceptualize culture by focusing on symbolic representations and signifying practices (see, e.g., Hall, ed. 1997). Drawing on poststructuralist theories about language, signs, and discourses, they claim to analyze and deconstruct what may be called the symbolic order of culture. I subscribe to these intentions by suggesting that for interactive constructivism, culture, in the first place, consists of discursive fields of symbolic practices where meanings are construed, articulated, and communicated between partakers. The cultural production of realities is therefore a matter of viable symbolic re- / deconstructions within discursive fields (see Neubert 2002). The question of cultural viability can of course be determined and interpreted quite differently by different observers, participants, and agents within a given society. To an increasing extent this seems to be the case in postmodern pluralist societies, in which a common denominator for partaking in culture is largely out of sight, and remaining claims to universal validity of cultural norms and standards are increasingly being overlaid by a diversity of heterogeneous, and partly even contradictory, claims to viability. However, there must be at least a minimum of symbolic resources common to the members of a cultural group or interpretive community—common enough, i.e., that they are able to conduct and partake in discourses. I agree with Georg Auernheimer's definition that "the culture of a society or social group . . . consists in their repertoire of symbolic meanings, i.e. their repertoire of means of communication and representation. The symbolic usage of things in everyday-life is certainly part of cultural practice, too" (Auernheimer 1996, 110, translation mine / S.N.).

Important in this connection is the poststructuralist thought that, with regard to Pragmatic usage in cultural practices, symbolic meanings, and representations, are in principle characterized by overdetermination.[5] That is to say, there is a movable and never wholly stabilized relationship between signifier and signified that allows for a potential excess of meaning in every cultural use of signs. The talk about the "sliding of the signifier" suggests that the re- / dearticulation of meanings in culture is a never-ending process that can at best be suspended for the time being, but never be halted lastingly. On the one hand, there is perhaps a tendency toward symbolic closure in every discursive event, an attempt to come to terms with what is to be said (and what is not), to attain a final articulation. But on the other hand, there is never a final point in discourses that could not as well be appropriated as a starting point for another discourse—i.e., there is always the possibility of rearticulations and dearticulations that reintrigue discourses where meanings had apparently been settled.

The following passage from an introductory text by Stuart Hall gives a basic illustration of what symbolic overdetermination implies, e.g., for the use of meanings in language: "if meaning changes, historically, and is never finally fixed, then it follows that 'taking the meaning' must involve an active process of interpretation. . . . Consequently, there is a necessary and inevitable imprecision about language. The meaning we take, as viewers, readers or audiences, is never exactly the meaning which has been given by the speaker or writer or by other viewers. And since, in order to say something meaningful, we have to 'enter language,' where all sorts of older meanings which pre-date us, are already stored from previous eras, we can never cleanse language completely, screening out all the other, hidden meanings which might modify or distort what we want to say" (Hall 1997, 32–33).

### IMAGINATIVE DESIRE

Interactive constructivism suggests that the analysis of culture be extended by taking into consideration the role of the imaginative. As expressions of imaginative desire, cultural representations involve processes of imaginative displacement and condensation (see Reich 1998b) that underlie the very dynamics of symbolic overdetermination. These imaginative processes cannot be separated from contexts of social interaction. That is to say, imaginative desire is always involved in mutual mirror-experiences between self and others. These mirrorings express a desire for the desire of the other that cannot be fully resolved by symbolic forms of recognition and understanding. Thus the imaginative appears as an internal limit of symbolic communication: with regard to imaginative desire, there is always something left.

Theories of dialogic imagination, e.g., following the Russian philosopher Mikhail Bakhtin, suggest an understanding that detects within the obstinacy of imaginative desire—i.e., within the experience of the radical otherness of the Other of desire—the very conditions that give birth to the possibility of dialogic interaction. Interactive constructivism similarly argues for an understanding of lived relationships (*Beziehungswirklichkeiten*) that acknowledges the imaginative fuzziness and indeterminacy of relations as an impulsion for, and simultaneously as a limit of, symbolic communication. As to the interactions of self and others, we distinguish between what we call (big) O—i.e., the Other who articulates herself within the orders of the symbolic—and (small) o—i.e., the imagined other of my desire as mirrored in the imaginative encounter with the other. And it is important to notice that, although the partakers in communicative interaction often aspire and imagine that they can directly reach each other's imaginative desire through ways of the symbolic, the two registers never completely coincide. This is because of two closely connected reasons. First, according to psychoanalysis, imaginative desire is deeply rooted in the unconscious phases of our inner lives. Secondly, imaginative mirrorings take place on a far more immediate and subliminal level than symbolic mediations. Here gestures and expressions of body-language often say more than a thousand words. Looks that "kill" can silence a conversation as easily as a friendly and encouraging gesture may move somebody to talk about things she would not have dared otherwise. To be sure, the point is not to argue that we cannot at all communicate about such imaginative processes on a symbolic level—this is precisely what the term "meta-communication" designates in therapeutic or pedagogical contexts (see Reich 2000a). But there remains a limit in that we can never completely absorb the imaginative encounter in symbolic understandings. With regard to this limit, interactive constructivism also employs the Lacanian term "language barrier" (*Sprachmauer*).

Insofar, then, as there is always a difference between (big) O and (small) o in any communicative relationship, the imaginative subverts our symbolic attempts to unambiguously clarify the meanings of cultural situations—e.g., by relying on purely rational ways of symbolic reasoning. Imaginative desire "in all its singularity and particularity of time and place renders all forms of symbolic understanding and communication incomplete" (Neubert and Reich 2001, 7). Thus the search for symbolic solutions of the questions of meaning in culture "can at no point evade the suspicion that observation and reflection have not yet been undertaken comprehensively enough" (ibid.).

Fissures and Gaps of the Real

Our imaginative and symbolic constructions of cultural realities can never be completely draught-proofed against forms of experience that interactive constructivism calls the intrusions of *the real* into culture. For interactive constructivism, "the real (as an event) has to be distinguished from reality (as constructed). The real enters experience as a tear or discontinuity, a lack of sense and meaning. We use the term 'real' to denote the contingency of the not yet symbolically registered or imaginatively expected lurking behind any construction of reality" (Neubert and Reich 2001, 8). Taking us by surprise and entering our experience and perception unexpectedly, *real* events time and again mark the boundaries of our symbolic and imaginative search for meaning and identity. "These events do not 'fit.' They are *the real* in its obstinate eventfulness that cannot be easily integrated and transformed into elements of a culturally viable understanding. They astonish us: there is something that could not be foreseen, something alien, strange, incomprehensible" (ibid.). They move us to change our symbolic thinking or imaginative horizon.

In a word, the fissures and gaps of *the real* represent important limiting conditions of any cultural re- / deconstruction of reality. However, we constructivists decidedly reject any attempt to devise an ontology of *the real*. We speak of *the real* strictly in the sense of a void signifier. We content ourselves with using this signifier to denote a limit of our constructive capacities as observers. We deny that any observer can transcend this limit and gain access to an overall perspective independent of his specific and limited cultural contexts and resources as an observer. Only a god could claim this position of the "ideal" or "absolute observer," but for us humans even the view of this god's eye remains but an imaginative projection of a wishful desire to escape the particularities and contingencies of our limited experiences.

For interactive constructivism, then, there is no best or final observer as to *the real*. That is to say, we cannot know what the real *really is* without incorporating and assimilating it into our symbolic and imaginative constructions of reality. The intrusions of *the real* that we encounter in our lives expose the *internal* gap, the *inner* fissure in the texture of our realities. They come to us as the unknown in our knowing, the mistaken twins of our expectations, the dark side of our moon. Therefore they are as much expressions of our cultural resources as are our re- / deconstructions of reality. What can (and cannot) enter our experience and observation as a *real* event may therefore differ quite considerably from culture to culture, from person to person, and even from situation to situation.

In other words, *the real* is but a construct that we devise in order to remind us that there is a world independent of our constructions, a world that is never totally absorbed by our observer perspectives, however sophisticated and refined these may be. Our relative openness to *the real* is a question of our being sensitive and vulnerable to the world in which we live. The intrusions of *the real* are often described as events of confusing, dumbfounding, perplexing loss, lack, or failure, like witnessing the unexpected death of someone we loved or feeling a sudden pain in our body without having any explanation. What these examples highlight is the dramatic extent to which *real* events may take us unawares and render us speechless, for a moment or even longer. But the beauty of a landscape that seizes the spectator or the sublime feeling that captures one in the presence of a work of art are as much expressions of our openness to *the real* as is the feeling of loss (or amusement) that follows the crash of a house of cards that we had built with care and love.

## Toward a Postmodern Theory of (Multi-)Culture

### CULTURE, DISCOURSE, AND POWER

Many of the aspects just indicated with regard to the constructivist perspectives of the symbolic, the imaginative, and the real in culture bear strong resemblances to insights of Deweyan Pragmatism. The Pragmatist theory of meanings as socially constructed in the process of symbolic interaction, e.g., implies an understanding of the work of cultural representations and signifying practices that in many respects is very similar to the one launched by Stuart Hall. Indeed, I guess that many Deweyan Pragmatists would more or less unreservedly subscribe to Hall's account of the use of meanings in language just quoted—i.e., to the historical changes of meanings, to the "taking of meaning" as a process of interpretation, to the ineradicable imprecision about language, and to the impossibility of attempts to completely cleanse language from hidden meanings stored up from previous eras. Likewise, there is a strong tendency in Dewey's thought that stresses the importance of the imaginative in culture. This holds true not only for his general account of human communication, his aesthetics and philosophy of art, but also for his account of the scientific method and, most importantly, his social and political theories. His claim that "Imagination is the chief instrument of the good" (LW 10:350) is a strong appeal against one-sidedly rationalistic attempts to found democracy on symbolically unambiguous principles of universal reasoning. Imagination, for Dewey, is like a window through which we may elicit "the possibilities that are interwoven within the texture of the actual" (LW 10:348)—possibilities, i.e., that exceed our so-far-constructed symbolic vocabularies as well as our established capacities to find descriptions of and devise reasons for the ways we conceive of "the good life." Finally, there is also a strong sensitivity in Dewey's writings for what I, from the perspective of interactive constructivism, have called the "intrusions of *the real.*" Especially in some of his major later works like "Experience and Nature" (LW 1) or "The Quest for Certainty" (LW 4), where he most penetratingly elaborates his complex concept of experience, there is an acute sense of the ineradicably precarious side of human existence. Contingency, in Dewey's view, is an inevitable trait of life that evades all attempts to construct symbolical orders and establish stability.[6] Life remains perilous, no matter how elaborated and sophisticated our symbolic systems of prediction and control may be. "For in any object of primary experience there are always potentialities which are not explicit; any object that is overt is charged with possible consequences that are hidden; the most overt act has factors which are not explicit. Strain thought as far as we may and not all consequences can be foreseen or made an express or known part of reflection and decision" (LW 1:28).

These obvious and important parallels notwithstanding, there are also points of divergence between Deweyan Pragmatism and interactive constructivism. I have pointed out in detail on another occasion (see Neubert 1998, 2001) that, to my mind, Dewey's holistic view of successful communication altogether tends to overestimate the symbolic dimension as compared to the level of imaginative mirror-experiences that, for interactive constructivism, imply a more radical limit to the symbolic possibilities of comprehensive understanding than Dewey often suggests; that his vision of free, full, and unconstrained communication sometimes neglects or at least underestimates the intricate power effects always at stake, given that the order of discourse, as Foucault so convincingly argues, largely rests on procedures of exclusion and restriction (Foucault 1981a); and that the claimed naturalistic realism that underpins his rich constructivist insights comes close to the search for an ontology of the real that ultimately tries to fill the void signifier with contents ("nature" in the Deweyan sense) independent of any specific observer position.[7]

I do not want to repeat these criticisms in detail here. Instead, I think it is more appropriate to focus at least briefly on some related issues that I think are of particular importance for present-day approaches to cultural theory. In doing so, I pick up a catchword from contemporary discussions about radical democracy. The poststructuralist "theory of hegemony," as developed, e.g., by Ernesto Laclau and Chantal Mouffe (see Laclau 1990; Laclau and Mouffe 1991; Mouffe 1996, 2000), conceives of present-day political struggles as largely being struggles over the power of interpretation.[8] Culture is seen as a field of highly contested meanings. While there are always hegemonic interpretations, e.g., about the meanings of nation, democracy, security, freedom, equality, gender, and ethnicity that temporarily prevail in a given society, they seldom succeed in establishing a complete and enduring victory over alternative interpretations. Since even the hegemonic discourse is characterized by overdetermination in the sense discussed above, there is always space for counter-discursive dearticulations and rearticulations that appropriate dominant meanings and reinterpret them in the new light of oppositional strategies. E.g., part of the victories of the feminist movement in twentieth-century Western societies was because it succeeded in appropriating the political meaning of "equality" so deeply rooted in

the political imaginations of modernity—albeit originally strongly associated with *fraternité* and thus designating the equality of men, first
of all. Feminism to a considerable extent succeeded in turning this
meaning of equality into a critical weapon against first political and
then economical and sexual forms of inequality and discrimination
hitherto largely taken for granted. This is what Laclau and Mouffe
call the articulation of an antagonism through the establishing of a
chain of equivalence. Similar examples could be found in the U.S.
Civil Rights movement, the green and ecological movements, or the
gay and lesbian movements in large parts of the Western world. And
one may guess that it is precisely the increasing proliferation, diversi-
fication, and social urgency of such oppositional and minority movements since the middle of the century—i.e., in the decades after
Dewey's death—that provide the historical background for the per-
suasive power of theories like Laclau's and Mouffe's. These theories
take the articulations of quarrel, dissent, and antagonistic interests
not as signs of deficit, but as the normal state in pluralist democracies,
provided that the very democratic attitudes and institutions that
guarantee the possibility of controversial articulations are not put at
risk (see Mouffe 1996). Instead of aspiring to the Great Community,
the one and overarching public sphere, the discourse free from domination, they put the stress on the vital necessity of a variety of discourses and counter-discourses, publics and counter-publics for the
prosperity of pluralist democracy (see also Fraser 1994). In doing so,
they construct a political discourse that, to my mind, expresses viable
perspectives for radical democracy in postmodern multicultural societies (Neubert 2002)—perspectives that at least articulate a shift of
emphasis as compared to the more holistic visions held by Dewey and
the early Pragmatists.[9]

## Incommensurability and Otherness

What is at stake here, in other words, is a partially new form of pluralist thinking in postmodernity that has become somewhat more cautious and modest, with hopes and visions of a *comm*-unity in

diversity, and puts more emphasis on a diversity of heterogeneous and in part even contradictory communities (although, as I said above, certain basic democratic beliefs should of course be made common). Although I think that this "new" brand of pluralism expresses but a shift of emphasis as compared to "older" versions like the ones held by Dewey and many of his fellow Pragmatists, I would say that this very shift has important implications for our understanding of difference and otherness that penetrates into postmodernist theories of culture. One strand of critical thought that to my mind makes an important contribution in this direction has become subsumed under the name of postcolonialism. Postcolonial deconstructions of the universalistic narratives of Western modernity open distant-observer perspectives that allow us to look and reflect more complexly on the uneven and overdetermined fields of action in multicultural societies. Concepts like *"différance"* (Hall), "hybridity," or "culture's in-between" (Bhabha) radicalize our understanding of cultural ambivalence in postmodernity. Articulated from the position of minority groups or marginalized communities (e.g., immigrants), they contest the dominant hegemonic narratives from *within*—by what Homi K. Bhabha calls an "'intersticial' agency" that emerges from "the outside of the inside: the part in the whole" (Bhabha 1996, 58). They attempt to deconstruct an easygoing liberal multiculturalism that proclaims universal recognition of difference on a "level playing field" of cultures: "'the presumption of equal respect' for cultural diversity" (ibid., 56).[10] Against this presumption they emphasize the subliminal persistence of power asymmetries that prevent the marginalized groups from articulating themselves right on time and attaining access to the "level fields" of equal recognition. In my view, this criticism aptly unmasks the often all-too-easy fancies of a multicultural *anything goes* in postmodernist societies. And what is more, it highlights an ambivalence that can make us more critical of the tempting but deceptive idea that there is or could be an ideal observer position somewhere in the cultural space from where to overlook and represent postmodern multiculture *in toto.* This possibility is what constructivists, as decisively as postcolonial authors like Hall and

Bhabha, do deny. From a constructivist viewpoint, this denial even expresses an essential claim for the project of radical democracy in postmodernity (see Neubert 2002). Culture should rather be seen as a space diversely folded in on itself—a space that displays discontinuities, ruptures, gaps, and interstices as well as continuities and transitions. As to the question of difference and otherness, this is to say that incommensurability is as marked and inevitable a trait of postmodern culture as are the possibilities of border-crossing and attaining commonalities and shared understandings.

Before I come to a close, I want to round out the chapter by commenting on a discussion of the problems of incommensurability and otherness that stems from a philosopher whose own border-crossings between different traditions and strains of contemporary thought seem to me to be very interesting for both (neo)Pragmatists and constructivists. Richard Bernstein, himself strongly affiliated with the Pragmatist tradition, has recently provided a critical appropriation of some of the main themes of so-called postmodernist thought. His insightful comments on postmodernist / poststructuralist figures like Foucault, Heidegger, Derrida, Levinas, and Rorty show an abundance of common theoretical interests as well as common theoretical references between his neo-Pragmatism and the program of Cologne interactive constructivism. In his discussion on "Incommensurability and Otherness Revisited" (see Bernstein 1995, 57–78), he critically draws upon the work of authors like Thomas Kuhn, Richard Rorty, Donald Davidson, Emmanuel Levinas, and Jacques Derrida. He gives a summery of his conclusions on each of his two topics in the form of provisional theses. I will conclude my essay by quoting at some length from Bernstein's theses on the problems of incommensurability.[11] I shall give a brief comment on each point, trying to interpret it from the perspective of interactive constructivism. Let me say in advance that what I basically think of as a strength in Bernstein's position is that he painstakingly tries to hold the precarious balance between recognizing incommensurable otherness on the one side and looking for possibilities (however far-reaching or limited) of establishing commonality and understanding across borders on the other.

"The controversies concerning incommensurability have challenged and raised serious doubts about the belief that there is—or must be—a determinate, universal, neutral, ahistorical framework in which all languages or 'vocabularies' can be *adequately* translated and which can enable us to evaluate rationally the validity claims made within these disparate languages. In this respect one of the most fundamental foundational claims of Western philosophy and epistemology has been called into question" (Bernstein 1995, 65).

For interactive constructivism, the discursive force of this calling into question rests on the pervasive impact on (post)modern thought of certain "movements of offended reason" (*Kränkungsbewegungen der Vernunft*) that mark the transitions from modernity to postmodernity. Basically, Kersten Reich has examined three such movements of offence that concern the relations between absolute / relative, self / other, and conscious / unconscious (see Reich 1998a). Postcolonial deconstructions like the ones indicated above may extend the scope of this analysis and provide suggestions for the elaboration of further implications for a postmodern theory of (multi)culture.

"The incommensurability of languages and traditions does not entail a self-defeating or self-referentially inconsistent form of relativism or perspectivism" (Bernstein 1995, 65).

Constructivists must be sensitive to this danger of self-referential inconsistency. Interactive constructivism suggests that the distinction between self-observer and distant-observer positions within discourses can help us to evade unqualified and naive forms of relativism or perspectivism. Focusing on the intricate interconnections between discourses of knowledge and power—i.e., validity claims and hegemonic struggles—constructivist discourse theory argues that the distant-observer who relativizes the validity claims of incommensurable "language games" is always already himself involved (as a self-observer) in a discourse that tends to generalize certain validity claims that are taken for granted. As far as self-observers are able to reflect upon themselves from a distant-observer position, then, relativization is always possible, but never total. And what is more, the statement that certain languages and traditions are incommensurable does *not* entail that the observation of this incommensurability is made from an absolute position that fixes insurmountable difference once and for all. The possibility of dialogue across differences inheres in the very overdetermination of discourses that implies that even the encounter of incommensurable languages can result in the construction of (limited) commonalities. This leads us on to another of Bernstein's theses.

"The concept of incommensurability is not to be confused with, or reduced to logical incompatibility or incomparability. Incommensurable languages can be compared and rationally evaluated in *multiple* ways. Practically, such comparison and evaluation requires the cultivation of hermeneutical sensitivity and imagination" (ibid.).

I should only like to add that, however cultivated our sensitivity and imagination may be, our standards for comparison and rational evaluation will never be taken from a realm beyond power relations. They express a hegemonic moment of encounter between our own and "alien" traditions. For interactive constructivism, the construction of inter- or transcultural comparisons and evaluations always implies power claims over the generalizability of one's own cultural standards—e.g., of rationality (see Neubert and Reich 2001).

"Incommensurable languages and traditions are not to be thought of as self-contained windowless monads that share nothing in common. ( . . . ) There are always points of overlap and criss-crossing, even if there is not perfect commensuration. ( . . . ) Our linguistic horizons are always open. This is what enables comparison, and even sometimes a 'fusion of horizons'" (Bernstein 1995, 65).

This point seems to me to be of particular importance. Drawing on poststructuralist theories of discourse, interactive constructivism has always argued that communities as well as discourses are no self-enclosed totalities, but show open sutures that can be turned into starting-points for interconnections and transitions to other communities and discourses. If, on the one hand, understanding that criss-crosses difference is not to be expected to entail complete commensuration—i.e., using the same vocabularies, applying the same standards, relying on the same methods, posing the same questions—incommensuration, on the other hand, is not simply to be understood as sheer and speechless Otherness. This can be further specified by coming back to the constructivist registers explained above. In the experience of *real* and genuine otherness, I encounter the Other in his obstinate and inaccessible otherness, the alien who delimits my capacity to grasp the world as the universalized sameness of my self. Wherever, yet, there is an encounter that implies a relationship, wherever, i.e., there is communication as inchoate, incomplete, or even faltering as it may be, there is also the imaginative other that expresses my desire to be mirrored, and there is the symbolic Other whose utterances contain a sense of their own—and be it only the sense of being senseless to me. The interactive constructivist theory of discourse further elaborates on these issues by introducing the "discourse of lived relationships" and the "discourse of the unconscious" as additional perspectives to the focus on relations of power and knowledge that characterizes many contemporary approaches to discourse (see Reich 1998b; Neubert and Reich 2000). "We can never escape the real practical possibility that we may fail to understand 'alien' traditions and the ways in which they are incommensurable with the traditions to which we belong" (Bernstein 1995, 65).

Incommensurability, indeed, denotes an indeterminate, fuzzy relationship wherein the lines between understanding and misunderstanding, reading and misreading, representing and misrepresenting are often shifting and fragile. For interactive constructivism, every communication implies a difference between the symbolic Other (O) and the imaginative other (o) that delimits the possibilities of complete symbolic understanding. The limit between the symbolic and the imaginative constitutes the very indeterminacy principle of communication, i.e., the "language barrier." This limit has to be reckoned with all the more intensely where communication takes place between languages or symbolic orders that are in one way or another incommensurable with each other. Here the most widespread imaginative fallacy in trying to understand "alien" communities and traditions is called "ethnocentrism." Interactive constructivism argues that the "ethnocentric view" is a cultural trap that cannot be abolished once and for all, e.g., by referring to a supposedly superior observer perspective of universal reasoning (see Neubert and Reich 2001). It is a "real practical possibility" that we should always be aware of—our very incapacity to recognize "the ways" in which "alien" traditions "are incommensurable with the traditions to which we belong."

"But the response to the threat of this practical failure—which can sometimes be tragic—should be an ethical one, i.e., to assume the responsibility to listen carefully, to use our linguistic, emotional, and cognitive imagination to grasp what is being expressed and said in 'alien' traditions. ( . . . ) Above all, we must always strive to avoid a false essentialism when we are trying to understand the traditions to which we belong or those alien traditions that are incommensurable with 'our' traditions" (Bernstein 1995, 65–66).

This criticism of "false essentialisms" is certainly one of the most fundamental affinities between Pragmatist and constructivist thought. Developed in both traditions first of all through their criticisms of knowledge, it has had a strong and powerful influence on their theories of culture, communication, and—as Bernstein aptly indicates—difference and otherness. It is a strong basis for their shared belief in the pluralist ethics of radical democracy—and their willingness to accept the precariousness of living in a pluralist universe.

"Learning to live with (among) rival pluralistic incommensurable traditions—which is one of the most pressing problems of contemporary life—is always precarious and fragile. There are no algorithms for grasping what is held in common and what is genuinely different. Indeed, commonality and difference are themselves historically conditioned and shifting. The search for commonalities and differences among incommensurable traditions is always a task and an obligation—an *Aufgabe*" (ibid.).

I wish to close by affirming Bernstein's belief that "it is only through an engaged encounter with the Other, with the otherness of the Other, that one comes to a more informed, textured understanding of the traditions to which 'we' belong. It is in our genuine encounters with what is other and alien (even in ourselves) that we can further our own self-understanding" (Bernstein 1995, 66–67) And I may add my own understanding that it is one of the chief intentions of the present volume to meet this claim on the modest level of theoretical exchanges between our different yet affine traditions of Pragmatism and constructivism and to rejoice in the adventure of philosophical border-crossings.

PART THREE

# DISCUSSION BY THE
# CONTRIBUTORS

# NINE

AFTER COLOGNE: AN ONLINE EMAIL
DISCUSSION ABOUT THE PHILOSOPHY
OF JOHN DEWEY
Larry A. Hickman, Stefan Neubert, Kersten Reich,
Kenneth W. Stikkers, and Jim Garrison

The following is an (edited) e-mail discussion based on the philosophical conversations at a conference held in Cologne, Germany, in December 2001. We will proceed in three steps. First, the
contributors will discuss selected questions about their contributions,
roughly following the sequence of the chapters in Part II of this book.
Second, we will ask more general questions about Dewey, Pragmatism, and constructivism. Finally, we will close with brief statements
about why Dewey is still an indispensible thinker for us.

*Discussion of the Contributions in This Volume*

Chapter 4: "Dialogue between Pragmatism and Constructivism in
Historical Perspective," by Kenneth W. Stikkers

**Kersten Reich:** In the history of German philosophy there is a relatively clear line that goes from *Phänomenologie* (Husserl, Schütz et
al.) to the *methodischer Konstruktivismus* of the Erlangen School. This

school has been very important in launching a cultural constructivist approach. It is presently represented by Peter Janich. From the perspective of interactive constructivism, this tradition is very valuable, especially because phenomenological concepts like "intentionality," "life-world," and "cultural world" are highly relevant for a constructivist understanding of the work of cultural reconstructions. What role would you, Ken, assign to implicit (or explicit) phenomenological tendencies in classical Pragmatism? What actual import do these tendencies have for present-day Pragmatism?

**Ken Stikkers:** The extent to which the empirical methodologies of the classical Pragmatists, most notably what William James termed "radical empiricism" and what John Dewey termed "the postulate of immediate empiricism," can properly be considered "phenomenologies," continues to be debated. What is clear, though, is that such methodologies undercut any assumption that some privileged perspective is securable in advance of inquiry, and the abandonment of such an assumption is the most important prerequisite for constructivism. The world is to be taken precisely as it is experienced, in its plurality, and through constructivist inquiry shared meanings emerge. Indeed, James already saw the profound political ramifications of his epistemology, and he connected it to his criticisms of United States imperialism, for which he was best known in his own time: i.e., United States imperialism justified itself, in part, upon the assumption that the form of science cultivated in the modern West enjoyed a privileged, viz., an "objective," access to the world, and, hence, the United States, as well as other Western powers, felt justified in imposing its Weltanschauung upon peoples it judged to be less enlightened. Clearly such imperialisms, epistemological and political, preclude the possibility of interactive constructivism, and their overcoming is essential for it even to start, and surely James's insights are chillingly applicable to current United States foreign policy: such policies make impossible any meaningful constructivist dialogue, with disastrous consequences.

Present-day Pragmatism to a significant degree fails to understand and appreciate adequately the phenomenological tendencies that one finds in classical Pragmatism, and that, I believe, is a significant loss. A number of present-day Pragmatists—viz., many of those who strive to be "thoroughgoing naturalists"—have not adequately understood, in my judgment, the importance of James's radical empiricism and Dewey's postulate of immediate experience for their Pragmatisms and thus too often fall, with their "naturalisms," into the sort of "naivety" that both James and Husserl believed plagued the sciences of their day; even Dewey is guilty of this in places. That is, they too uncritically accept the categories of natural science, e.g., the categories of evolutionary biology, as universally valid; impose them upon human experiences in realms where they simply do not belong; and thereby participate in the sort of epistemological imperialism that earlier Pragmatists, and classical phenomenologists, criticized. I am thinking especially of current tendencies, among a number of American Pragmatists, to want to disregard, in the name of naturalism, religion, and matters of spirituality generally. Such reductionist trends clearly pose a major barrier to constructivist dialogue between religious and nonreligious people. Thus I believe that contemporary Pragmatism could benefit from a recovery of the phenomenological tendencies of earlier Pragmatism.

**Stefan Neubert:** In the Cologne program of interactive constructivism there is a clear distinction between the concepts "real" and "reality." Reality, for constructivists, is always constructed by observers, agents, and participants in the context of interpretive communities. The real is understood as a border concept, a "void signifier" that denotes the limits and open sutures of our reality constructions. As constructivists, though, we reject any attempt to devise an ontology of the real. We emphasize the eventfulness of the real and use the term "real events" to denote situations in which something unexpected, unforeseen, or dumbfounding enters and often disturbs our reality constructions. Ken, could you briefly explain the usage of the term "real" in the classical Pragmatist approaches of Peirce, James, and Dewey? Is there an (implicit or explicit) ontology of the real in these philosophers? Does the constructivist distinction between "the

real" and "reality" make sense from your Pragmatist perspective? Do
you see a difference between classical and present-day Pragmatism on
these issues?

**Ken Stikkers:** The distinction is one I learned especially from
Scheler and have found it extremely applicable to Pragmatism, although I do not think that Pragmatists themselves have maintained
it consistently. As my essay suggests, Peirce seemed to use the phrases
"reality" and "the independently real" synonymously. However,
there does appear to be some equivocation in his use of these terms,
along the lines of the distinction that Stefan Neubert has articulated.
On the one hand, and as I indicated in Chapter 4, Peirce defines "reality" as "the object represented" in the "opinion which is fated to be
ultimately agreed to by all who investigate," and Dewey endorses this
definition in his *Logic.* Clearly Peirce's use of "fated" suggests a non-
constructed, metaphysical conception of the "real," and, furthermore—something I did not discuss in my contribution—he tells us
that the existence of independent reals is evident from the fact that
we all admit to making mistakes: that is, if reality were merely constructed, we would never err but only change our minds. Inquiry is
guided not merely by the desire for consensus, viz., "the social impulse," but also by the desire to learn "the truth" of the matter, viz.,
to square oneself, as a living organism, with the real constraints and
resistances of one's environment. This use of these terms seems to
coincide with what you term "the eventfulness of the real." However,
Peirce also tells us that the reality that inquiry seeks to know is not
fixed in advance and merely awaiting discovery, but contingent upon
the opinions and decisions of the community of inquirers. So clearly
there is also a constructivist element to his notions of "reality" and
"the real," coinciding with the Cologne constructivist use of "reality." What Peirce definitely wants to avoid is the extreme position
that reality is *merely* constructed, i.e., made up: rather, the construction of reality takes place within an environment, which exerts limits
and constraints, "external" to the processes of constructivist inquiry
themselves. Much of neo-Pragmatism, e.g., Richard Rorty, seems to

want to ignore such "external" constraints. (I place "external" in quotation marks here to indicate that the term is to be taken phenomenologically and does not presuppose some sort of metaphysical distinction between inner and outer: the constraints are experienced by the inquirers *as* "external" to their activities.) The Cologne program of constructivism, however, like Peirce, avoids such an extreme with its use of "the real," as explained by Stefan Neubert: constructivism, along with the classical Pragmatists, recognizes constraints "external" to its own processes of inquiry. Moreover, the Cologne program and classical Pragmatists, following Peirce, seem to agree that recognition of such external limits does not require a metaphysical theory of *what* "the real" is—that is what I take Neubert to mean when he characterizes the constructivist conception of "the real" as "a border concept," a "void signifier." Rather, it is sufficient to let "the real" stand for an indefinite something that continuously challenges, resists, and disrupts our constructivist efforts and with which inquiry must constantly contend.

Chapter 5: "Dewey's Constructivism . . . ," by Jim Garrison

**Kersten Reich:** Constructivist critique of knowledge generally rejects naturalism as a foundation of truth claims. We concede that there is a world beyond human constructions, but the linguistic turn and other movements in modern and postmodern theories of knowledge (e.g., Wittgenstein and his successors) have shown that truth claims are always part of language games and discourses and that there is no way of simply copying nature into culture and knowledge. Thus, if we speak about nature, this is always already a culturally informed talk. Here the most famous neo-Pragmatist critique is, of course, Richard Rorty's *Philosophy and the Mirror of Nature*. In this context I'd like to ask you, Jim: Doesn't any form of naturalism eventually imply an ontological tendency and lead us to the fallacies of correspondence theories? How would you describe the import and the limits of Pragmatist naturalism in the Deweyan sense? Do you see a tension between Dewey's naturalistic concepts of "existence / essence" and (post)modern theories of discourse? How would you defend the Deweyan naturalistic concept of "existences" and "essences" in the face of (post)modern anti-essentialist criticisms in both Pragmatism and constructivism?

**Ken Stikkers:** Let me interject that Kersten Reich's excellent question gets, in a different way, at the very point I made previously about "naturalism" in certain Pragmatist contexts. I, too, will be very interested to hear Jim Garrison's reply.

**Jim Garrison:** Dewey was well-versed in the history of philosophy. Twice in *The Collected Works*, Dewey invokes the classical Greek concept of *"phusis"* (also spelled *physis*). In *Experience and Nature*, he uses it to criticize modern notions of "nature" that convert the physical into the material, something the classical Greeks never did. He reminds us that the Latin *"natura"* is a translation of the Greek *phusis*, and that *natura* is associated with growth and change. Dewey finds much to applaud in the Greek and Medieval concepts as opposed to the modern notions of "nature," though he rejects the notion of antecedently existing fixed ontology as the predetermined end of the process of growth (see LW 1:348).

Wolfgang Schadewaldt points out two interesting things about *physis*; first, *"Physis* is never that 'nature' out there where people make Sunday excursions, 'in' which this and that occurs or this and that is such and such." Second, he observes that "like all Greek constructions ending is *sis, physis* does not mean some object or material thing, but a coming-to-pass, an event, a directing activity, a *Wesen*—if we understand this word in its original active meaning, which is preserved in *verwesen"* (Hickman, 1992, 220). Dewey rejects any sense of directing activity insofar as that implies a predetermined essence or being. In this way, Dewey reconstructs the classical Greek sense of nature. For Dewey, experience is always the experience of existence, and existence is always an *event* (not a thing, subject, ontology, etc.). William James's idea of a stream of consciousness is a good metaphor to express our experience of nature not as a place of things, but an event of events. Dewey explicitly argues that the law of excluded middle does not apply directly to existence, only to the ontology and essences that are the constructed products of the process of inquiry.

Dewey completely deontologizes the very concept of nature. In his 1938 *Logic*, he again invokes *phusis* to explicitly reject talk of "the nature of things," in the metaphysical sense of "unchanging substances with their fixed essential characters or 'natures'" (LW 12:88). With this comment, he sweeps away the entire metaphysics of substance (i.e., what Derrida calls the metaphysics of presence) that has dominated Western thought from the beginning of philosophy through the modern age so influenced by science. Dewey's theory of nature is not reductionistic; rather, it is a *process* theory in which organic, biological beings *emerge* from mechanical, physical beings, and mental beings emerge from organic, biological beings through social-linguistic practice. Ontology, essences, etc., are always the product of inquiry carried out by mental beings; they are never something that subsists antecedently in existence. Indeed, the very concept of "nature" is, like all meanings, itself a cultural construction.

Once we acquire language, we can never experience "nature" beyond the limits of language. We have a "sense" of existence, nature, etc., beyond the limits of language, but we cannot say anything about it. One might designate it using the "void signifier;" that is a good word for it, but after we exhaust words we may only gesture toward what cannot be said. After that, we gesticulate with "OOOHH!" and "AHH!" or "UGH!" After that there is only awe, wonder, and reverence for that beyond our control, our comprehension, and yes, our construction. It is a reminder that not even a god can construct something from nothing. Sometimes, the experience of nonontological existence beyond the limits of language should simply leave us all speechless before the holy.

**Stefan Neubert:** I find your answer very interesting. Generally, it is clear that Pragmatism and constructivism share a pluralistic understanding of truth. However, there are also minor differences at specific points, e.g., in connection with their different assessment of the relevance of naturalism. Doesn't even a modest Deweyan naturalism like the one you support imply the tendency to establish a realm of superior observation and truth claims? Could you explain again what

understanding of truth characterizes your Pragmatism and constructivism? What role does experimentalism in Dewey's sense play in this
connection?

**Jim Garrison:** I will focus on how Dewey understands truth, and
its relevance to constructivism. First, there are no intuitive, immediate, or self-evident truths for Dewey. Second, truth is not a matter of
the correspondence of a proposition to a state of affairs such as we
find in the classical correspondence theory of truth. It is a functional
correspondence of means to ends, which is very different from the
standard correspondence theory. Here is a statement of what Dewey
means by truth: "Sometimes the use of the word 'truth' is confined
to designating a logical property of proposition; but if we extend its
significance to designate character of existential reference, this is the
meaning of truth: processes of change so directed that they achieve
an intended consummation. Instrumentalities are actually such only
in operation. . . . The means is fully a means only in its end" (LW
1:128). Truth in its existential sense is a course of constructed operations yielding the same consequences every time and everywhere. To
avoid entanglement with the usual theories of truth, Dewey will turn
to warranted assertion in his 1938 *Logic.* There, knowledge is simply
the product of a process of inquiry. Now, warranted assertion concerns knowledge here; not truth per se, but knowledge is the end of
inquiry, and we may warrant a knowledge claim if the same operations using the same means produce the same end of knowledge every
time (given the constraints of context). I like to take constructivism
very literally. We construct meanings in our sociolinguistic practices
and we construct truth as the product of the operations in a process
of inquiry (i.e., the formation of judgment). That Dewey often refers
to industrial operations and the like when explaining what he means
by operations seems very significant to me. To say we socially construct meaning and from meanings we construct warranted assertions
(knowledge, things we assert as true with warrant) does not mean
we can make anything true we want. It is usually very hard to find
constructions that, in fact, succeed in transforming some problematic

situation. If we can figure out a course of operations that are stable, repeatable, and reliably produce the same end every time, then we have good warrant to say we have worked out "processes of change so directed that they achieve an intended consummation." I think what Larry Hickman has written on Dewey's philosophy of technology bears much more on this question than it seems. We produce warranted assertions in the process of forming judgment, much as we produce automobiles that run well.

**Larry Hickman:** Peirce, James, and Dewey had somewhat different notions of truth, or at least they expressed the core ideas of Pragmatism's treatment of the subject somewhat differently. In a 1941 reply to Bertrand Russell, Dewey is quite clear. Truth is defined as warranted assertibility. Truth is not subjective, but objective in the sense that there are many things that are assertible with warrant whether or not we wish them to be so. Truth is not the correspondence of an idea with a preexisting, extra-mental fact, nor is it the coherence of an idea within a system of thought. Truth is backward-looking in the sense that what is true is so because of the experimental work that has led to its status as warranted. It is also forward-looking in the sense that what is true is assertible. A warranted idea can be asserted in a context in which it is relevant and so serve to resolve a problematic situation.

**Stefan Neubert:** Jim, how would you position your own Pragmatist constructivism with regard to (post)modern anti-essentialist criticisms? E.g., do you agree (and how far) with the criticisms of essentialism contained in Richard Bernstein's 1992 book *The New Constellation*?

**Jim Garrison:** One of the things I like about Richard Bernstein's book is that it puts contemporary Pragmatism in creative dialogue with contemporary European thinkers, especially postmodernists and poststructuralists. I also like this aspect of the Cologne program of interactive constructivism. I believe Pragmatism has much to learn from Cologne constructivism in this regard.

In response to postmodern incredulity toward metanarratives and recognition of fragmentation, Bernstein accentuates the pluralism of

Pragmatism. Nonetheless, once we acknowledge the inevitability of fragmentation, we must also acknowledge the importance of unity as well. How to achieve *dynamic* unity in diversity will probably prove the most important topic of the twenty-first century. Another thing Bernstein does well is acknowledging not only the falsifiability of philosophical positions, but also their contingency. In general, Bernstein does a good job at noting the plurality of essences along with their falsifiability and contingency.

What Bernstein says about essences also applies to the human essence and personal identity. Essences endure, but are not eternal. We need to construct enduring essences and identities that allow us to survive and thrive. For Pragmatists, this means we should constantly evaluate the *consequences* of our constructions of meanings, essences, identities, etc., to see whether they contribute to human well-being and growth. Interestingly enough, both Peirce and Dewey refer to Matthew 7:20 of the Christian Bible: The passage reads, "By their fruits ye shall know them." Here the task is to distinguish false from true prophets. Peirce, the founder of Pragmatism, asserts that this is the core of Pragmatism. An emphasis on consequences not only delineates false and true prophets, but it is how we work out meaning, truth, essence, and value. In the present case, we are talking about essences. Further, while the working out of the truth and value of an essence, or anything else, is forward-looking, it is also experimental. Given the extensive experimentation with totalitarianism in the twentieth century, those living in the twenty-first century have good warrant for believing that it knows the essence of totalitarianism and that it is false prophesy.

Chapter 6: "Observers, Participants, and Agents in Discourses," by Kersten Reich

**Ken Stikkers:** Postmodernist discourses are often criticized for their seeming self-referential inconsistencies, and Stefan Neubert, in Chapter 8, warns constructivists to be sensitive to such dangers. Various postmodern writers have offered responses to such criticisms, which generally I find unsatisfying. Several of your claims seem to lend themselves readily to charges of self-referential contradictions, and so I wonder how you respond to such accusations. How, generally, does constructivism's "anti-universalist stance" not end up being itself a disguised universalism, proclaiming "Thou shalt renounce all universals"? More specifically: (a) What is the position from which the plurality of perspectives is viewed and the lack of a privileged perspective proclaimed—i.e., that the queen's mirror is not "the final and best observer"? How is *that* position not itself a privileged one? Or, put another way, what is the status of the language game that announces the plurality of language games? And (b), you claim, along with Pragmatism and constructivism, that "a universal, ultimately transcendental, final, or best truth valid for all humans . . . is no longer achievable." How is that claim itself *not* "a universal, ultimately transcendental, final, or best truth valid for all humans?"

**Kersten Reich:** Constructivism frequently encounters this critical reproach for alleged self-referential contradictions. Emphasizing issues like the relativity of contexts, the viability of argumentations, and majority of opinions as conditions for laying claims to truth, constructivists take an anti-universalist stance. The objection then indeed often holds that this anti-universalism can only be based on another (but hidden and unacknowledged) universalist claim. "Thou shalt renounce all universals!" or "Do anti-universalism!" seems itself to be a universalist assertion. But such objections presuppose the very theoretical attitude that constructivism contests. The position from which Cologne constructivism speaks cannot itself be a meta-position in the sense of knowing everything in advance or being able to tell with sufficient completeness how all others have to decide on issues of truth claims. We are at the same time more modest and more radical here. Modest, because we recognize that the plurality and diversity of scientific argumentations and validity claims are relative with regard to the succession and juxtaposition of discourses, the scope of their validities (majority decision reached through interpretive communities) and their viabilities (success in deployment). In science, however, majority decisions alone are never sufficient warrants of truth claims. They have to be qualified by proof of viability and practical success that legitimate the claims made by an interpretive community. We know from the history of science how precarious an issue this can be, because interpretive communities repeatedly tend to make up their own world according to their own manners of thinking, thus securing their own presuppositions and prejudices. Therefore it is important in science to take both perspectives, taking into account the majority decisions made by specific interpretive communities, but also the quality of their argumentations (what Dewey emphasizes as warranted assertibility) and the scope of validity of their truth claims. And this implies also that one take into account the concrete viability of their claims in empirical practices, an issue that presupposes the deployment of experimental methods as crucial for the discernment of success or failure of specific hypotheses. If we critically reflect on science, then, we always have to specify for whom, why, and in what situation (practices) claims to validity and truth are laid. And what does that involve with regard to other approaches? What implications does it have, what effects does it produce in other and different contexts? This position does not preclude the possibility that we often succeed in achieving consensus and establishing generalizations thereafter largely taken for granted. Especially in the field of techno-sciences we find such agreements across cultures, because the workings of specific techniques are alike in different cultures (although their meaning can be understood and interpreted quite differently, e.g., as to their risks and dangers). We are modest here, because we cannot identify any privileged position from which to maintain for all others equally and universally what in all respects is appropriate and true for them. We at the same time abandon any attempt to claim universal validity for our own view. Our modesty of necessity entails that we abandon the talk about performative self-contradictions, because it does not make sense for us anymore—for it imposes on us the belief in the possibility of universalizing our truth claims, which is the very belief that we have already abandoned. This is why the objection does not affect us so much as it confirms our critics. Therefore this misunderstanding will not move us to abandon our constructivism only because it seems illogical and contradictory to them. To us those very critics seem illogical, because they do not understand that universal reasoning does not apply in the frame of constructivism. This is a truly radical move, for it implies that science can no longer by itself develop true discourses with universalizable results that apply to everyone and each and any situation. Scientific discourses are always relative to time and culture, because they stem from a particular time with its particular practices; they generalize, e.g., viable solutions and majority decisions, but they cannot ever claim complete and eternal validity. Even if it may seem that in some fields there are universalizable assertions (e.g., logical equations in mathematics), we must concede that such universalizable assertions are only valid within their particular scope of application—which in turn is largely influenced by culture. It is one of the great conceits of Western culture and its techno-sciences that its own claims to truth and warrants of assertion are applicable to everyone and everywhere. Although they are valid wherever the attendant technologies are employed, those technologies do not escape relativization (as to their limits and risks). Their validity is always restricted to the narrow field of functional deployment. The risks produced by their deployment, as well as the circular cumulative effects of their interaction with other practices and forces in a given culture, always relativize the technologies as well. For example, if cell phones are employed worldwide, the respective technology seems to be universal (the technical rules and procedures are the same everywhere). But the attendant risks (e.g., with regard to possible health problems caused by rays) point to the relativization of this viable solution through unforeseeable consequences. The perception of these very risks, however, depends on different cultural and subjective contexts and expectations. This is precisely what distinguishes the constructivist viewpoint. We are so skeptical of universalizations because they are always enforced by omissions. In the euphoria of the feasible we become neglectful of the reductions that have enforced the universal. To sum up my answer to your question, Ken: (1) the reproach for self-referential contradictoriness does not apply to constructivism, because it concedes that even its own truth claims are relative with regard to viability and majority decisions (i.e., there must be people who consider constructivism to be true and viable); (2) constructivists can well admit that there are seemingly universal truths, especially in the techno-sciences, but given the omissions and necessary reductions and abstractions implied in such statements they turn out to be generalizable at best; they must always be critically considered in the context of cultural practices; (3) to achieve plausible analyses, then, constructivists have to distinguish and critically reflect at least two levels of truth validity: (a) the majority decisions of interpretive communities that succeed in having certain truths prevail for a certain smaller or larger period of time (this has been emphasized, e.g., by Thomas S. Kuhn); (b) the viability of assertions and claimed truths that can be tested by experiments, investigations, inquiries into the working of hypotheses, and empirical methods in many ways; it must be critically and repeatedly reexamined as a counter-balance to majority decisions.

**Jim Garrison:** I find your distinction between observers, participants, and agents quite valuable. I would like to learn more. As a beginning, please say more about how the three stances interact to construct personal identity. The position also seems to have implications for our relation to "the other" and dialogues across differences of culture, gender, etc. Could you say something about these possibilities?

**Kersten Reich:** The three concepts are not meant to represent identities in the sense of a copy theory of representation—concepts can't do that. Rather, they are meant to help us understand the complexity of the cultural construction and negotiation of identities. I think that we can use these three perspectives today as an interpretive orientation for explaining the formation of identities and discussing the issues of balancing our identities. And I think that the three perspectives are especially helpful for approaching these issues in an open as well as critical manner. However, as theoretical concepts or perspectives they do not stand for themselves, but are continuous with other concepts and models that they in turn supplement. As to the formation of identities, traditional models of explanation often resort to dualisms. Then we have a world "out there" as opposed to an "inner world" in our minds, and the individual is supposed to appropriate as much as possible from "outside" and to provide proof of interest and persistence as "inner qualities." As experienced learners we know that this image is far too simple. Not only that, but our learning and our emerging identities are always open and incomplete constructions that represent snapshots, as it were, of our own narrations. They moreover depend on our constant—and always situated—efforts at balancing out forces and influences. We may count ourselves lucky anticipating successfully the roles, expectations, and challenges that we encounter. Nevertheless, even after such success life remains perilous. But a multilayered assessment from the perspectives of the observer, participant, and agent may at least help us to participate better in the developments of our own lives and to deliberately develop our identities in a balanced way. Take, as an example, possible difficulties implied in the role of the participant. How often have we been told, as a child, that the world "is" such and such. They have offered us conventions, and if we were lucky, some of those conventions allowed for observations that approached the world experimentally, as Dewey conceived it. But very seldom was participation itself discussed or critically considered. Why do we think the way we think? What makes us proceed the way we proceed? Here there is the important distinction between convergent and divergent thinking. Educators are often tempted to reduce divergent thinking conventionally and thus promote convergent thinking. Too much divergence, diversity, and plurality seem to hinder the learning process. They are admitted only in very limited fields of observation. But what do we get in return? Our conception of humans will be characterized by the dominance of rather passive forms of participation, content with having things be the way they "are." But they "are" not really "so," but we have constructed a universe of learning that renders them the way we then do experience and see them. If, however, you want to facilitate your learner's own development of their chances and opportunities to achieve identity and agency in a broad democratic sense, you have first to change the learning process and organize thoroughgoing forms of participation that balance out the participations, observations, and actions of learners. This, indeed, implies a reconstructed understanding of the other and of culture. Here I tie on to what, to my mind, is so valuable in Dewey: democracy is the basis of all education, and only through education will we succeed in furthering and improving democracy. Mere observation is not sufficient here, but we need to act. This is why Dewey strives for immediately democratic communications (e.g., in the school)—a democracy in miniature, as it were—to provide everyday situations for learning to act and cooperate in democratic ways. Otherwise democracy remains but the name of a program that turns out to be more and more unachievable. This implies opportunities for real participation on the part of every learner. And this in turn means that every learner who does not yet know about the conditions of participations he's getting involved in must have the opportunity to learn about the reasons for getting involved and to assess alternatives. Here our constructivist approach coincides with American theories of "situated learning," which rightly insist that it is only through communities of social practice that learning gains meaning. And I should like to add that it is crucial, therefore, to give every learner opportunities for reflecting on this meaning. This may even change our understanding of otherness, the alien, different cultures, the other sex. Balancing out our own identities, we have to concede that others, too, create their life-worlds within their culturally constructed contexts. Deviation from standardized expectations is nothing arbitrary; it has become normal in our present world. We may provide opportunities for appreciation, if as observers we recognize differences, as participants we talk about the limits of our cultural horizons, and as agents we reflect on our own doings as well as those of others. And only such appreciation can lead us out of the arbitrariness of well-meaning understanding for everything and everybody. For we cannot simply understand and appreciate everything whatsoever, but have to take our stand, e.g., as to cultures that enforce undemocratic participations, restrict the freedom of observations, or use violence and power to compel agents to do certain things. Constructivists here take a decidedly democratic stand that they defend against opponents, even if they try to understand alien cultures in the light of their different contextualities, for this does not dispose of critical engagement wherever democratic participation is put at risk or rendered impossible. For interactive constructivism, democracy is the precondition of its very discourse, the condition of its own possibility as a theoretical approach (although constructivists admit that this very precondition is itself ethnocentric). Therefore it calls for participation and democracy in miniature, following John Dewey. I have tried to elaborate the consequences of these ideas for the theory of teaching, too, and have made some suggestions of how they might work out in constructivist classroom practice (see Reich 2002b).

**Larry Hickman:** Kersten's contribution raises a number of interesting issues, not the least of which concerns what he sees as the differences between Pragmatism and interactive constructivism. It is in this connection that he discusses two pairs of concepts as they relate to knowing: the permanent versus the temporary and the universalist versus the anti-universalist. In each case he opts for the second member of the pair—the temporary in the first case and the anti-universalist in the second. If I have understood him correctly, I would agree that there are some significant differences between interactive constructivism and the classical Pragmatism of John Dewey.

First, there seem to me to be two types of permanence factored into Dewey's theory of inquiry. First, there is a quasi- or *functional* permanence, in the sense that some things are (legitimately) *treated as* permanent as long as they are not called into question by some unstable situation. Our experimentally derived belief that the Earth revolves about the Sun provides a good example of such a functionally permanent belief. And second, there is what is permanent because it has been so thoroughly abstracted from concrete affairs that it has become fixed. The value of *pi* to fifty places is a good example of this type of permanence. Neither of these types of permanence undercuts Dewey's well-known fallibilism, however, since he also held that ideas are *in principle* open to revision, that is, should the need arise. But what he wanted to do was avoid the extreme positions on this issue—on the one side the Platonic notion that all truth worthy of the name is timeless and immutable, and on the other side the view that all truths are subjective or relative to a particular culture.

So my first question for Kersten is whether he can accept the idea that there are some beliefs that are in fact permanent in these two senses, functionally and abstractly. That is, can he accept the idea that there are some truths that are (legitimately) *treated as* permanent as long as they are not called into question by some unstable situation and other truths that are permanent because they have been so thoroughly abstracted?

Regarding the second pair, I should point out that this is precisely the matter I discussed in Chapter 7 of this volume. To put matters succinctly, I doubt that Kersten's distinction between the universalist and the anti-universalist is fine-meshed enough to capture the subtlety of Dewey's account of the kind of knowing exhibited by the techno-sciences. That is why I introduced a distinction between two types of universalization—what has been universal*ized*, on the one hand, and what is universal*izable*, on the other. I believe that this distinction allows us to maintain the type of cultural relativism that Kersten wants to hold and at the same time avoid the type of disaster that would ensue if we were to say that the major successes of the techno-sciences are just arbitrary, or even just geographically or culturally limited in terms of their applicability.

So I have two questions for Kersten on this point. First, does he think that the melting point of a sample of pure tin at one standard atmosphere is culturally determined? The question is not whether tin *is* melted in every culture, since that is clearly not the case. The question is rather whether, *if* tin were to be melted in any particular culture, the melting point would be variable based on cultural differences.

And second, I wonder whether the issue Kersten raises about Chinese medicine really does the work he wants it to do. Of course he is correct that there are what he terms "certain limits and indeterminacies," in any situation in which we speak or act across cultures that have different histories and practices. But I would argue that one of the strengths of the methods of the techno-sciences as we now practice them is that at their best they are thoroughly instrumental / experimental and therefore self-correcting. One only need consider the rapidity with which the SARS virus was isolated, especially when that research is compared to the years of research that went into the isolation of the Human Immunodeficiency Virus.

What this means in practice is that there is not one science for Europe and another, different science for China. There is only one science that is at least in principle capable of taking into account new information, whatever its origin, as long as that data is capable of being assessed instrumentally and experimentally. That this instrumental / experimental method was developed first in Europe is just an historical accident. To say that its results are culturally bound, thus, seems to me to go too far (even freely admitting, of course, that certain problems and not others have been chosen as the subject of inquiry). Otherwise it would be impossible for the World Health Organization to mount effective vaccination programs, to take just one example. It is a fact that smallpox vaccinations work whether one is in Kansas City, Cologne, or Kandahar.

**Kersten Reich:** In my view, all constructions of truths or realities involve social contextuality—i.e., they are always, among other aspects, historically and socially determined. In science we often tend to neglect this because we follow the more specific lines of our specific research programs. And here the cultural contextuality of our scientific practices often does not seem to be of any specific import for our research questions. It is easy for me to concede, in reply to Larry's first question, that functional and abstract types of permanence are indeed useful in the context of specific scientific constructions. We have to consider, though, that even the claim to permanence is itself a specific construction. And, what is more, this construction is often readily used against critics in order to deny their potentially new ideas in advance. Thomas S. Kuhn, in his *Structure of Scientific Revolutions*, has repeatedly stressed that paradigm shifts in science are mostly prompted not by better observations or insights—even in the case of significant empirical findings; rather, they occur only after new scientists have occupied the crucial power positions and thus gained opportunities for promoting new ideas. Now the idea of permanence is much more sustainable in the techno-sciences than in the humanities and social sciences. We might begin an endless game of telling the true and trustworthy claims to permanence existing in our culture from other, more problematic or doubtful claims. The constructivist position is unequivocal here: informed by cultural history and the history of sciences, constructivists tend to understate the idea of permanences, because they fear the thread of overgeneralizing habits and resorting to untrustworthy universalizations. In specific practical cases, however, they have to concede the applicability of warranted methods and results of science, lest they themselves resort to untrustworthy and esoteric tenets. But the constructivist claim is nevertheless sustainable without committing the fallacy of sheer arbitrariness that all truth claims are relative to the constructions within a culture or society. And this claim applies to the techno-sciences as well. In their present and globally successful manner, they are the very product of a Western habitus that expresses a thirst for new knowledge characteristic of an enlightened and industrial culture. This habitus tends to project its own way of life and patterns of thinking onto every other culture in this world—i.e., to universalize them on a global scale. We must not confuse the success of this project with the idea that this success corresponds to the wishes of mankind in general. There *is* no such "in general," one might be tempted to say, or, more precisely: it is again but one cultural construction that some have established in order to suggest that their viewpoints and interests—namely, Western viewpoints and interests—are generally valid. This culturally relative perspective can prevent us from representing, without a break, the West as a model for the rest of the world. Rather, it helps us to stop and rethink the risks and dangers of this procedure:

e.g., the vanishing of whole cultures that have no resources for resisting the techno-sciences and the attendant processes of industrialization and globalization. The development of technologies and material ways of life characteristic of the industrial age has not only added to the extinction of certain animal species; it has destroyed whole cultures as well. This fact alone underscores the viability of a cultural relativism that does not confine its views on everything we do to the advantages of producing permanences in the longer run. Such permanences are often Janus-faced in that the technologically successful society involves the risk society as its other (and often neglected) side. And the risks are dispersed quite unequally according to the societal position of those concerned.

Now I turn to Larry's other questions. He asks how far the melting point of pure tin is culturally determined. To answer this question is not as easy as it first may seem. Of course it is clear that insofar as we presuppose the technology of melting tin, the melting process according to that technology is an equal or at least similar procedure, independent of culture or location. With regard to this technology, then, the melting point is unequivocal and can be generalized. Therefore it seems to be free from cultural determination. But we must also concede that culture is already involved in this very technology—namely, the history of the techno-sciences. In the context of particular cultural practices and on the basis of particular cultural conditions, was it possible in the past to discover and theoretically elaborate that, and how, tin can be melted? This presupposes a technological context, a cultural context of application and usage of knowledge that makes the process of melting tin meaningful to those involved and responds to their interests. If we only look at technological functionality, we neglect this cultural context of creation. But for what reasons should we consider that "contexts of creation"? In the German discussion, the program of so-called "*methodischer Konstruktivismus*" launched by Kamlah and Lorenzen (1967) and Janich's (1996) approach of "*Kulturalismus*" have put particular emphasis on these issues. Their historical reconstructions of the practical contexts of creation that underlie the developments of science (especially the natural sciences and techno-sciences) show what presuppositions are involved in scientific inventions, how far the historical situation and specific practices of distribution, production, and means of production have been crucial determinants, what logical forms and abstractions were generated on that basis, and also what omissions took place. Science should not only know how things happen, but also reconstruct the "why" and the cultural contexts of inventions. The *"Kulturalismus"* approach puts special emphasis on analyzing (rethinking) the technological presuppositions that are always already implied before inventions are made (e.g., the invention of the toothed wheel presupposes the invention of the wheel). This applies to our example of the melting point of tin as well. The melting process alone presupposes quite a number of other technologies before we arrive at the process itself. Significantly, though, the sciences themselves have never shown much interest in the analyses of *"methodischer Konstruktivismus"* and its attempts at accurate cultural analyses. There can be no doubt that "know-how" is the dominant interest in the techno-sciences. And I think there are reasons for doubting that the painstaking analytical work done in the program of *"methodischer Konstruktivismus"* can at all prompt a sufficiently critical discussion within the sciences. But I would at least suggest that we take their basic idea seriously—namely, that the foundation of our truth claims is culturally relative and that we should not simply take the feasible for the real only because it can be controlled readily and transferred to each and every location. Replying to Larry's question, then, I think that we must reflect every scientific truth claim contextually—and this always implies reflection on cultural conditions as well.

Larry's further question touches the experimental and instrumental dimension of scientific research. Here I think that he overestimates the self-corrective powers of inquiry. Contemporary research practice shows that researchers are not completely free in choosing their subjects and methods. They work under strong profit interests of those who fund their researches. These interests have long since reached even into the universities, although, as a rule, freedom of inquiry still has a stronger traditional and institutional support here than else-where. Interactive constructivism takes up these issues and tries to critically rethink and understand what they imply in the way of re-search perspectives and a possible narrowing of approaches. From this viewpoint, globalization, e.g., does not only imply technological progress (in that we learn to identify pathogenic agents more quickly and devise medical counterstrategies). It may also imply, on the other hand, that we generate and proliferate diseases by exposing more and more people to what ecological critics denounce as "out-door experi-ments" that try out the feasible in the fields of genetic manipulation, electromagnetic transmission, traffic, etc., without sufficiently identi-fying the attendant risks for live creatures in advance. What seemed so readily universalizable may turn out quite the reverse in effect once it has been universalized. And then we'll have to reverse the universal-ization again and dispose of its effects. This is why constructivists avoid the term universalization and on principle speak only of gener-alizations. They claim but temporary validity and remind us of the fallibility of our knowledge—although some of those generalizations may remain valid for a very long period of time without refutation or even serious contestation, like the proposition that the earth circles around the sun. This critical stance is so important to us that we pre-fer concepts that relativize without entailing arbitrariness.

Chapter 7: "Pragmatism, Constructivism, and the Philosophy of Technology," by Larry A. Hickman

**Kersten Reich:** Larry Hickman has developed a comprehensive argu-mentation for avoiding the relativism of neo-Pragmatism that he finds, e.g., in Rorty—or also in those aspects of interactive construc-tivism that he criticizes. But I wonder whether this criticism is as easy as his examples suggest. There are two different figures of argumenta-tion: (1) The example of the melting temperature of pure tin is taken from techno-science, and it refers to a technological context that is already determined for all those who work with pure tin in technical or scientific procedures. The apparatus constructed for conducting these procedures has proven reliable in repeatable intersubjective testing. I would regard this as a generalization that is valuable and useful for these interpretive communities characteristic of industrialized societies. Its universalizability is restricted to precisely these pragmatic aims of application, which seem universal because we live in such a society. However, there is a double cultural conditionality that the narrow focus on these pragmatic aims all too readily tends to neglect, namely the emergence of those techniques from the larger developments of culture on one side and the deployment of those techniques in a given culture on the other side. (2) The example of the mangoes is more complicated, though. For it simply assumes the context that mangoes are actually eaten, just as it is useful to melt tin when working scientifically or technically with it. But in the case of the mangoes it is more obvious that this assumption is culturally dependent. Edibility is conditioned not only on physiology—i.e., that which we can eat—but also on taste and disgust—i.e., that which we like to eat. I think that John Dewey already saw this when he wrote, in *Context and Thought*: "We grasp the meaning of what is said in our own language not because appreciation of context is unnecessary but because context is so unescapably present. It is taken for granted; it is a matter of course, and accordingly is not explicitly specified. Habits of speech, including syntax and vocabulary, and modes of interpretation have been formed in the face of inclusive and defining situations of context" (LW 6:4). Cannot we take this account of Dewey's as also providing a key for the interpretation of our habit to look for universalizations? I wish to put to Larry two more specific questions: Isn't it better to give up the concept of universalization altogether, i.e., even in the techno-sciences, in order to draw attention to the fact that even these sciences have constructed their knowledge, and will continually have to reconstruct and prove it anew? Isn't it necessary to avoid universalizations with regard to problems whose contexts are themselves ambiguous, multilayered, ambivalent—which as a rule is the case in all cultural affairs?

**Larry Hickman:** Kersten asks if it would not be better to give up the notion of universalization altogether so that we can honor the fact that the techno-sciences have a history of construction and a future of reconstruction. I believe that the notion of universalization does not capture the finer distinction between what has been universalized and what is universalizable.

Kersten is correct to point out that a part of the process by means of which the melting point of a sample of pure tin was experimentally determined involved generalization. Generalization is a part of the logic of discovery, and therefore a part of the history of science. I would disagree, however, that the melting point of tin just "seems universal" (as he puts it) because we live in a society in which tin is melted. This is why I used the term "universalizable." First, I distinguished that term from the term "universalized" in order to reflect the fact that there are cultures in which tin has never been (and perhaps never will be) melted. And second, the suffix "-able" in "universalizable" indicates that the term contains an implicit conditional. *If* tin were ever to be melted in a culture in which it had never before been melted, *then* a pure sample would melt at 232 degrees Celsius at one standard atmosphere. We would in fact be shocked to find a case in which that did not occur, since it would upset much of what we know about chemistry. The chances of this happening are so small as to be not worth considering. (This is an example of *functional permanence*.)

My point was that the physical law by means of which we describe the melting of tin is not just apparent, but real: it has effects that are uniform and therefore predictable across cultures. In answer to the first question, therefore, I'm ready to give up the notion of *universalization*, since it is overly vague in any event. But I'm not ready to give up the notions of having been *universalized* and being *universalizable*, since they do important work for us. (This example of the melting point of tin was Dewey's own, by the way, and is consistent with his brand of constructivism.)

Kersten's second question is more difficult. *Prima facie*, it seems unexceptional to say, as he does, that we should "avoid universalizations with regard to problems whose contexts are themselves ambiguous, multilayered, ambivalent—which as a rule is the case in all cultural affairs." But matters may not be as simple as they first appear. In order to respond to his question, I must once again emphasize the difference between what is universal*ized* and what is universal*izable*.

I raise here an example that involves a very unpleasant cultural practice—but it is the type of example that must be raised because it is precisely the type of cultural practice that is at issue—of female genital mutilation as it is practiced in certain parts of sub-Saharan Africa. This is a cultural issue that is profoundly "ambiguous, multilayered, ambivalent." From the standpoint of good medical practice, however, we are justified in making a claim that is universalizable: regardless of the various cultural, religious, or even utility claims advanced by the proponents of that particular cultural practice, it should be stopped. Our claim is universal*izable*, moreover, since it applies where and everywhere the practice may be encountered. Prohibition of the practice has clearly not been universal*ized*, however, since it persists. This is not just a matter of one cultural value opposed to another, as if we were trying to decide whether to order a plate of sausage or a plate of sushi. It is a matter of good medical practice, good health, and promotion of the values of human flourishing against their opposites, namely, bad medical practice, bad health, and the subjugation of women as a class. I simply don't see any grounds on which an informed person could deny this.

**Stefan Neubert:** I think I can understand Larry's reasons for objecting to what he calls "cognitive relativism" quite well. As far as what he has in mind is the menace of arbitrariness and the danger of attendant theoretical and methodological fallacies like the pseudo-scientific discourse of "creationism," I am frankly and fully on his side—although my theoretical "back-up" of this position would read somewhat differently. In the first place, I would argue that from a constructivist perspective, any form of "cognitive relativism," lest it become naive, must be qualified by a theory that takes cultural contextuality into account. Interactive constructivism here suggests a constructivist theory of discourses, among other things. We distinguish and combine four major theoretical perspectives on discourses, namely power, knowledge, lived relationships, and the unconscious. Without going too much into details here I would like to argue that, first, it is our very involvement in discourses that basically delimits arbitrariness for constructivists, too. For in discourse we cannot simply make *anything go*, but only those solutions that prove viable for a relevant interpretive community. Secondly, to come back to the example of "creationism," discourses of knowledge always imply methodologies and interpretations that represent the "state of the art" and provide criteria for excluding some solutions as irrelevant or outdated. This is part of the hegemonic contextuality that characterizes even scientific discourses, for good or bad. And here it is clear that Western scientific discourses on human nature have long since generated a cultural context of knowledge production that denounces creationist ideas as mythological. If we do not want to ignore or abandon this scientific context altogether, we will have to reject the knowledge claims of creationism as pseudo-scientific. This is not to deny that creationist ideas are cultural constructions, too, which seem to be viable for some people or communities. But it is to deny that these ideas fit the cultural context they want to impose as the only legitimate and authoritative interpretation. As constructivists, we will reject such attempts and criticize the intolerant and anti-democratic tendencies that become evident when, e.g., creationism takes the form of a discourse of educational indoctrination. And this is to say that we will have to ask what creationism as a cultural construction implies in the way of discursive dimensions of power, lived relationships, and maybe also unconscious desires.

**Kersten Reich:** I, too, can understand Larry's objections against cognitive relativism insofar as he wants to defend himself against the menace of arbitrariness and to counter dangerous developments, like the movement of creationism and its attempt to do away with the Darwinian theory of evolution on the basis of flimsy reasons. There is no dissent between our positions on these issues, although the way of our argumentation may be different. So let me add one further question to Larry. His criticism notwithstanding, I would like to know whether he, as a contemporary Pragmatist, may also find some positive traits in "cognitive relativism." If we for the moment disregard quarrels in our own Pragmatist-constructivist camp, shouldn't we say that this relativism is an important ally against much greater adversaries on the outside: ontologies, idealistic metaphysics, scientism, narrow realism, foundational universalisms that fight against both Pragmatism and constructivism?

**Larry Hickman:** I believe that Stefan's position and the one I advanced in Chapter 7 are quite close. There is one matter that I would emphasize, however, that does not seem to get sufficient emphasis in Stefan's contribution: beneath all the talk about discourse and interpretative communities, there must be an experimental, behavioral platform if we are to make informed decisions that reflect the actual pushes and pulls of problematic situations. As we well know, there have been situations in which many terrible things have been deemed acceptable by certain interpretive communities (the mass hysteria of certain medieval religious communities comes to mind, as well as other, more recent events in Europe during the first half of the twentieth century). Now it may be that Stefan's use of the term "viable" in this context is designed to cover the cases I just mentioned. But if that is the case, then I would suggest that the term "viable" lacks the muscle—the vigor—of the term "experimental." There is an instrumental / experimental component that is missing (or at least so deeply submerged that it becomes invisible) in talk of discourse and interpretive communities.

So I would just suggest once again, as I did in Chapter 7, that the difference between the classical Pragmatism of Dewey and interactive constructivism seems to lie in Pragmatism's commitment to experimentalism in the strong sense, whereas interactive constructivism seems more at home with postmodernist notions of "discourse."

Since Kersten has added another question, I should respond to that one as well. He asks whether postmodern cognitive relativists and Pragmatists should not form an alliance against various types of foundationalists. To this I would respond that one of the central virtues of Dewey's brand of Pragmatism, as I understand it, is precisely its rejection of both extremes: absolutism and extreme relativism. His account of inquiry gives us the tools to come to terms with both the scientific realists and the religious fundamentalists, on one extreme, and the cognitive relativism of the postmodernists, on the other. The problem with taking a position that is too far toward the postmodernist end of the spectrum, at least as I see it, is that one loses the ability to mount credible arguments against the fundamentalists. The question for interactive constructivism, I think, is just how far in the direction of cognitive relativism it is prepared to go. If it goes too far, it may perforce be unable to communicate with the techno-sciences. There are French philosophers who have already plunged over this precipice, I regret to say, as Alan Sokal demonstrated several years ago with his famous hoax and then his book *Fashionable Nonsense*.

**Kersten Reich:** As to Sokal, one could as well take an opposite position and claim with warrant that he has largely distorted the positions of the French philosophers he refers to. Furthermore, I think that by relativism Dewey means an extreme position that is far away from interactive constructivism. We do not at all see ourselves as mere subjectivists. Rather, we attempt to rethink theoretical claims including their relativization over time, for especially in cultural matters there is nothing permanent or eternal. At this point I would like to add another question. Dewey is very clear as to experience, inquiry, and progress in science. But his thinking is also influenced by claims to modernity that we today see somewhat differently and more critically. We certainly may recognize the risks of modernity more clearly now than Dewey could anticipate in his day. We even call the world we live in a "risk society." What to my mind is largely missing here in Dewey is an understanding of the ambivalence of modernity that, e.g., Zygmunt Bauman elaborates in his works. According to the theory of ambivalence, all technological progress and all progress in the increase of liberties in democratic societies is Janus-faced: they grant us some opportunities, but they simultaneously deny us others. In this connection outsiders often insinuate that Pragmatism shortsightedly focuses on the successes of modernity and neglects its dark sides. A similar criticism can be seen in Habermas's objections to Rorty. But is this criticism warranted? And has Pragmatism further developed her positions in these matters?

**Larry Hickman:** Kersten rightly points out the "Janus-faced" character of so-called "technological" progress. Dewey was not unaware of this double effect, and even discussed it as a part of his treatment of his well-known categories of the precarious and the stable. But Dewey was also clear that where tools and techniques fail, it is only techno*logy*, in the sense of inquiry into tools and techniques, that has the possibility of resolving the difficulty. I'm afraid I would have to say that the standard critiques of Pragmatism as narrow utilitarianism or straight-line instrumentalism are little more than caricatures. Dewey in fact had a rich treatment of ends-means relationships, and he was well aware of the need for continual improvement of tools and techniques as a means of adjustment to changed and changing situations.

Chapter 8: "Pragmatism, Constructivism, and the Theory of Culture," by Stefan Neubert

**Ken Stikkers:** I concur especially strongly with two points you make. First, I support your suggestion that constructivist theory needs to be developed within the context of the philosophy of culture—Scheler held the same with respect to his "sociology of knowledge." Second, and as I already indicated in my response to your question to me, I very much appreciate your articulation of the constructivist notion of "the real," which is so important in saving it from naive relativism, but which much of neo-Pragmatism is without.

You characterize the Cologne program as *"interactive* constructivism," and other constructivists similarly describe their projects as "interactive." Is there any reason constructivism would resist substituting "transactional" for "interactive"? In many contexts I would raise no objection to the use of "interactive," but in several places you seem to illustrate why a Deweyan modification of terminology might be in order, and I wonder if you would accept my Deweyan suggestion in this regard. In *Knowing and the Known*, coauthored with Arthur Bentley, Dewey distinguished between "interactional" and "transactional" theories of communication and interpretation. Interactional models assume the interacting elements to be, more or less, already given or constituted in advance of their constructivist interactions, while transactional models describe how the elements themselves are co-constituted, co-constructed, with increasing definiteness, along with their shared meanings, through their constructivist activities. Thus, from the latter perspective, self and Other do not merely come together to construct common truths, meanings, and values, but rather in the constructive event, self and Other too emerge, are themselves constructed. I fully agree with you that observers are better understood as also participants and agents in culture, but from a transactional perspective, observers / participants / agents do not merely engage in sets of symbolic cultural practices, as your account suggests, but are constituted through them. So, again, my question is, do you have any objection to this Deweyan shift from "interactive" to "transactional constructivism"?

**Stefan Neubert:** I know the conceptual distinction in *Knowing and the Known*, and I must confess that I myself have been thinking for some time of the conceptual change you suggest when I first read the concerned passages in Dewey's and Bentley's book. However, this is a pragmatic question of linguistic usage, in the first place, and in German the term *"Transaktionismus"* is far less usual than the term *"Interaktionismus."* But I fully agree with you as to the theoretical contents. The meaning of "transactional" that you have just described is precisely what Cologne constructivism means by *"interaktionistisch."* *"Interaktionismus"* here not only refers to the interactions and interchanges between discrete entities whose identities are already completely constituted; rather, the term refers to the comprehensive processes of co-construction from which meanings and identities first emerge. By the way, there are many references as to this viewpoint between Cologne constructivism and the approach of

*"Symbolischer Interaktionismus"* in the wake of George Herbert Mead that similarly shows a very "transactional" conception of "interaction." Furthermore, in Chapter 8, I have indicated some basic assumptions of Cologne constructivism's theory of discourse that build partly on poststructuralist approaches. Among other things, these theories hold the crucial view that discourses are not only articulated by subjects, but conversely, subjectivity or so-called "subject positions" are also first constituted in and through discourse. This view also expresses a basically "transactional" perspective that of course also underlies our constructivist understanding of the terms "observer," "participant," and "agent." Hence it would be misleading to think that observers / participants / agents do merely engage in "sets of symbolic cultural practices" as already fully constituted entities or identities respectively. Rather, they are constituted as identities only in the very process of their observations, participations, and actions. Cologne constructivism particularly emphasizes the continual and always unfinished construction processes of self and others in their interactions, which are always of a "transactional" character in the sense described. With regard to the imaginative dimension of human communications, this view is especially expressed in the concept of "mirrorings" that underlie every construction of identities.

**Kersten Reich:** Considering the distinction between "interactional" and "transactional" we have to take account of the contextuality of our discourses and their connections to other discourses. Working out the foundations of interactive constructivism, I have studied and discussed intensely the work of George Herbert Mead and so-called "symbolic interactionism." Already in Habermas we find a differentiated discussion of "interaction," which he incorporates into his theory of communicative action. In none of these approaches related to and inspired by Mead can the term "interaction" be reduced to a mere interaction between fixed objects or persons. This would indeed be a very narrow interpretation of its meaning. Rather, it always already implies what Bentley and Dewey have called transaction. I think that in the English-speaking world, too, the term "interaction" is very often used in this transactional sense, and that the usage of "transaction" is largely restricted to specific circles (e.g., Dewey scholars). Important for us, as Stefan has just explained, is indeed a transactional understanding of "interaction."

**Jim Garrison:** Stefan, you say a great deal about Dewey's holism in your contribution, but little about his pluralism, including his pluralistic metaphysics, theory of knowledge, and theory of democracy. After pointing out that Dewey took the linguistic turn long before Wittgenstein, the famous analytic philosopher W. V. O. Quine used both philosophers to construct a theory of "ontological relativity," a strong version of the underdetermination of meaning leading to a radical pluralism. Quine did this without discussing some of the observer's contributions Dewey emphasizes, including the importance of selective attention. Our experience is limited to what we attend to, and our interpretive forestructure, needs, desires, interests, and purposes influence to what we attend and into what we inquire. Indeed, every meaning, essence, object, and value construct depend upon the concerns and actions of the inquirer. Can you help me better understand why you say Deweyan Pragmatism tends to ignore the observer in the interaction of knower and known, subject and object, etc.?

**Stefan Neubert:** I didn't mean to underestimate, much less neglect, Dewey's pluralism. As I indicated at the very outset of my contribution—in my maybe all-too-brief remarks about the cultural dimensions in his theory of experience—I see his approach as a genuinely pluralistic philosophical position. His pluralism is not restricted to his political theory and vision of democracy, but is rooted in his generous understanding of human experience as rich, diversified, resourceful, and abundant in meanings. His repeated and forceful comments on themes like qualitative individuality, originality, creativity, and incommensurability as inextinguishable traits of experience, his insistence on the necessity of taking into account the vague, obscure, and twilight phases of existence, and his frequent reminder that we always have to inquire into concrete and unique situations as providing touchstones for our judgments and beliefs all testify to the genuine pluralism that is at the very heart of his philosophy. Indeed, the relevance of pluralism in Dewey's philosophy seemed so obvious to me that I maybe didn't underscore it enough in my contribution. So I'm very grateful, Jim, that you mentioned this point because this gives me the opportunity to make it more explicit. Actually, I should be tempted to say that the centrality of pluralist thinking in Dewey's philosophical perspectives is one of the general traits that make his Pragmatism so attractive for present-day constructivists.

What I wanted to say in the passage to which you probably refer was that in a certain field, namely the field of political discourse and radical democracy, there has been a shift of emphasis in recent decades from a more "holistic" brand of pluralist thinking—holistic in the sense that it focuses at least ideally on comprehensive solutions like "Socialism," the "Great Community," or "A Common Faith" —to more "antagonistic" versions of plural democracy that are cautious as to comprehensive expectations and put more stress on the necessity of quarrel, dissent, and the articulation of unresolved antagonisms. Over the twentieth century, faith in comprehensive reconciliation has somewhat waned in Western democratic societies. Promises of reconciliation have too often betrayed us. But to say that this disillusionment is expressed in a somewhat different emphasis is not to claim that only now have we arrived at genuine pluralism. The tensional relationship between consensus and dissent, commonality and difference, conciliation and struggle is implied in Dewey's political pluralism no bit less (or more) than in the one launched by Ernesto Laclau and Chantal Mouffe, even if they construct somewhat different perspectives as to where to look for (and what to expect of) viable solutions. To be sure, these different perspectives imply different theoretical backgrounds for thinking pluralist democracy, namely poststructuralist deconstruction of Marxism in Laclau and Pragmatist social theory in Dewey. However, from a Pragmatic standpoint it seems to me that these theoretical differences are far less important than the continuity of democratic struggles that underlies discursive variations. And certainly no bit less than in Dewey's time do we today need "democracy" as a signifier for our hope and vision that our solutions shall not ultimately collapse on one pole or the other, distorting consensus to totalitarian conformity or oppositional struggle to anarchic terrorism. In some aspects we, at the beginning of the twenty-first century, have a somewhat different but still continuous "democratic imagination" (Thomas Alexander 1995) with the one Dewey advocated in his time. But I think that Deweyans should *expect* that democratic imagination changes over time.

As to the role of observation and the observer, I would not say that Dewey's theory and criticism of knowledge generally neglects the observer. Quite the contrary, I would hold that there is a deep understanding in Dewey of what interactive constructivism calls the intimate interconnection between the roles of observer, participant, and agent. (Kersten Reich has elaborated at large on these issues in Chapter 6.) In Dewey, this understanding is sometimes more implicit than explicit, but there are also places where it finds a pretty direct expression. Of course, I would not say that Dewey systematically develops a constructivist theory of observer and observation as we hold such a theory today. But neither would I expect him to do so. As a present-day constructivist, I am deeply impressed by the extent to which his philosophy of experience, way ahead of his time, anticipates and articulates perspectives that point in that direction. And I would add that his focus on "experience"—in the rich Deweyan sense of that term—may today well serve as a reminder for many constructivists that their focus on the "observer" has to be qualified by cultural contexts of participation and action, lest they become naive as to the concrete conditions and limits of human reality constructions. In this sense, I would indeed maintain that Dewey is still ahead of many more subjectivist versions of constructivism today.

The only aspect in which I would say that Dewey does not, and not even implicitly, rely on a sufficiently constructivist observer theory is in his claim to naturalistic metaphysics. To my mind, this claim at least partially tends to cover the cultural constructivity of his own views about nature, i.e., the constructivity (and contextuality) of his

own observation of "the generic traits of existence." The constructivist counterclaim here would be that any attempt to detect "generic
traits of existence" goes hand in hand with omissions and a search
for viability that is culturally dependent. And I must admit that I cannot free myself from the suspicion that even Dewey's subtle and rich
notion of "nature" partly tends to universalize aspects of the cultural
context of American progressivism in which he himself lived and
worked, e.g., aspects like dynamic development, resolution of conflicts through reorganization and readjustment, or evolutionary progress. Of course "generic traits" like "the precarious and the stable,"
"contingency and need," "movement and arrest" are very good can-
didates for indicating basic characteristics of an open and pluralist
universe that allows for an abundance of constructivist insights. This
is what makes it pretty hard to criticize Dewey's naturalism from a
constructivist viewpoint. But what about those cultural categories
that are omitted? To give only one example: shouldn't we say that a
metaphysical account of "nature" that does not explicitly and extensively elaborate on the relevance of cultural gender norms to the social construction of concepts about "nature" is therefore neglectful
of its own contextuality? In a word, I think that Dewey's claim to
"naturalistic metaphysics" does not fully realize the cultural dependence of his own position as an observer. But then, throughout his
work and condensed in an essay like "Context and Thought," Dewey
would develop very good arguments that point to the contextuality
of *all* philosophical reflection. I suggest that we encounter an internal
tension in his rich philosophical thinking—a tension that we today
may make productive use of. And I am willing to concede that in his
time Dewey's very naturalism, expressed, e.g., in *Experience and Nature*, was a far better means for countering his philosophical opponents than a constructivist observer theory that only now seems
viable to us, but would probably have been dismissed then as an un-
duly, weak brand of relativism. After all, you always only go as far as
your contemporary adversaries would let you go.

**Larry Hickman:** I've already commented on Stefan's contribution
in Chapter 7, but I do have a couple of additional questions for him.

First, he says that there is a difference between Dewey's classical Pragmatism and the program of interactive constructivism, in the sense that Dewey is interested in "experience," and interactive constructivism is interested in "the observer." This is further broken down into self-observers and distant-observers. As we know, however, Dewey relied very heavily on the work of G. H. Mead, who had worked out something similar to this observer theory. Dewey even built Mead's ideas into his own notion of experience. I wonder then, whether Stefan may not have found some differences (at least in this regard) where there are only nuances of emphasis.

However, there appear to be some real differences between the two positions. I have discussed Stefan's cognitive relativism at length in Chapter 7. But I wonder if there is not also a significant difference in the two positions when it comes to what C. S. Peirce called "the final and veritable logical interpretant of a sign." Stefan holds the position that there is "never a final point in discourses that could not as well be appropriated as a starting point for another discourse," and there is a certain obvious truth in that. But from the standpoint of classical Pragmatism, there are termination points—final interpretants—that stay put because a problem has been solved for all the world except those who enjoy chewing over an issue long after it has been settled. (The melting point of a sample of pure tin at one standard atmosphere is one such final interpretant.) So I wonder if Stefan would care to elaborate on the force of his remark that there is never a "final" point in discourse. I suspect that this issue goes to the matter that I have been emphasizing, that is, the importance of the instrumental / experimental factor in fixing belief.

**Stefan Neubert:** With the one exception indicated in my answer to Jim (the issue of metaphysical realism), I would agree with Larry that most differences between our experience- and observer-orientations are so small that they may be called "nuances of emphasis." For example, the observer theory of Cologne constructivism indeed bears many connections to the theoretical approach of George Herbert Mead. There are many affinities and similarities, even if Mead's approach is mainly focussed on the level of symbolic interactions, while

Cologne constructivism, next to the symbolic, also puts specific emphasis on the dimensions of imaginative mirrorings and the real that delimits our capacities for symbolic understanding. But one can certainly learn much from such differences in focus or emphasis, because they express less stressed implications of your own positions.

For example, what gives me stuff to think about is Larry's insistent emphasis on "the experimental" and its relationship to the constructivist concept of "viability." He has made this point twice, in his question to me and in his former remarks to Kersten's and my questions to Chapter 7. It gives me stuff to think about because I have always believed that Dewey's thoroughgoing experimentalism is one of the greatest achievements of his philosophical approach. In my view, constructivists can learn much from Dewey's classical Pragmatism here. They may profit largely from critically rethinking their own understanding of cultural viability with regard to the basic assumptions of a cultural experimentalism in Dewey's sense. Maybe I can put it this way: I agree with Larry that "viability" is a weaker claim as compared to "experimental validity" or "warranted assertibility," to use the Deweyan term. But the concession of this very weakness, from my constructivist perspective, reflects the recognition that experimentalism, after all, is but one discourse among others. To say this is not meant to devalue experimentalism. Quite the contrary, in the cultural discursive universe in which we live, experimentalism is, to my mind, one of the most valuable discourses that we have at our disposal. It stands for openness, plurality, and our hope for (relative) progress in a world that is in dire need of amelioration. The Pragmatist idea of meliorism is one of our most valuable social visions, which indeed expresses the vigor and vitality that Larry wishes to defend. Like him, I would not like to give it up to mere "language games" and arbitrary discourses that might involve us, behind the screens, in premodern and anti-democratic power relations that go unchecked by methods of peer-review as comprehensive and democratically inclusive, as far as it gets. Control through experiments and methods of democratic communication and deliberation as comprehensive and inclusive as possible is, to my mind, a basic claim that constructivists as well as Pragmatists must defend, because it represents, to both approaches, a fundamental precondition for the (post)modern diversity of discourses they welcome. I think the term "democratic experimentalism" is a very good name for this basic stance, which strongly relates Pragmatism and constructivism. And I hope that my earlier comments on the issue of "creationalism" have helped to make clear that there's no substantial difference on this point between constructivism, as I understand it, and Larry's "productive Pragmatism."

But then we also have to take into account that "experimentalism" as a concrete historical discursive formation always implies power relations and power effects, even if these effects are often rather hidden or subliminal (e.g., as an expression of Western and male-centered scientific practice). And I think it is here where Larry's position and mine are partially different. From the viewpoint of interactive constructivism, I would argue that experimentalism, as a concrete discursive practice taking place in historically specific institutions, has in the past repeatedly and all too often fostered not only communities, but also exclusions (e.g., of female or other marginalized articulations) and that, given this legacy of excluding others, we can no longer call it an "innocent discourse" that disposes us of the responsibility for reflecting on the intricate power relations always at stake when we make truth claims (even in the sense of "experimental validity"). The constructivist concept of viability acknowledges this responsibility, in that it recognizes from the start that every concrete realization of experimentalism (as a specific discursive formation) is but one form of reality construction viable to an interpretive community—which may of course be a very large and comprehensive interpretive community, as in the case, e.g., of many transculturally valid applications in the field of the techno-sciences. But even then, "viability-to-us" is not the same as ultimate validity, in the sense of a best or final observer position obligatory for all others, too. If we concede that in our so-far-established discourse of "experimentalism" (which always builds on presupposition, e.g., about proper methods and procedures as well as proper ways of reasoning and types of rationality), we may as yet not even have seen what other possible viable perspectives we have excluded, we will not be surprised if sometimes one of our "final interpretants" turns out to be too narrow or one-sided once we have discovered a new viability through the invention of a new discourse. "Cultural viability," in this sense, may serve as a corrective principle to "experimental validity." Emphasizing the cultural contextuality of experimentalism, it might contribute to its internal self-corrective potentials.

## A Discussion of General Issues

*What understanding of discourse characterizes Pragmatism and / or constructivism to your mind? And if you'd like to be more specific: What importance do you assign, in this connection, to the following: (a) classical Pragmatist conceptions of community (e.g., the scientific community); (b) theories of discourse ethics; (c) poststructuralist theories of discourse; (d) the liberal ironist following Rorty?*

**Larry Hickman:** Briefly, I would say that "discourse" now seems to have almost as many meanings as there are individuals who employ the term. Habermas, of course, has emphasized the role of discourse in coming to consensus within a community seeking democratic solutions to its disagreements. As I read some poststructuralist writers, discourse seems to be almost an end in itself, or at least an occasion for the exhibition of high literary style, with an emphasis on the infinite interpretability of the signs that advance discourse. Rorty has been influenced by the poststructuralists in this regard. He seems to view the function of discourse as similar to that of poetizing, which he characterizes as "making things new" in ways that allow the liberal ironist to work on his or her own (secular) salvation.

For Dewey, I would argue, discourse in the sense of verbal communication among human beings is part of a larger pattern of inquiry with nonverbal instrumental or experimental aspects that he thinks are able to stand behind and warrant the claims that are a part of discourse. This is to say that Dewey's notion of inquiry is considerably broader than the three notions of discourse listed. On my reading, his notion of inquiry is able to include those types of discourse as aspects or moments that are more or less pertinent to some particular sequence of inquiry. But his notion of inquiry is much broader than discourse in any of the senses discussed above.

**Jim Garrison:** For Dewey, to have a mind is to have meaning, and meaning is, most basically, a functional coordination between two or more emergent centers of action with regard to some emergent object. More fully, to have a mind is to participate in the sociolinguistic practice of some community, and to have a self is to take the stance of another in regard to one's own acts. Meanings are made; they are socially constructed and involve the larger world of events. Once we construct them, they may serve in the production of warranted assertions. (For example, "there is a large snake right behind you about to strike" is meaningful; hopefully, a brief inquiry will prove it is false. "The Top Quark exists" is also meaningful, but the last I read, quantum physicists were still looking for it.) The coordination is achieved through discourse in its most expanded sense. The discourse between adult and child, for instance, may involve only gestures. Likewise, writing, including cuneiform, pictographs, etc., are discourse.

There are disturbing consequences here that Pragmatists and constructivists tend to ignore. For one thing, indoctrination is inevitable. Infants are born without a mind, and unless they participate without skepticism in the discourse practices of the community, they cannot acquire a mind or self. At some level, therefore, indoctrination is inevitable. It is easy to synthesize a discourse ethics from Dewey's opus. For instance, it is clear that Dewey champions pluralistic, communicative democracy in which as many people as possible should have the right to speak. Because having the right to speak does not matter if no one is listening, I have developed a theory of listening in dialogues across difference using Dewey's philosophy. Indeed, if we replace Gadamer's interpretive "prejudices" with Dewey's habits, we can also quickly get a hermeneutics of behavior and conduct with implications for discourse. It is also easy to extend Dewey's discussion of virtues in *Democracy and Education* and his *Ethics* to communication, as well.

Dewey is poststructuralist in that he rejects the metaphysics of substance (or what Derrida calls the metaphysics of presence). There are no fixed and final essences (*eidos*) in Dewey; there are only the essences we have constructed (produced) in the process of inquiry—hence, they are always subject to deconstruction. The word "species" is simply the Latin for the ancient Greek word *eidos*; Dewey does for all essences what Darwin did for species. Since there are no eternal, immutable essences for Dewey, there is no ultimate origin or foundation (*arche*) or substance (*ousia*), or perfect telos (*entelecheia*). In Derrida's terms, there is no transcendental signified. Both Dewey and Derrida owe a great deal to Peirce for their thinking. It is easy to see why Derrida ends up saying things like "I recall that from the beginning the question of the trace was connected with a certain notion of labour, of doing, and that what I called 'Prasrammatology' tried to link Pragmatism and grammatology." The notion of labor here is something like "endlessly working out the consequences." Now, Larry Hickman has taught me to take Peirce's notion of ultimate interpretant (roughly, a habit under our self-control) very seriously. Derrida says little about the body, even the body as a sign, which is one reason he has trouble translating his work into ethical-political action. Meanwhile, Foucault has a great deal to say about the body. While I think Rorty goes too far by claiming that the only difference between Foucault and Dewey is over for what we may hope, nonetheless, the similarity is substantial. Lakoff and Johnson (1999) dedicate *Philosophy in the Flesh* to Merleau-Ponty and John Dewey, the two philosophers of the body in the twentieth century. Merleau-Ponty immensely influences Foucault and has a close intellectual affinity to Dewey (and George Herbert Mead). I do think that Foucault's emphasis on the micropolitics of power and the body (power *over*) is a valuable supplement to Dewey, but then Dewey has a lot of things to say about power *to* do things, and power *with* others that Foucault ignores, and certainly Dewey has insightful things to say about power over as well.

Rorty's liberal ironist is interesting largely for what such an ironist says about one's final vocabulary. To expand one's final vocabulary involves encountering "the Other" and having the Human Eros. I will comment on this more below.

**Stefan Neubert:** Jim, you said that Foucault's emphasis on the micropolitics of power and the body (power *over*) might be a valuable supplement to Deweyan Pragmatism. What specific aspects of supplementation do you have in mind? Foucault's concept of power has also a strong productive side that exceeds the mere "power-over" perspective. How do you think these productive aspects of the Foucaultian power concept accord with what Dewey has to say about "power *to* do things" and "power *with* others"? Do you find critical perspectives in Foucault here, too, that might supplement classical Pragmatism? For example, do Foucaultian concepts like "discursive formation," "episteme," "dispositive," or "technologies of the self" have a bearing on Pragmatism?

**Jim Garrison:** First, I would like to admit I understated the positive contributions Foucault makes to our understanding of power relations. This underestimation, though, is not entirely my fault. As Bernstein 1992, 148–52, shows, Foucault moves toward a radical skepticism that eventually leaves him in performative contradiction; that is, he cannot sustain his own discourse once we turn his skepticism on him. Foucault desperately needs something to help us distinguish good from bad forms of power. Personally, I do not require some fixed, final, and eternal essence, but I need more than Foucault provides. Pragmatism's emphasis on working out the consequences of meanings (e.g., discursive formations, etc.) allows Foucault to avoid flirting with vicious relativism, which we should never confuse with pluralism. Finally, Foucaultian concepts like "discursive formation," etc., should inform a reconstructed Pragmatism.

**Kersten Reich:** I, too, wish to give a brief answer to the general question raised above. From the viewpoint of interactive constructivism, discourses are symbolic orders by which interpretive communities construct interpretations of their realities for a certain time.

These constructions contain, first of all, rules that determine certain intentions and procedures of interpretation. As discourses, Pragmatism and constructivism reject final and absolute metaphysical positions or a "god's eye view." Interactive constructivism takes up discursive perspectives from classical Pragmatism as well as poststructuralism and postmodernism, which support philosophical criticisms of a metaphysics or ontology of the "final word." These perspectives become crucial if we concede that humans construct their realities as well as their scientific methods of knowledge production. But, as said before, this is not to say that everything collapses into discursive arbitrariness. Constructivist interpretive communities, too, delimit arbitrariness in and through their interpretations. For example, let's consider the political implications that are characteristic and decisive for the discursive positions of Pragmatism and constructivism. Of necessity, these are democratic claims. It is interesting to see so many affinities between the two approaches here. Pragmatism and constructivism not only need democracy as a precondition of their own open-mindedness to plurality and a tensional relationship between consensus and dissent with regard to interests and decisions, but they also positively stress the opportunities of reconstruction, innovation, and development in humane living together implied in democratic ways of life. The political intentions of both approaches depend on existing democratic societies that provide spaces for their realization. This is why the work of Michel Foucault is so important for interactive constructivism. His focus on the analysis of power suggests that we neither forget to critically address external and delimitating power relations nor neglect the power effects entailed in our own discourses. In this connection I think it is very helpful to remember Dewey's understanding of democracy and to reinterpret it for our own present situation.

*What do you think is the enduring import of Dewey's theory of democracy for contemporary Pragmatism and/or constructivism? Which*

*newer perspectives or suggestions (after or beyond Dewey) do you find in contemporary discussions?*

**Jim Garrison:** Dewey gave us an image of communicative, pluralistic democracy that emerges out of what it means to have a mind and a self. It satisfies what Thomas M. Alexander calls "the Human Eros"; that is, the desire to live a life of expanding meaning and value. I believe Dewey sought spiritual democracy in the tradition of Walt Whitman (whom Dewey calls "the seer of democracy") in that Dewey shows us how to live in intimate relation with the rest of existence (the social and physical environment) in such a way that our creative acts matter in the course of events. It is a grand vision that relates well to Habermas. It does not relate well with those who would replace government *by* the people with technocratic and elitist government *for* the people. Ultimately, Deweyan democracy is not about government, except as a technology and instrument for translating the will of the people and administrating to that will. The role of education in democracy is now all but forgotten. We are only interested in training human capital for the production function. The emphasis everywhere on standards is really about turning people into standardized, interchangeable parts.

I think all of Dewey's theory of democracy continues to serve the discourse of democracy well, though democracy itself is rapidly declining internationally. In my own work, I have begun to follow Richard Bernstein in taking Levinas's question of "the Other" seriously. While the conversation about violence and the Other has been very important to Continental thought, Deweyan scholars and constructivists have yet to pay it much attention. One of the things I especially like most about Cologne constructivism is its ability to thematize alterity, otherness, and difference. Dewey's pluralism and rejection of the metaphysics of presence makes him amendable to the idea of alterity. Dewey takes most of the elements of classical metaphysics, e.g., *eidos*, *arche*, *ousia*, and *entelecheia*, and turns them over to logic. However, he does retain the classical metaphysical categories of potentiality (*dynamis*) and actuality (*energeia*), though he rejects the notion of "latent" potential. For instance, acorns do not become oak trees because that is their developmental *eidos* and *entelecheia*. What they become depends on their interactions (most acorns simply rot, many become food for squirrels, while very few become oak trees). Dewey writes: "When the idea that development is due to some in-dwelling end which tends to control the series of changes passed through is abandoned, potentialities must be thought of in terms of consequences of interactions with other things. Hence potentialities cannot be known until after the interactions have occurred. There are at a given time unactualized potentialities in an individual because and in as far as there are in existence other things with which it has not as yet interacted" (LW 14:109).

If the Other to us did not exist, change and growth would be im-possible. The connection to the human Eros is clear. Pluralistic de-mocracy not only passively tolerates the Other, it actively relies on it. Let me add that Dewey does not believe in linear developmental stages, although he does believe in development in an unfinished and unfinishable universe.

**Kersten Reich:** And what do you, Jim, think about Richard Rorty's hypothetical Dewey in this connection? Do you have your own hypo-thetical Dewey? If so, what newer lines of thought would he follow in the present situation? Would he reconstruct or revise some of his clas-sical positions?

**Jim Garrison:** I do not care much for Rorty's hypothetical Dewey. Most of what he says that is useful is already in Dewey (likewise for Wittgenstein and Heidegger). Rorty's dualisms, such as the private versus public dualism, are unsustainable, though a useful distinction. What I said about "the Other" must suffice on this occasion to an-swer what new lines Dewey might follow. Dewey is a philosopher of reconstruction that reconstructed himself many times in the course of his long career. The appropriate use of Dewey today is to recon-struct him for our context.

**Larry Hickman:** Dewey inter-defined democracy, education, and (techno-)science. He did not think democracy identifiable with any particular form of government or any set of results, just as he did not think education or (techno-)science identifiable with any particular method or set of results. Instead, he emphasized the ways in which human organisms interact with their natural and social environments so as to promote the determination of what is valuable and the means by which it can be secured. That would seem to be a solid constructivist position. As for the "newer perspectives," so much has happened in the field of social and political philosophy since Dewey's time that it is difficult even to list the major players in a brief comment such as this one. Habermas's important work is just one example among many. The same can be said of advances in the philosophy of education, and here the works of Howard Gardner and Jonathan Kozol come to mind. In the (techno-)sciences, Bruno Latour and Andrew Pickering come to mind.

**Stefan Neubert:** I think that Dewey's philosophy of democracy is still highly relevant in many respects. One piece of evidence for this, to my mind, is the number of inspiring new perspectives that have emerged from Dewey scholars in recent years that show the actuality of Pragmatist cultural and political criticisms; I mean studies like Jim Campbell's *The Community Reconstructs* (Campbell 1992), Mike Eldridge's *Transforming Experience* (Eldridge 1998) or Charlene Haddock Seigfried's Deweyan Pragmatist feminism (see Seigfried 1996, 2002). Larry has just indicated one crucial strength of Dewey's political approach—namely, that he did not identify democracy with any specific form of government or set of results. Democracy as a way of life has to be continually reinvented. For Dewey, political forms and ideas are tools for solving particular problems—tools that are themselves reshaped in the very process of political reconstruction. Hence we should always ask ourselves what a political idea like democracy might mean in our present situation, and we should be open to finding new implications resulting from the changed conditions of human beings now living together in community. For example, Dewey and his fellow leftist liberals, in the first half of the twentieth century, particularly emphasized the economical and educational aspects of democracy and developed a strong criticism of predatory capitalism based on their understanding of democracy. I agree with Judith Green (2002) that Pragmatists (and constructivists) today should continue this kind of criticism, while at the same time enlarging it by taking into account more recently developed perspectives as to the implications of democracy—e.g., issues like the legislation of sexual relationships or the political challenges of an increasingly globalized economical, social, and cultural world. To my mind, then, thinking about democracy in our own day of necessity means that we go beyond Dewey—partly *with* Dewey, in that we attempt to apply (and thereby reconstruct) his approach to our own situation, but partly also *without* Dewey, in that we now see more clearly some of the limitations of his political thought and try to overcome them. For example, I think there is some truth in Charlene Haddock Seigfried's feminist criticism that Dewey, by "locating conflicts in different approaches to life and not in struggles for power, . . frequently underestimates what is required to overcome them" (Seigfried 2002, 55). Here I think it would be worthwhile, on the theoretical as well as on the practical side, to try to complement and critically enlarge Dewey's political philosophy by comparing it with more recently developed approaches to "radical democracy" that put more emphasis on questions of antagonism and hegemony (see Laclau and Mouffe 1985). A more penetrating analysis of power relations seems to be crucial for advancing Pragmatist social thought today. And from the perspective of interactive constructivism, I should like to add, again, that this also implies taking more seriously the critical work of Michel Foucault.

*It is evident that there are a great number of affinities between present-day Pragmatism and constructivism. What difference do you see between the two approaches?*

**Larry Hickman:** As I understand Cologne constructivism, it appears to have a great deal in common with Dewey's brand of Pragmatism. Dewey was, after all, a thoroughgoing constructivist in matters

of knowledge and value. But it appears to me that Cologne constructivism may be closer to Rorty's neo-Pragmatism in at least one important sense, namely its embrace of what I take to be a type of
cognitive relativism. My contribution to this volume does not go into
great detail regarding the many similarities between Cologne constructivism and classical Pragmatism, because I wanted to get to the
more difficult issue of contrasting what I take to be their two different
concepts of truth. I argued that Dewey's notion of truth as warranted
assertibility—which I illustrate in terms of the universalizability of
certain claims—is stronger and more defensible than what I take to
be the weaker form of truth advanced by interactive constructivism,
based on cognitive relativism.

**Stefan Neubert:** There are of course differences, but I think we
should not overemphasize them, because, compared with the affinities between the two approaches, the differences are altogether small.
Sometimes they turn out to be rather conceptual or linguistic in nature, and the more you discuss what is different, the more the difference itself seems to disappear or diminish. For example, Jim's use of
the Deweyan concepts of "existence" and "essence" and the constructivist distinction between "the real" and "reality" at first sight
seem to be far apart, but if we look closer, there are more similarities
between the two distinctions than we might have expected. However,
there remain some substantial differences, and I think the discussions
in this volume have shown that taking these differences seriously can
be an enrichment for both sides. One of these more substantial differences concerns the status of universalizations (in science, philosophy,
ethics); another is the relevance of naturalism and metaphysics; a
third expresses our perspectives on discourse and power. And I find it
interesting that, concerning all three of these issues, there is at present
considerable dissent among contemporary (neo)Pragmatists themselves, if we consider positions like Rorty's, Bernstein's, Putnam's,
and many others referred to in the contributions of this volume.
Maybe we should welcome these controversies as exemplifying the

more paradoxical aspects implied in both Pragmatism and constructivism—as well as in so many other projects of knowledge criticism
in (post)modernity.

**Jim Garrison:** There are many kinds of constructivism. I have tried
to show that Dewey is incompatible with those forms deriving from
von Glasersfeld and the Kantian approach generally. Various kinds of
social constructivism and activity theory are compatible to different
degrees. Cologne constructivism makes an especially exciting dialogue partner for Dewey's constructivism, because the two share so
many basic assumptions. I think Cologne constructivism's attention
to the struggle for cultural hegemony (e.g., Gramsci), discursive
constitution (e.g., Foucault), and multiple publics (e.g., Fraser) are
valuable additions compatible with a reconstructed Deweyan constructivism. What to make of Dewey's event realism need not be a
point of crucial contention; clearly, events are not lumpy substances.
At some point, I do think the idea of a "void signifier" advocated by
Cologne constructivism is a good linguistic way of indicating that we
have arrived at the limits of linguistic construction and can say no
more. Finally, I do think there is much for constructivism to learn
from returning to early German social constructivist thinking, as indicated by Ken Stikkers. This would do all parties good.

**Kersten Reich:** As to Larry's approach, I think that Pragmatism,
too, can claim but partial universalizations in limited fields, e.g., of
means-ends relations. Especially in his later works, Dewey himself repeatedly observed that scientific generalizations depend on their contexts. I concede that, for constructivists, it is always a difficult task
to determine objective degrees of necessary generalizations. This is a
practical question, after all. And unfortunately, scientific generalizations are often used in social practices, routines, and institutions on
behalf of hegemonic purposes, struggles for power and (re)distribu-
tion, and the defence of vested interest and properties. As to Jim's
contributions, I can largely support his positions. I believe that interpreting Dewey today, we need a clear and definite constructivist turn
in order to expand his approach for our contemporary interests. To

my mind, though, these interests are basically informed by the dismissal of naturalism and realism, because both approaches tend all too much toward the fallacies of a copy or mirror approach to "reality." Here interactive constructivism takes a clear-cut counter position. Not only does it recognize different versions of world making that human observers claim as viable according to different contexts and interests, but it also recognizes that the rules of such world making—e.g., objectified procedures in science—are human constructions. This viewpoint enhances the ethical demands and standards to be claimed from science. It is becoming more and more important to take scientific legitimations out of a narrow discursive field of specialized reasonings and to discuss them in public discourses that provide broad participation of all those who are concerned—as human agents—by the consequences of scientific solutions and technological decisions. To claim that values and norms are human constructions is not, after all, to invalidate them. Rather, it is to increase the importance of deliberations, efforts at legitimation, and attempts to provide plausible reasons in human experience—and this, I think, is completely in accord with the heritage of Dewey's philosophy.

*We close with a final question to all of us: Why do we think that John Dewey is still an indispensable thinker in our present time?*

**Ken Stikkers:** I wish to identify three points. First, Dewey remains *the* philosopher of democracy insofar as he demonstrated how democracy, in order to have abiding significance, must manifest itself in everyday life, and not just on election day: it needs to be a way of life, entailing habitual participation in the governance of those institutions affecting our lives. I know of no other thinker who has made this point more eloquently and forcefully. Also in this regard, his notion of "publics" is a subtle but profound contribution to sociopolitical theory generally and to the theory of democracy in particular, because it opens up the vast but neglected middle landscape between the realm of the interpersonal, well studied by psychology, and theories of the state, the focus of traditional political philosophy; it is in this middle world where individuals and groups come together to address their common problems and, as Dewey shows, so much of the real work of democracy takes place. Second, he, along with William James, challenged the deeply held assumption in Western epistemologies and theories of communication that we must first clearly identify the proper conditions for the possibility of knowing and communicating before we can understand these activities adequately. James and Dewey demonstrated that a firmly secured (transcendental) starting point is not a prerequisite for constructivist inquiry, but that we can start simply in the middle of things, i.e., with the world just as it is experienced and with the plurality of perspectives that we find ourselves to have. Some have criticized Dewey recently, especially in light of the work of Michel Foucault in this regard, for not being sufficiently attuned to the power dimension of human discourse, but regardless of the merits of such criticisms, Dewey did much to disrupt traditional epistemological games of power: one of the traditional strategies of epistemological power has been the laying claim to proper starting points for knowing and communicating, and this is a strategy that James and Dewey deny. Third, Dewey radically rethinks the very meaning of philosophy and philosophical rigor by insisting, in such works as "The Need for a Recovery of Philosophy," that philosophy be accountable to the concrete, everyday lives of human beings. Philosophy is most rigorous, not when it retreats from experience into the sterility of its abstract formalisms, but in its fidelity to that experience.

**Jim Garrison:** Dewey, like Heidegger and Wittgenstein, took the linguistic turn so decisive for twentieth-century Western philosophy on either side of the Atlantic. Significantly, all three of these philosophers never lost sight of the role played by concrete social practices in language acquisition. Dewey and Heidegger also emphasized mood, feeling, and emotion as fundamental to our being in the world. For Dewey, our emotionally charged selective attention determines the world to which we respond. Intelligence, in the Latin sense of *intellectus* ("inter," among, and "legere," to choose) begins here. What we do not *interact with* is not *our* environment. Only our environment provides the raw materials for the construction of stimuli, meaning, truth, and value. Dewey also emphasized embodiment; beliefs for him are embodied habits evincing emotions. Habits are part of the meaning function for Dewey's three-term schema of meaning. They are, in Peirce's sense, interpretants of the sign and signified while the sign and signified are often external to the skin. The result is that Dewey describes a semiotic "world without withins" (as J. E. Tiles so aptly puts it). In Dewey's functionalism, events occur wherever they have consequences. The embodied three-term semiotics Dewey inherits from Peirce is already poststructuralist, yet is able to deal with embodiment and the use of tools (including language, "the tool of tools") in ways poststructuralists such as Derrida cannot, which is why, in part, *Derrida* often has difficulties with ethical-political issues. Dewey provides a holistic philosophy that integrates thought, feeling, and action, which contemporary philosophy leaves disintegrated. Dewey is relevant for almost any topic of contemporary cultural concern.

**Kersten Reich:** To my mind, Dewey's philosophy is important in many respects. I wish to confine my answer to one of his many achievements that seems to me especially pioneering. Dewey freed himself from the philosophical tradition that regarded knowledge and truth as the "copy" of an independent outer reality. Therefore, he clearly saw that humans construct the meanings and interpretations that then have an import for them. These processes, however, are very complicated. Thus they easily overlook and forget the ways they arrived at those meanings and interpretations. To liberate the development of people's agencies of inquiring into the preconditions and presuppositions of their practices and the opportunities for further constructive solutions, we need fundamentally new ways of education. In no way must we reduce learning to simply "copying" or imitating. Introducing experience into education, Dewey has given us a key for our future. And the last hundred years have confirmed the viability of his vision. Education is nothing that we can leave to accident, but deliberate and intentional education is a key for making the societies we live in more just, free, and democratic. This is an issue that Pragmatists and constructivists alike have to bear in mind. I'm sure they time and again will find inspiring suggestions in Dewey's broad and rich work.

**Larry Hickman:** First, Dewey had a rare talent for isolating the polar extremes on issues of philosophical importance. From each extreme he would then take what worked and jettison what didn't. If you accept the idea, as I do, that the underlying issues of human life can be expressed in terms that are broadly philosophical, and if you think, as I also do, that over time there are pendulum swings that tend through some fashion or another to overemphasize one or the other of those extreme positions, then it is an easy matter to see the contemporary relevance of Dewey's thought. He was very good at taking the measure of the swings of the pendula, and this from the vantage point of someone who was constantly looking for ways to reconstruct what he considered a solid middle position. I believe that the pendula are still swinging back and forth between some of the same extreme philosophical positions, even though those extremities keep getting new names. That is one of the reasons Dewey's thought is still relevant. Second, Dewey was a comprehensive thinker in a manner that is quite unusual in our own time. He was a public intellectual who was active in progressive causes, and yet he was able to write influential books on ethics, philosophy of education, theory of inquiry, the place of the arts in human experience, and religion. He even constructed what might be called a metaphysical naturalism. These are still areas of enormous importance, especially in a time during which our experiences are increasingly "globalized."

**Stefan Neubert:** The broad Renaissance of Dewey scholarship that has taken place in the English-speaking world in the last decades shows how much his philosophy has to say that is still relevant half a century after his death. In Germany, we are just beginning to recognize this relevancy. To my mind, his philosophy of education, his vision of democracy, and his theory of culture and communication are of supreme importance today—to name but a few of the manifold themes developed in his comprehensive and multilayered work. In all of these fields, I see Dewey not only as a founder of Pragmatism, but also as one of the most important (and comprehensive) forerunners of present-day constructivism. And if we expand our focus from his work to his life, I think we will realize that we are in dire need of the kind of model of the public intellectual that Dewey in his time invented, lived, and represented.

# Notes

CHAPTER ONE

JOHN DEWEY: HIS LIFE AND WORK

*(Larry A. Hickman)*

1. Even if these technologies exposed his innate shyness, as is apparent in the clip.

2. Hull House was a widely known example of the late-nineteenth-century social settlement movement in major American cities that reacted, among other things, to the great migration and urbanization processes that followed the Civil War. Hull House provided solidarity and support for marginalized parts of the citizenry and a forum for progressive thinking and social reform. Great importance was attached to social education and political work, especially with female immigrants. Addams tried to establish political coalitions among urban workers, peasants, socialists, and other progressive intellectuals and to support legislative amelioration of the situation of industrial workers and better urban services (see Westbrook 1991, 85). Most of its work was carried out by women. Hull House is also often cited today as an outstanding example of pioneering work in Pragmatist feminism (see Seigfried 1996, 57ff.). For further information see http://www.uic.edu/jaddams/hull/hull_house.html. Retrieved July 31, 2007.

3. See Jim Garrison's extensive discussion in Chapter 5 of this volume.

4. It is important to note that by "adjustment" Dewey does not simply have in mind the passive acceptance of an environment. In "The Need for a Recovery of Philosophy" (1917), e.g., he writes: "as life requires the fitness of the environment to the organic functions, adjustment to the environment means not passive acceptance of the latter, but acting so that the environing changes take a certain turn. The 'higher' the type of life, the more adjustment takes the form of an adjusting of the factors of the environment to one

another in the interest of life . . ." (MW 10:8). See also the distinction between passive and active adaptation in his "Contributions to *Cyclopedia of Education*" (MW 6:364f), where he notes that in "progressive societies . . . activities are to an extent directed toward securing an adaptation of the environment to the individual's needs and ends, rather than vice versa."

CHAPTER TWO
PRAGMATISM: DIVERSITY OF SUBJECTS IN DEWEY'S PHILOSOPHY
AND THE PRESENT DEWEY SCHOLARSHIP
*(Stefan Neubert)*

1. There are, however, already in Dewey's *Middle Works* a number of minor writings in which his mature concept of experience is already prefigured and progressively worked out. Compare, e.g., the writings indicated by the key words "experience" and "immediate empiricism" in the index of MW 3, the essay "The Subject-Matter of Metaphysical Inquiry" (MW 8:3–13), Chapter 11 of *Democracy and Education* (MW 9:146–58), and Chapter 4 in *Reconstruction in Philosophy* (MW 12:124–38).

2. Compare in this connection Dewey's important 1931 essay "Context and Thought" (LW 6:3–21), where he criticizes "the habit of philosophers of neglecting the indispensability of context, both in particular and in general," and suggests that "the most pervasive fallacy of philosophic thinking goes back to neglect of context" (LW 6:5).

3. In addition to *Experience and Nature* compare especially his two books *Reconstruction in Philosophy* (MW 12:77–201) and *The Quest for Certainty: A Study of the Relation of Knowledge and Action* (LW 4).

4. It deserves attention, too, that Dewey eventually explicitly renounced the term "metaphysics" with regard to his own philosophy. His student and colleague Sidney Hook reports in his introduction to the *Collected Works* edition of *Experience and Nature* that Dewey "vowed on the eve of his ninetieth year 'never to use the words [metaphysics and metaphysical] again in connection with any aspect of my own position' because, he complained, his use of the terms had been assimilated to the sense they bear 'in the classic tradition based on Aristotle'" (LW 1:viii). In a late draft for a new introduction of *Experience and Nature* that Dewey wrote in the years before his death (1949–51; see "The Unfinished Introduction," LW 1:329–64), he was even prepared to jettison the term "experience" and replace it by the term "culture," because his specific use of the word "experience" had led to misunderstandings (LW 1:361f.).

5. There is no doubt that this dimension had already been emphasized in earlier works like *Experience and Nature* (LW 1), but Dewey's elaboration

in *Art as Experience* is more systematic and takes place on a considerably broader scale. As to the qualitative and aesthetic dimension of experience, with specific regard to thinking, see also Dewey's important 1930 essay "Qualitative Thought" (LW 5:243–62).

6. Dewey's own contributions to the *Studies* of 1903 can be found in MW 2. His *Essays* collectively published in 1916 are scattered about several volumes of the *Middle Works* in the critical edition. It is easy to find them with the help of the edition's Index.

7. For a more extended discussion see Larry A. Hickman's contribution in Part II of this volume.

8. See also the essay "Three Independent Factors in Morals" (1930 / 1966; LW 5:279–88) as well as Dewey's extraordinarily subtle discussion of the relation of means and ends—e.g., in his 1939 *Theory of Evaluation* (LW 13:189–251, esp. 226ff: "The Continuum of Ends-Means")—which completely refutes the still-existing misunderstanding of his Pragmatism as a narrow utilitarianism.

9. See also examples given in Dewey's *Art as Experience* (e.g., LW 10:49f.).

10. The quote is taken from the essay "Three Independent Factors in Morals."

11. This means no rejection of representative structures, but rather the combination of forms and methods of direct and representative democracy.

12. The quote is from Dewey's 1937 statement "Democracy is Radical" (LW 11:296–99), first published in *Common Sense*, the "unofficial organ" of the "League for Independent Political Action" (LIPA). The LIPA was one of the most important organizations in which "Dewey's political activism was centered" at that time (Westbrook 1991, 445–52). See also the address Dewey wrote on the occasion of the celebration of his eightieth birthday (1939), "Creative Democracy—The Task Before Us" (LW 14:224–30).

13. Part of Dewey's political activities in the early 1930s was the attempt to establish a new political party in the United States, partly resembling the model of the European social-democratic parties of the time. The (ultimately failed) attempt was meant to disrupt the encrusted two-party system and its entanglement with vested economical interests and influential lobbies (see LW 6:156–81; Westbrook 1991, 443ff.).

14. Important work in present Dewey scholarship is focused on Dewey's correspondence. Especially with regard to his journalistic work and commentary to the current political affairs of his day, this work reveals important details on the personal and sociocultural backgrounds of his involvements in public life.

15. Dewey's Chicago School experiment, afterwards often labeled as the "Dewey School," existed until 1904, when he moved to Columbia University in New York City.

16. For further information on SAAP, see http://www.american-philosophy.org (retrieved July 31, 2007).

17. For further information on the Dewey Center, see http://www.siu.edu/~deweyctr (retrieved July 31, 2007).

18. A German branch of the Dewey Center was established at the University of Cologne in 2005. For further information see http://dewey.uni-koeln.de (retrieved July 31, 2007).

19. For further information, see the Web site of the Center for Dewey Studies.

CHAPTER THREE

CONSTRUCTIVISM: DIVERSITY OF APPROACHES AND
CONNECTIONS WITH PRAGMATISM
(Kersten Reich)

1. The three terms belong to the basic categories of the Cologne program of interactive constructivism (see my contribution in Chapter 6 of this volume).

2. Singularity of events implies, among other things, that these events change in repetition.

3. From an explicitly constructivist standpoint in Germany; cp. Fischer et al (1992). The title of the two most important conferences on constructivism in Germany in the 1990s, *Weisen der Welterzeugung*—i.e. "Versions of World Making"—used Goodman's phrase to draw attention to the plurality of multiple versions as against the *one* comprehensive narrative.

4. I have discussed this at length in my analysis of three important "movements of offended reason" characteristic of modernity / postmodernity (see Reich 1998a).

5. See, e.g., Ernst von Glasersfeld, http://www.umass.edu/srri/vonGlasersfeld/publications.html (retrieved July 31, 2007).

6. A broad diversity of constructivist approaches can also be found in the field of education.

7. For a survey of the approach and for publications cf. to the Heinz von Foerster web page URL: http://www.univie.ac.at/constructivism/HvF.htm (retrieved July 31, 2007).

8. For a survey of the approach and for publications cf. to the Ernst von Glasersfeld web page URL: http://www.umass.edu/srri/vonGlasersfeld/ (retrieved July 31, 2007).

9. For an instructive position as to the dispute between realism and constructivism in the natural sciences, see, e.g., Hacking (1999).

10. The approach has been developed in the last decade at the University of Cologne and is occasionally referred to in the present volume as the Cologne program or Cologne constructivism.

11. I have discussed three important "movements of offended reason" (*Kränkungsbewegungen der Vernunft*) that underlie the transition from modernity to postmodernity and the appearance of explicit constructivist approaches to knowledge criticism on another occasion (see Reich 1998a, 1998b).

12. An English introduction can be found at the Web site of interactive constructivism; see Neubert and Reich URL: http://www.uni-koeln.de/ew-fak/konstrukt/english/index.htm (retrieved July 31, 2007).

13. For further publications, refer to URL: http://www.stanford.edu/~rorty/ (retrieved July 31, 2007).

14. In *Knowing and the Known* (LW 16:1–294), a book coauthored with Arthur F. Bentley, interaction means the mutual operation of persons or objects upon each other as already established identities, whereas transaction also implies the very emergence and co-evolution of identities within interactive affairs. See the discussion in Chapter 9 of this volume.

CHAPTER FOUR

DIALOGUE BETWEEN PRAGMATISM AND CONSTRUCTIVISM
IN HISTORICAL PERSPECTIVE
*(Kenneth W. Stikkers)*

1. May 2, 1909, in Papers of William James, Houghton Library, Harvard University, MS 450.

2. See 1–146; expanded and revised in *Die Wissensformen und die Gesellschaft* (Leipzig: Der Neue Geist Verlag, 1926), 1–229.

3. Earlier, Boutroux wrote a long and highly sympathetic Preface to the French translation of James's *Varieties of Religious Experience, L'Expérience religieuse*, translated by F. Abauzit (Paris: Alcan, 1905), and an article, "William James et l'expérience *religieuse*," for the *Revue de métaphysique et de moral* 16 (1908):1–27, which formed a chapter of his book *Science et Religion dans la philosophie contemporaine* (Paris: E. Flammarion, 1908).

4. Translated by Bruno Jordan (Leipzig: Veit, 1912).

5. This formulation lends support to Scheler's first criticism of Pragmatism, viz., that it is a disguised correspondence theory, if one extends Pragmatism, as did James, into a theory of truth.

6. I am grateful to Professor Manfried S. Frings, editor of Scheler's *Ge-sammelte Werke*, for bringing this letter to my attention.

7. Scheler borrows the Latin expressions from James.

8. Michael D. Barber (1993) develops this point very well.

9. I am grateful to Professor Frings for bringing this notebook to my attention.

10. E.g., Mills (1940a, 316–30) explores the relevance of Peirce's, Dewey's, and Mead's Pragmatisms for the sociology of knowledge. See also Mills (1939, 670–78).

CHAPTER FIVE

DEWEY'S CONSTRUCTIVISM: FROM THE REFLEX ARC
CONCEPT TO SOCIAL CONSTRUCTIVISM
*(Jim Garrison)*

1. This fact has an immediate and important educational implication. Dewey insists: "Not only is social life identical with communication, but also all communication (and hence all genuine social life) is educative. To be a recipient of a communication is to have an enlarged and changed experience. One shares in what another has thought and felt and in so far, meagerly or amply, has his own attitude modified. The one who communicates is also affected. Try the experiment of communicating, with fullness and accuracy, some experience to another, especially if it be somewhat complicated, and you will find your own attitude toward your experience changing; otherwise you resort to expletives and ejaculations. . . . All communication is like art" (MW 9:8–9).

Any teacher who has actually practiced the art of teaching and reflected upon the experience knows Dewey's observation here is true.

2. Similarly, Richard Rorty (1979) lauds Dewey's "epistemological behaviorism." Unfortunately, for Quine, he eventually chose the individualistic, reductive behaviorism of B. F. Skinner, rather than the emergent social behaviorism of Dewey and Mead. Ontological relativity assures the possibility that various parties may contend over the proper interpretation of reality.

CHAPTER SIX

OBSERVERS, PARTICIPANTS, AND AGENTS IN DISCOURSES:
A CONSIDERATION OF PRAGMATIST AND CONSTRUCTIVIST
THEORIES OF THE OBSERVER
*(Kersten Reich)*

1. In the discourse theory of interactive constructivism, discourses of knowledge are seen in intimate interrelation with discourses of power, lived relationships, and the unconscious (see Reich 1998b; Neubert and Reich

2000). Although I cannot go too much into detail here, these different perspectives on discourses should always be taken into account in postmodern discourse analyses.

2. Janich's approach, which goes by the name of "*methodischer Kulturalismus*," develops an interesting perspective on methodological constructivism.

3. Richard Rorty discusses a variety of similar approaches in philosophy that, each in its specific manner, testifies to a Pragmatic understanding of truth.

4. Dewey discusses the role of observation in contexts of learning, e.g., in *How We Think* (comp. MW 6:328ff., LW 8:315ff.). The role of observation in inquiry is developed in *Experience and Nature* (LW 1) and *Logic* (LW 12).

5. See Larry Hickman's defense of universalistic claims in Chapter 7 of this volume.

CHAPTER SEVEN

PRAGMATISM, CONSTRUCTIVISM, AND THE

PHILOSOPHY OF TECHNOLOGY

*(Larry A. Hickman)*

1. If these are postmodernist insights, then of course Dewey was a postmodernist as well.

2. Thanks to John Hartmann for calling my attention to this wonderfully concise statement of the position.

3. This is, I take it, an example of the "inherent paradox of the absolute and the relative in the field of truth claims." It involves an absolute assent to the relativity (or contextual nature) of truth claims.

4. I freely admit that bananas *qua* food have been socially constructed, as have fossils *qua* records of previous life on earth.

5. Repeatability of an experiment should not be confused with the repeatability of an event that is the object of the experiment. Otherwise, geology and other sciences that deal with unique past events would be impossible. Alvin Plantinga appears to commit this simple error when, in his essay "Methodological Naturalism?" he confuses the Big Bang *qua* an unrepeatable event with experiments that have led to the hypothesis of the Big Bang. He utilizes this confusion to question Michael Ruse's otherwise unremarkable claim that scientific claims rest on repeatability (a claim that is so unremarkable, in fact, that without it the satire in *The Journal of Irreproducible Results* wouldn't have any point). Plantinga's essay, a defense of a Christian version of creationism, can be found at http://www.arn.org/docs/odesign/od182/methnat182.htm.

6. Source: http://www.cs.uwaterloo.ca/~alopez-o/math-faq/mathtext/node18.html, retrieved July 31, 2007.

7. As Dewey uses these terms, qualities are existential, immediately experienced. Traits are mediated: they are qualities that have become involved in inference.

8. See Dewey's claim, for example, in LW 12:434–35. "Application of conceptions and hypotheses to existential matters through the medium of doing and making is an intrinsic constituent of scientific method. No hard and fast line can be drawn between such forms of 'practical' activity and those which apply their conclusions to humane social ends without involving disastrous consequences to science in its narrower sense."

9. Dewey's 1938 *Logic* provides excellent examples of the lack of isomorphism between linguistic and logical forms.

10. Between the abstracting and the applying we have the global reliability of the abstraction. It is both abstracted and ready to be applied.

11. By this I mean, of course, all existential material except the material qualities of the expression.

12. "One standard atmosphere" is of course a construction. From the standpoint of the judgment under discussion, it has the form of an intermediate judgment.

13. Here is another example of a locally reliable judgment. "Milk is not edible" is locally reliable among Australian aborigines. That population is almost entirely lactose-intolerant.

14. Another final judgment that this judgment (qua intermediate) supports is that women should be afforded the means of reproductive choice. This matter is particularly pertinent in the light of the recent statement by Karen P. Hughes, the senior presidential advisor in the current U.S. administration, that it is the administration's view that "improving education, improving access to health care and improving economic opportunity are an important part of making a nation [such as Afghanistan] more stable" (Bumiller 2001, B2). The irony is that she speaks for an administration that is opposed to reproductive choice insofar as it may involve abortion.

CHAPTER EIGHT

PRAGMATISM, CONSTRUCTIVISM, AND THE THEORY OF CULTURE
*(Stefan Neubert)*

1. See also Chapter 5 of this volume.

2. See also Chapter 7 of this volume. For an interesting interpretation of the constructive and critical potentialities of Deweyan "cultural instrumentalism," see also Eldridge (1998).

3. This is not a plea to abandon the concept of "experience" altogether, but only to reconstruct it as an observer-perspective in the constructivist sense.

4. See also Chapter 6 of this volume.

5. The term "overdetermination" has been imported into poststructuralist thought from Freudian psychoanalysis (in particular from the *Traumdeutung*).

6. Compare Dewey's 1919 essay "Philosophy and Democracy," where he argues that "[a] philosophy animated . . . by the strivings of men to achieve democracy will construe liberty as meaning a universe in which there is real uncertainty and contingency, a world which is not all in, and never will be, a world which in some respect is incomplete and in the making, and which in these respects may be made this way or that according as men judge, prize, love and labor" (MW 11:50). We can interpret Dewey's radical understanding of the meaning of contingency as a trait that links his philosophy to postmodernity.

7. This criticism also applies to Dewey's claim to a naturalistic metaphysics as he formulated it, e.g., in *Experience and Nature*—i.e., the "cognizance of the generic traits of existence" (LW 1:50), or "a statement of the generic traits manifested by existences of all kinds without regard to their differentiation into physical and mental" (LW 1:308). In Dewey, the metaphysical quest for these "generic traits" is not a transcendental move, but always remains within the realm of experience. From a constructivist perspective, the naturalistic-metaphysical argument nevertheless all too much tends to neglect the dependence on observer positions in the very foundation of Dewey's philosophy.

8. Laclau and Mouffe have developed their theories by way of a critical reinterpretation and deconstruction of Marxism. In particular, they borrow the core concept of their approach, hegemony, from a critical poststructuralist reading of the work of the Italian Marxist Antonio Gramsci.

9. That there are—despite this contrast—many affinities between present-day theories of hegemony, like the one launched by Laclau and Mouffe, and the political philosophy of Pragmatism (especially in the wake of Dewey) could be shown in detail, e.g., with the help of Jim Campbell's (1992) book *The Community Reconstructs: The Meaning of Pragmatic Social Thought*. In particular, the chapter entitled "Politics and Conceptual Reconstruction" (ibid., 59–70) offers many implicit connections to the theory of hegemony. This applies, e.g., to Campbell's critique of the neo-conservative "rhetoric of restoration" in the 1980s and early-1990s political debates in the

U.S. When Campbell argues that political concepts like "democracy," "free-dom," and "individualism" are always open constructs of meanings that cannot be reduced to *one* single correct, true, or legitimate interpretation, he actually underscores the importance of hegemonic struggles in democratic societies. In this connection, the engagement for democracy implies that "we must offer new conceptions of what *democracy, freedom,* and *individualism* can and should mean here and now so that these terms can continue to function as useful symbols in our attempts at social reconstruction" (Camp-bell 1992, 69). Compare also Dewey's own observation about the vagueness of terms like "liberty, equality and fraternity," which partly involves that these terms represent politically contested ideas (MW 11:49).

10. The quote within the quote refers to Bhabha's criticism of Charles Taylor.

11. In passing, I wish to indicate that, with regard to a theory of the in-commensurable, one also finds interesting suggestions in Dewey. There are a lot of places in Dewey where he particularly stresses the uniqueness of con-crete human experience and the limits of the possibility of reducing it to or equating it with something else by means of a common denominator. See, e.g., his "Construction and Criticism" (LW 5:125–43), as well as the follow-ing passage from "Philosophy and Democracy," in which Dewey interprets the meaning of the democratic principle of equality: "In social and moral matters, equality does not mean mathematical equivalence. It means rather the inapplicability of considerations of greater and less, superior and infe-rior. It means that no matter how great the quantitative differences of ability, strength, position, wealth, such differences are negligible in comparison with something else—the fact of individuality. . . . It means, in short, a world in which an existence must be reckoned with on its own account, not as some-thing capable of equation with and transformation into something else." It means, so to speak, a world of "the incommensurable in which each speaks for itself and demands consideration on its own behalf" (MW 11:53). It is perhaps noteworthy, too, that the leading present-day Pragmatist feminist, Charlene Haddock Seigfried, uses this passage as a key reference in her own reconstruction of "Dewey's Pragmatist Feminist Theory" (see Seigfried 2002, esp. 62–65).

# Bibliography

The List of Abbreviations at the front of this volume contains references to *The Collected Works of John Dewey*. In addition to works cited in this volume, the following bibliography also lists selected titles relevant to John Dewey, pragmatism, constructivism, and related topics.

Alexander, Thomas M. 1987. *John Dewey's theory of art, experience, and nature: The horizons of feeling.* Albany: State University of New York Press.
———. 1995. John Dewey and the Roots of Democratic Imagination. In Langsdorf, Lenore, and Andrew R. Smith, eds. *Recovering pragmatism's voice: The classical tradition, Rorty, and the philosophy of communication.* Albany: State University of New York Press.
Auernheimer, Georg. 1996. *Einführung in die interkulturelle Erziehung.* Darmstadt: Primus.
Bakhtin, Michail. 1981. *The dialogic imagination.* Austin: University of Texas Press.
———. 1984. *Rabelais and his world.* Bloomington: Indiana University Press.
Barber, M. D. 1993. *Guardian of dialogue: Max Scheler's phenomenology, sociology of knowledge, and philosophy of love.* Lewisburg, Penn.: Bucknell University Press.
———. 2002. *Mind and nature.* Cresskill, N.J.: Hampton Press.
Bataille, Georges. 1997. *Theorie der Religion.* Hrsg. u. Nachw. v. Gerd Bergfleth. Batterien Bd. 59. Berlin: Matthes and Seitz.
Bateson, Gregory. 2000. *Steps to an ecology of mind.* Chicago: University of Chicago Press.
Bauman, Zygmunt. 1993. *Postmodern ethics.* Cambridge, Mass.: Blackwell.
———. 1997. *Postmodernity and its discontents.* New York: New York University Press.

————. 1998a. *Work, consumerism and the new poor.* Philadelphia: Open University Press.

————. 1998b. *Globalization: The human consequences.* New York: Columbia University Press.

————. 1999. *Culture as praxis.* Thousand Oaks, Calif.: Sage.

————. 2000. *Liquid modernity.* Cambridge: Polity Press.

Beck, Ulrich. 1992. *Risk society.* London: Sage.

Becker, Howard. 1927–28. Review of *Wesen und Formen der Sympathie*, by Max Scheler. *American Journal of Sociology* 33:637–42.

————. 1931. Some forms of sympathy: A phenomenological analysis. *Journal of Abnormal and Social Psychology* 26:58–68.

Becker, Howard, and Harry Elmer Barnes. 1952. Phenomenology and Scheler and the forms of knowledge and society. In *Social thought from lore to science*, 906–13. Washington, D.C.: Harren Press.

Becker, Howard, and Helmut O. Dahlke. 1942. Max Scheler's sociology of knowledge. *Philosophy and Phenomenological Research* 2:309–22.

Berger, P. L., and T. Luckmann. 1966. *The social construction of reality.* Garden City, N.Y.: Doubleday.

Bernstein, Richard J. 1967. *John Dewey.* New York: Washington Square Press.

————. 1983. *Beyond objectivism and relativism.* Philadelphia: University of Pennsylvannia Press.

————. 1992. *The new constellation: The ethical-political horizons of modernity/postmodernity.* Cambridge, Mass.: MIT Press.

————. 1998. Community in the pragmatic tradition. In *The revival of pragmatism*, ed. M. Dickstein, 141–56. Durham: Duke University Press.

Bettelheim, Bruno (1980). Kinder brauchen Märchen. München: DTV Deutscher Taschenbuch.

Bhabha, Homi K. 1994. *The location of culture.* London and New York: Routledge.

————. 1996. Culture's in-between. In *Questions of cultural dentity*, ed., Stuart Hall and Paul Du Gay, 53–60. London: Sage.

Bittner, Stefan. 2001. *Learning by Dewey? John Dewey und die Deutsche Pädagogik 1900–2000.* Bad Heilbrunn and Obb: Klinkhardt.

Bohnsack, Fritz. 1976. *Erziehung zur Demokratie: John Deweys Pädagogik und ihre Bedeutung für die Reform unserer Schule.* Ravensburg: Otto Maier.

Boisvert, Raymond D. 1988. *Dewey's metaphysics.* New York: Fordham University Press.

————. 1992. Metaphysics as the search for paradigmatic instances. In *Transactions of the Charles S. Peirce Society* 28:189–203.

Boutroux, E. 1911. *William James*. Paris: Colin.

Browne, Malcolm. 1999. Lene Vestergaard Hau: She puts the brakes on light. *New York Times*. March 30.

Bruner, Jerome S. 1983. *Child's talk—learning to use language*. Oxford: Oxford University Press.

———. 1984. Vygotsky's zone of proximal development: The hidden agenda. In *Children's learning in the "zone of proximal development,"* ed. B. Rogoff and J. V. Wertsch, 93–97. San Francisco: Jossey-Bass.

———. 1990. *Acts of meaning*. Cambridge, Mass.: Harvard University Press.

———. 1996. *The culture of education*. Cambridge, Mass.: Harvard University Press.

Bruner, J. S., and H. Haste. 1987. *Making sense: The child's construction of the world*. London: Methuen.

Bumiller, Elisabeth. 2001. White House letter: The politics of plight and the gender gap. *New York Times*. November 19.

Burckhart, H., and K. Reich. 2000. *Begründung von Moral: Diskursethik versus Konstruktivismus—eine Streitschrift*. Würzburg: Könighausen und Neumann.

Burke, Thomas. 1994. *Dewey's new logic: A reply to Russell*. Chicago: University of Chicago Press.

Burr, V. 1995. *An introduction to social constructivism*. London: Routledge.

Butler, Judith. 1990. *Gender trouble*. London: Routledge.

———. 1993. *Bodies that matter*. London: Routledge.

———. 1997. *Excitable speech*. London: Routledge.

Campbell, James. 1992. *The community reconstructs: The meaning of pragmatic social thought*. Urbana: University of Illinois Press.

Carter, Elliott. 1993. Expressionismus und amerikanische Musik. In *Amerikanische Musik seit Charles Ives: Interpretationen, Quellentexte, Komponistenmonographien*, ed. Hermann Danuser, Dietrich Kamper, and Paul Terse, 275–87. Laaber: Laaber.

Clancey, W. J. 1997. *Situated cognition: On human knowledge and computer representation*. Cambridge: Cambridge University Press.

Cobern, W. 1993. Contextual constructivism: The impact of culture on the learning and teaching of science. In *The practice of constructivism in science education*, ed. K. Tobin, 51–69. Hillsdale, N.J.: Lawrence Erlbaum.

Cuffaro, Harriet K. 1995. *Experimenting with the world: John Dewey and the early childhood classroom*. New York: Teachers College Press.

Dahlke, Helmut Otto. 1940. The sociology of knowledge. In *Contemporary social theory*, ed. Harry Elmer Barnes, Howard Becker, and Frances Bennett Becker, 64–89. New York: D. Appleton-Century.

Dalton, Thomas C. 2002. *Becoming John Dewey*. Bloomington: Indiana University Press.

Davidson Films. 2001. *John Dewey: His life and work*. Davidson Films, Inc. San Luis Obispo, Calif. (http://www.davidsonfilms.com/giants.htm# DEW).

Dewey, John. 1980. *Kunst als Erfahrung*. Frankfurt am Main: Suhrkamp.

———. 1993. *Demokratie und Erziehung*. Hrsg. v. Jürgen Oelkers, übers. v. Erich Hylla. Weinheim and Basel: Beltz.

———. 1995. *Erfahrung und Natur*. Übers. v. Martin Suhr. Frankfurt am Main: Suhrkamp.

———. 1998. *Die Suche nach Gewissheit: Eine Untersuchung des Verhältnisses von Erkenntnis und Handeln*. Übers. v. Martin Suhr. Frankfurt am Main: Suhrkamp.

———. 2001. *Die Öffentlichkeit und ihre Probleme*. Hrsg. v. Hans-Peter Krüger, übers. v. Wolf-Dietrich Junghanns. Berlin and Vienna: Philo.

———. 2002. *Logik—die Theorie der Foschung*. Übers. v. Martin Suhr. Frankfurt am Main: Suhrkamp.

———. 2003. *Philosophie und Zivilisation*. Übers. v. Martin Suhr. Frankfurt am Main: Suhrkamp.

Dickstein, Morris, ed. 1998. *The revival of pragmatism: New essays on social thought, law, and culture*. Durham: Duke University Press.

Driver, R., and J. Easley. 1978. Pupils and paradigms: A review of literature related to concept development in adolescent science students. In *Studies in Science Education* 5:61–84.

Driver, R., and V. Oldham. 1986. A constructivist approach to curriculum development in science. In *Studies in Science Education* 13:105–22.

Dubs, R. 1995. Konstruktivismus: Einige Überlegungen aus der Sicht der Unterrichtsgestaltung. In *Zeitschrift für Pädagogik* 41:889–903

Dykhuizen, George. 1973. *The life and mind of John Dewey*. Carbondale and Edwardsville: Southern Illinois University Press.

Eldridge, Michael. 1998. *Transforming experience: John Dewey's cultural instrumentalism*. Nashville: Vanderbilt University Press.

Engler, Ulrich. 1992. *Kritik der Erfahrung: Die Bedeutung der ästhetischen Erfahrung in der Philosophie John Deweys*. Würzburg: Königshausen & Neumann.

Fischer, Hans Rudi. 1995. *Die Wirklichkeit des Konstruktivismus*. Heidelberg: Auer.

Fischer, Hans Rudi, ed. 1991. *Autopoiesis: Eine Theorie im Brennpunkt der Kritik*. Heidelberg: Auer.

Fischer, Hans Rudi, et al., eds. 1992. *Das Ende der großen Entwürfe*. Frankfurt am Main: Suhrkamp.

Fish, Stanley. 1998. Truth and toilets: Pragmatism and the practices of life. In *The revival of pragmatism*, ed. M. Dickstein, 418–34. Durham: Duke University Press.

Fishman, Stephen M., and Lucille McCarthy. 1998. *John Dewey and the challenge of classroom practice*. New York: Teachers College Press.

Fosnot, C. T. 1993. Rethinking science education: A defence of Piagetian constructivism. In *Journal of Research in Science Teaching* 30:1189–201.

Fosnot, C.T., ed. 1996. *Constructivism: Theory, perspectives, and practice*. New York: Teachers College Press.

Foucault, Michel. 1981a. The order of discourse. In *Untying the text—A poststructuralist reader*, ed. Robert Young, 48–78. Boston: Routledge and Kegan Paul.

———. 1981b. *Archäologie des Wissens*. Frankfurt am Main: Suhrkamp.

Fraser, Nancy. 1994. Rethinking the public sphere: A contribution to the critique of actually existing democracy. In *Between borders: Pedagogy and the politics of cultural studies*, ed. Henry A. Giroux and Peter McLaren, 74–98. New York and London: Routledge.

———. 1998. Another pragmatism: Alain Locke, critical "race" theory, and the politics of culture. In *The revival of pragmatism*, ed. M. Dickstein, 157–75. Durham: Duke University Press.

Furth, Hans G. 1990. *Wissen als Leidenschaft: Eine Untersuchung über Freud und Piaget*. Frankfurt am Main: Suhrkamp.

Garnier, C., N. Bednarz, and I. Ulanovskaya, eds. 1991. *Après Vygotski et Piaget: Perspectives sociale et constructiviste*. Brussels: De Boeck.

Garrison, Jim. 1996. A Deweyan theory of democratic listening. In *Educational Theory* 48:429–51.

———. 1997a. *Dewey and eros: Wisdom and desire in the art of teaching*. New York: Teachers College Press.

———. 1997b. An alternative to Von Glasersfeld's subjectivism in science education: Deweyan social constructivism. In *Science and Education* 6:301–12.

———. 1998a. Toward a pragmatic social constructivism. In *Constructivism and education*, ed. M. Larochelle, N. Bednarz, and J. Garrison, 43–62. Cambridge: Cambridge University Press.

———. 1998b. John Dewey's philosophy as education. In *Reading Dewey—Interpretations for a postmodern generation*, ed. Larry A. Hickman, 63–81. Bloomington: Indiana University Press.

Garrison, Jim, ed. 1995. *The new scholarship on Dewey*. Dordrecht, Boston, and London: Kluwer Academic Publishers.

Gavin, William J., ed. 2003. *In Dewey's wake: Unfinished work of pragmatic reconstruction*. Albany: State University of New York Press.

Geelan, D. R. 1997. Epistemological anarchy and the many forms of constructivism. In *Science and Education* 6:15–28.

Gergen, K. J. 1991. *The saturated self*. New York: Basic Books.

———. 1994. *Realities and relationships: Soundings in social construction*. Cambridge, Mass.: Harvard University Press.

———. 1999. *An invitation to social construction*. London: Sage.

Gergen, K. J., J. Shotter, and S. M. Widdicombe, eds. 1987–2005. *Inquiries in social construction*. London: Sage.

Gethmann, C. F. 1979. *Protologik*. Frankfurt am Main: Suhrkamp.

Gethmann, C. F., ed. 1991. *Lebenswelt und Wissenschaft*. Bonn: Bouvier.

Giddens, Anthony. 1991. *Modernity and self-identity: Self and society in the late modern age*. Stanford, Calif.: Stanford University Press.

Giroux, Henry A. 1992. *Border crossings: Cultural workers and the politics of education*. New York and London: Routledge.

———. 1993. *Living dangerously: Multiculturalism and the politics of difference*. New York: Lang.

———. 1994. *Disturbing pleasures: Learning popular culture*. New York and London: Routledge.

Giroux, Henry A., and Peter McLaren, eds. 1994. *Between borders: Pedagogy and the politics of cultural studies*. New York and London: Routledge.

Goffman, Erving. 1979. *Gender advertisements*. New York: Harper.

———. 1981. *Forms of talk*. Philadelphia: University of Pennsylvania Press.

Goodman, Nelson. 1978. *Ways of worldmaking*. Indianapolis: Hackett.

Green, Judith M. 1999. *Deep democracy*. New York: Rowman and Littlefield.

———. 2002. Deepening democratic transformation—Deweyan individuation and pragmatist feminism. In *Feminist interpretations of John Dewey*, ed. Charlene H. Seigfried, 260–77. University Park: Pennsylvania State University Press.

Grundmann, M., ed. 1999. *Konstruktivistische Sozialisationsforschung*. Frankfurt am Main: Suhrkamp.

Hacking, Ian. 1999. *The social construction of what?* Cambridge, Mass.: Harvard University Press.

Hall, Stuart. 1992. Race, culture and communications: Looking backward and forward at cultural studies. In *Rethinking Marxism* 5:10–18.

———. 1997. The work of representation. In *Representation: Cultural representations and signifying practices*, ed. Stuart Hall, 13–74. London: Sage Publications and Open University.

Hall, Stuart, ed. 1997. *Representation: Cultural representations and signifying practices.* London: Sage.

Hall, Stuart, and P. du Gay, eds. 1996. *Questions of cultural identity.* London: Sage.

Hall, Stuart, and B. Gieben, eds. 1992. *Formations of modernity.* Cambridge: Polity Press.

Hall, Stuart, D. Held, and A. McGrew, eds. 1992. *Modernity and its futures.* Cambridge: Polity Press.

Hartmann, Dirk, and Peter Janich, eds. 1996. *Methodischer Kulturalismus: Zwischen Naturalismus und Postmoderne.* Frankfurt am Main: Suhrkamp.

———. 1998. *Die Kulturalistische Wende: Zur Orientierung des philosophischen Selbstverständnisses.* Frankfurt am Main: Suhrkamp.

Hau, L. V., et al. 1999. Light speed reduction to 17 meters per second in an ultracold atomic gas. *Nature* 397:594–98.

Hickman, Larry A. 1992. *John Dewey's pragmatic technology.* Bloomington: Indiana University Press.

———. 2000. Habermas' unresolved dualism: *Zweckrationalität* as *Idée Fixe.* In *Perspectives on Habermas,* ed. Lewis E. Hahn, 501–13. Chicago and La Salle, Ill.: Open Court.

———. 2001. *Philosophical tools for technological culture: Putting pragmatism to work.* Bloomington and Indianapolis: Indiana University Press.

Hickman, Larry A., ed. 1998. *Reading Dewey—Interpretations for a postmodern generation.* Bloomington: Indiana University Press.

Hickman, Larry A., and Thomas M. Alexander, eds. 1998. *The essential Dewey.* 2 vols. Bloomington: Indiana University Press.

Hitchcock, H. Wiley. 1993. Charles Ives und seine Zeit. In *Amerikanische Musik seit Charles Ives: Interpretationen, Quellentexte, Komponistenmonographien,* ed. Hermann Danuser, Dietrich Kamper, and Paul Terse, 21–30. Laaber: Laaber-Verlag.

Horlacher, Rebekka, and Jürgen Oelkers, eds. 2002. *John Dewey: Pädagogische Aufsätze und Abhandlungen 1900–1944.* Zürich: Pestalozzianum.

Jackson, Philip W. 1998. *John Dewey and the lessons of art.* New Haven, Conn.: Yale University Press.

James, William. 1908. *Der Pragmatismus: Ein neuer Name für alte Denkmethoden.* Leipzig: Klinkhard.

———. 1958. *Talks to teachers on psychology and to students on some of life's ideals.* New York: Holt.

———. 1975. *Pragmatism.* In *The works of William James,* ed. Frederick H. Burkhardt, et al. Cambridge, Mass.: Harvard University Press.

———. 1981. *The Principles of psychology.* In *The works of William James,* ed. Frederick H. Burkhardt, et al. Cambridge, Mass.: Harvard University Press.

Janich, Peter. 1996. *Konstruktivismus und Naturerkenntnis.* Frankfurt am Main: Suhrkamp.

———. 1999. *Wechselwirkungen: Zum Verhältnis von Kulturalismus, Phäno-menologie und Methode.* Würzburg: Könighausen und Neumann.

———. 2001. Vom Handwerk zum Mundwerk: Grundzüge von Konstruktivismus und Kulturalismus. In *Konstruktivismen,* ed., F. Wallner and R. Angnese, 1–14. Vienna: Universitätsverlag.

Jerusalem, Wilhelm. 1908. *Der Pragmatismus: einer neuer Name für alter Denkmethoden.* Leipzig: W. Klinkhard.

———. 1909. Soziologie des Erkenntnis. *Die Zukunft* 67:236–46.

———. 1921. Bermerkungen zu Max Schelers Aufsatz "Die positivistic Geschichtsphilosophie des Wissens und die Aufgaben einer Soziologie der Erkenntnis." In *Kölner Vierteljahrsheften für Sozialwissenschaften* I, 3:28–34.

Joas, Hans. 1989. *Praktische Intersubjektivität: Die Entwicklung des Werkes von G. H. Mead.* Frankfurt am Main: Suhrkamp.

———. 1992. Amerikanischer Pragmatismus und deutsches Denken: Zur Geschichte eines Mißverständnisses. In Hans Joas, *Pragmatismus und Gesellschaftstheorie,* 114–45. Frankfurt am Main: Suhrkamp.

———. 1993. *Pragmatism and social theory.* Chicago: University of Chicago Press.

———. 1996. *Die Kreativität des Handelns.* Frankfurt am Main: Suhrkamp.

———. 1997. *Die Entstehung der Werte.* Frankfurt am Main: Suhrkamp.

Joas, Hans, ed. 2000. *Philosophie der Demokratie: Beiträge zum Werk von John Dewey.* Frankfurt am Main: Suhrkamp.

Jörke, Dirk. 2003. *Demokratie als Erfahrung: John Dewey und die politische Philosophie der Gegenwart.* Wiesbaden: Westdeutscher Verlag.

Kamlah, W., and P. Lorenzen. 1967. *Logische Propädeutik.* Mannheim: Bibliographisches Institut.

Kaplan, Robert. 2000. *The nothing that is: A natural history of zero.* Oxford: Oxford University Press.

Kelly, G. A. 1955. *Principles of personal construct theory.* New York: Norton.

Kestenbaum, Victor. 1977. *The phenomenological sense of John Dewey: Habit and meaning.* Atlantic Highlands, N.J.: Humanities Press.

Kleinespel, Karin. 1997. *Schulpädagogik als Experiment: Zur Theorie und Praxis der Universitäts-Versuchsschulen in Jena, Chicago und Bielefeld.* Weinheim: Beltz.

Kloppenberg, James T. 1998. Pragmatism: An old name for some new ways of thinking? In *The revival of pragmatism*, ed. M. Dickstein, 83–127. Durham: Duke University Press.

Knorr-Cetina, K. 1981. *The manufacture of knowledge: An essay on the constructivist and contextual nature of science.* Oxford: Pergamon.

———. 1999. *Epistemic cultures: How the sciences make knowledge.* Cambridge, Mass.: Harvard University Press.

Kuhn, Thomas S. 1976. *Die Struktur wissenschaftlicher Revolutionen.* Frankfurt am Main: Suhrkamp.

Laclau, Ernesto. 1990. *New reflections on the revolution of our time.* London: Verso.

Laclau, Ernesto, and Chantal Mouffe. 1985. *Hegemony and socialist strategy: Towards a radical democratic politics.* London: Verso.

———. 1991. *Hegemonie und radikale Demokratie.* Vienna: Passagen.

Lakoff, G. and M. Johnson. 1999. *Philosophy in the Flesh.* New York: Basic Books.

Lambert, L., et al. 1995. *The constructivist leader.* New York: Teachers College Press.

———. 1996. *Who will save our schools? Teachers as constructivist leaders.* Thousand Oaks, Calif.: Sage and Corwin Press.

Langsdorf, Lenore, and Andrew R. Smith, eds. 1995. *Recovering pragmatism's voice: The classical tradition, Rorty, and the philosophy of communication.* Albany: State University of New York Press.

Larochelle, M., N. Bednarz, and J. Garrison, eds. 1998. *Constructivism and education.* Cambridge: Cambridge University Press.

Lave, J. 1988. *Cognition in practice: Mind, mathematics and culture in everyday life.* Cambridge: Cambridge University Press.

Lave, J., and E. Wenger. 1991. *Situated learning: Legitimate peripheral participation.* Cambridge: Cambridge University Press.

Law, L. C. 2000. Die Überwindung der Kluft zwischen Wissen und Handeln aus situativer Sicht. In *Die Kluft zwischen Wissen und Handeln. Empirische und theoretische Befunde,* ed. H. Mandl and J. Gerstenmeier, 253–87. Göttingen: Hogrefe.

Lemert, Charles, and Ann Branaman, eds. 1997. *The Goffman reader.* Cambridge, Mass.: Blackwell.

Levine, Barbara. *Works about John Dewey,* 1886–2006. Carbondale: Southern Illinois University Press, 2007.

Loenhoff, Jens. 1992. *Interkulturelle Verständigung: Zum Problem grenzüberschreitender Kommunikation.* Opladen: Leske und Budrich.

Lorenzen, P. 1974. *Konstruktive Wissenschaftstheorie*. Frankfurt am Main: Suhrkamp.

Lorenzen, P., and O. Schwemmer. 1975. *Konstruktive Logik, Ethik und Wissenschaftstheorie*. Mannheim: Bibliographisches Institut.

Luhmann, Niklas. 1988. *Erkenntnis als Konstruktion*. Bern: Benteli.

Lyotard, Jean-Francois. 1984. *The postmodern condition*. Manchester: Manchester University Press.

Marlowe, B. A., and M. L. Page. 1998. *Creating and sustaining the constructivist classroom*. Thousand Oaks, Calif.: Sage and Corwin Press.

Martin, Jay. 2002. *The education of John Dewey: A biography*. New York: Columbia University Press.

Maturana, Humberto R. 1978. Biology of language: The epistemology of reality. In *Psychology and Biology of Language and Thought*, ed. G. Miller and E. Lenneberg, 26–73. New York: Academic Press.

Maturana, Humberto R., and Francisco L. Varela. 1988. *The tree of knowledge*. Boston: Shambhala New Science Library.

McDermott, J. J., ed. 1967. *The Writings of William James*. New York: Random House.

Mills, C. Wright. 1939. Language, logic, and culture. In *American Sociological Review* 4:670–80.

———. 1940a. Methodological consequences of the sociology of knowledge. In *The American Journal of Sociology* 46:316–30.

———. 1940b. Bibliographical Appendix. In Harry Elmer Barnes, Howard Becker, and Frances Bennett Becker, eds. *Contemporary social theory*. New York: D. Appleton-Century.

Mittelstraß, J. 1974. *Die Möglichkeit von Wissenschaft*. Frankfurt am Main: Suhrkamp.

———. 1998. *Die Häuser des Wissens*. Frankfurt am Main: Suhrkamp.

Mouffe, Chantal. 1996. Deconstruction, pragmatism and the politics of democracy. In *Deconstruction and pragmatism*, ed. Chantal Mouffe, 1–12. London: Routledge.

———. 1997. *The return of the political*. London: Verso.

———. 2000. *The democratic paradox*. London: Verso.

Neubert, Stefan. 1998. *Erkenntnis, Verhalten und Kommunikation: John Deweys Philosophie des "experience" in interaktionistisch-konstruktivistischer Interpretation*. Münster: Waxmann.

———. 1999. John Deweys "Kunst als Erfahrung": Anmerkungen zu einer mißlungenen Übersetzung. In *Jahrbuch für Historische Bildungsforschung*, Bd. 5:289–300. Bad Heilbrunn and Obb: Klinkhardt.

————. 2001. Pragmatism and constructivism in contemporary philosophical discourse. http://konstruktivismus.uni-koeln.de.

————. 2002. Konstruktivismus, Demokratie und Multikultur: Konstruktivistische Überlegungen zu ausgewählten theoretischen Grundlagen der anglo-amerikanischen Multikulturalismusdebatte. In *Multikulturalität in der Diskussion: Neuere Beiträge zu einem umstrittenen Konzept*, ed. Stefan Neubert, Hans-Joachim Roth, and Erol Yildiz, 63–98. Opladen: Leske and Budrich.

Neubert, Stefan, and Kersten Reich. 2000. Die konstruktivistische Erweiterung der Diskurstheorie: eine Einführung in die interaktionistisch-konstruktive Sicht von Diskursen. In *Die Idee des Diskurses. Interdisziplinäre Annäherungen*, ed. Holger Burckhart, Horst Gronke, and Jens Peter Brune, 43–74. Markt Schwaben: Eusl.

————. 2001. The ethnocentric view: Constructivism and the practice of intercultural discourse. In *Learning for the future, proceedings of the learning conference 2001*, ed. Bill Cope and Mary Kalantzis. Melbourne and Sydney, Australia: Common Ground Publishing (www.theLearner.com).

Niquet, Marcel. 1999. *Nichthintergehbarkeit und Diskurs*. Berlin: Duncker and Humblot.

Oelkers, Jürgen, and Heinz Rhyn, eds. 2000. *Dewey and European education: General problems and case studies*. Dordrecht, Boston, and London: Kluwer.

Parker, S. P., ed. 1992. *McGraw-Hill Encyclopedia of Science and Technology* Vol. 6, 7th ed. New York: Columbia University Press.

Peirce, Charles S. 1972. *Pragmatism and pragmaticism*. Vol. 5 of *Collected papers*, ed. Charles Hartshorne and Paul Weiss. Cambridge, Mass.: Harvard University Press.

————. 1984. *1867–1871*, Vol. 2 of *Writings of Charles S. Peirce: A chronological edition*, ed. Edward C. Moore. Bloomington: Indiana University Press.

————. 1986. *1872–1878*, Vol. 3 of *Writings of Charles S. Peirce: A chronological edition*, ed. Christian J. W. Kloesel. Bloomington: Indiana University Press.

Perry, R. B. 1935. *The thought and character of William James*. Boston: Little, Brown.

Pines, A. L., and L. H. T. West. 1986. Conceptual understanding and science learning: An interpretation of research within sources-of-knowledge framework. In *Science Education* 70:583–604.

Putnam, Hilary. 1992. Irrealism and deconstruction. In *Renewing philosophy (The Gifford Lectures)*. Cambridge, Mass.: Harvard University Press.

Quine, Willard van Orman. 1969. Ontological relativity. In *Ontological relativity and other essays*, 26–68. New York: Columbia University Press.

Reich, Kersten. 1998a. *Beobachtung und die Unschärfen der Erkenntnis*. Band 1 of *Die Ordnung der Blicke*. Neuwied: Luchterhand.

———. 1998b. *Beziehungen und Lebenswelt*. Band 2 of *Die Ordnung der Blicke*. Neuwied: Luchterhand.

———. 1998c. Das Imaginäre in der systemisch-konstruktivistischen Didaktik. In *Schul-Visionen*, ed. Reinhard Voß, 189–98. Heidelberg: Auer.

———. 1998d. Die Kindheit neu erfinden. In *Familiendynamik*, Heft 1:6–24.

———. 2000a. *Systemisch-konstruktivistische Pädagogik: Einführung in Grundlagen einer interaktionistisch-konstruktivistischen Pädagogik*. Neuwied, Kriftel, and Berlin: Luchterhand.

———. 2000b. Interaktionistisch-konstruktive Kritik einer universalistischen Begründung von Ethik und Moral. In *Begründung von Moral. Diskursethik versus Konstruktivismus—eine Streitschrift*, Holger Burckhart and Kersten Reich, 88–181. Würzburg: Königshausen and Neumann.

———. 2001a. Konstruktivistische Ansätze in den Sozial-und Kulturwissenschaften. In *Wie kommt Wissenschaft zu Wissen?* ed. Theo Hug, Bd. 4:356–76. Baltmannsweiler: Schneider Verlag Hohengehren.

———. 2001b. Konstruktivismen aus kultureller Sicht—zur Position des Interaktionistischen Konstruktivismus. In *Konstruktivismen*, ed., F. Wallner and R. Angnese. Vienna: Universitätsverlag.

———. 2002. *Systemisch-konstruktivistische Pädagogik*. Neuwied: Luchterhand.

———. 2004a. *Konstruktivistische Didaktik*. Neuwied: Luchterhand.

———. 2004b. Experimental truth and context. URL: http://konstruktivismus.uni-koeln.de.

Reich, Kersten, and Yuquing Wei. 1997. *Beziehungen als Lebensform: Philosophie und Pädagogik im alten China*. Münster: Waxmann.

Rockefeller, Steven C. 1991. *John Dewey: Religious faith and democratic humanism*. New York: Columbia University Press.

Rorty, Richard. 1979. *Philosophy and the mirror of nature*. Princeton, N.J.: Princeton University Press.

———. 1989. *Contingency, irony, and solidarity*. Cambridge: Cambridge University Press.

———. 1991. *Objectivity, relativism, and truth*. Cambridge: Cambridge University Press.

———. 2000. *Philosophy and social hope*. New York: Penguin.

———. 2003. *Wahrheit und Fortschritt*. Frankfurt am Main: Suhrkamp.

Ryan, Alan. 1995. *John Dewey and the high tide of American liberalism*. New York: W. W. Norton and Company.

Sandbothe, M., ed. 2000. *Die Renaissance des Pragmatismus*. Weilerswist: Velbrück Wissenschaft.

Scheler, Max. 1924. *Versuche zu einer Soziologie des Wissens*. Munich: Duncker and Humboldt.

———. 1926. *Die Wissensformen und die Gesellschaft*. Leipzig: Der Neue Geist Verlag.

———. 1954a. *Vom Ewigen im Menschen* (1920), 4th ed. In *Gesammelte Werke*, ed. Maria Scheler. 5:286, 324fn. Bern: Francke Verlag.

———. 1954b. *Der Formalismus in der Ethik und die materiale Wertethik: neuer Versuch der Grundlegung eines ethischen Personalismus*, 3rd ed. *Gesammelte Werke*, ed. Maria Scheler, Vol. 2. Bern: Francke Verlag.

———. 1963a. Über die positivistische Geschichtsphilosophie des Wissens (Dreistadiengesetz) (1921). *Gesammelte Werke*, ed. Maria Scheler, 6:27–35. Bern: Francke Verlag.

———. 1963b. Zu W. Jerusalems "Bermerkungen" (1921). In *Gesammelte Werke*, ed. Maria Scheler, 6:327–30. Bern: Francke Verlag.

———. 1971. *Frühe Schriften*. Vol. 1 of *Gesammelte Werke*, ed. Maria Scheler and Manfried Frings. Bern: Francke Verlag.

———. 1972a. Zur Rehabilitierung der Tugend (1913). In *Gesammelte Werke*, ed. Maria Scheler. 3:23–25. Bern: Francke Verlag.

———. 1972b. *Das Ressentiment in Aufbau der Moralen* (1915). In *Gesammelte Werke*, ed. Maria Scheler. Vol. 3. Bern: Francke Verlag.

———. 1973. *Formalism in ethics and non-formal ethics of values: A new attempt toward the foundation of an ethical personalism*. Trans. Manfried Frings and Roger L. Funk. Evanston, Ill.: Northwestern University Press.

———. 1979. Erkenntnislehre und Metaphysik. In *Schriften aus dem Nachlass*. Vol. II. *Erkenntnislehre und Metaphysik*, ed. Manfried Frings. Vol. 11. Bern: Francke Verlag.

———. 1980. Erkenntnis und Arbeit. In *Gesammelte Werke*, ed. Maria Scheler, 8:191–382. Bern: Francke Verlag.

Scheunpflug, A. 1998. Systemtheorie und Pädagogik. In *Zeitschrift für Erziehungswissenschaft* Heft 1:619.

Schiller, F. C. S. 1912. *Humanism: Philosophical essays*. London: Macmillan and Co.

Schilpp, Paul A. 1926. American neglect of a philosophy of culture. In *Philosophical Review* 35:434–46.

———. 1927a. The "formal problems" of Scheler's sociology of knowledge. In *The Philosophical Review* 36:101–20.

————. 1927b. The doctrine of "illusion" and "error" in Scheler's phenomenology. In *Journal of Philosophy* 24:624–33.

————. 1929. Max Scheler 1874–1928. In *Philosophical Review* 38:547–88.

Schilpp, Paul A., ed. 1951. *The philosophy of John Dewey*. New York: Tudor.

Schlippe, Arist von, and Jochen Schweitzer. 1996. *Lehrbuch der systemischen
Therapie und Beratung*. Göttingen: Vandenhoeck und Ruprecht.

Schmid, Wilhelm. 1991, 2000. *Auf der Suche nach einer neuen Lebenskunst:
Die Frage nach dem Grund und die Neubegründung der Ethik bei Foucault*.
Frankfurt am Main: Suhrkamp.

————. 2001a. *Philosophie der Lebenskunst: Eine Grundlegung*. Frankfurt am
Main: Suhrkamp.

————. 2001b. *Schönes Leben? Einführung in die Lebenskunst*. Frankfurt am
Main: Suhrkamp.

Schmidt, Siegfried J. 1994. *Kognitive Autonomie und soziale Orientierung:
Konstruktivistische Bemerkungen zum Zusammenhang von Kognition,
Kommunikation, Medien und Kultur*. Frankfurt am Main: Suhrkamp.

Schmidt, Siegfried J., ed. 1987. *Der Diskurs des radikalen Konstruktivismus*.
Frankfurt am Main: Suhrkamp.

————. 1992. *Kognition und Gesellschaft: Der Diskurs des radikalen Konstruktivismus*, Vol. 2. Frankfurt am Main: Suhrkamp.

Schreier, Helmut, ed. 1994. *John Dewey: Erziehung durch Erfahrung*. Stutt-
gart: Klett-Cotta.

Schütz, Alfred, and T. Luckmann. 1991. *Strukturen der Lebenswelt*. Vol. 2.
Frankfurt am Main: Suhrkamp.

Science and Education. 1997. *Philosophy and constructivism in science education*. Vol. 6, nos. 1–2, January.

Searle, J. R. 1997. *Die Konstruktion der gesellschaftlichen Wirklichkeit: Zur On-
tologie sozialer Tatsachen*. Reinbek: Rowohlt.

Seigfried, Charlene Haddock. 1996. *Pragmatism and feminism: Reweaving the
social fabric*. Chicago: University of Chicago Press.

————. 2002. John Dewey's pragmatist feminism. In *Feminist interpretations
of John Dewey*, ed. Charlene H. Seigfried, 47–77. University Park: Pennsylvania State University Press.

Seigfried, Charlene Haddock, ed. 2002. *Feminist interpretations of John
Dewey*. University Park: Pennsylvania State University Press.

Sen, Amartya. 1999. *Development as freedom*. New York: Anchor Books.

Shotter, J. 1994. *Conversational realities: Constructing life through language.
Inquiries in social construction*. London: Sage.

Shusterman, Richard. 2000. *Pragmatist aesthetics: Living beauty, rethinking
art*. New York: Rowman and Littlefield.

Siebert, Horst. 1999. *Pädagogischer Konstruktivismus*. Neuwied: Luchterhand.

Sleeper, Ralph W. 1986. *The necessity of pragmatism: John Dewey's conception of philosophy*. New Haven, Conn.: Yale University Press.

Small, Albion. 1921. Review of *Kölner Vierteljahrshefte für Sozialwissenschaften*, ed. Max Scheler, et al. In *American Journal of Sociology* 27:92–94.

————. 1925–26. Review of *Versuche zu einer Soziologie des Wissens*, ed. Max Scheler. In *The American Journal of Sociology* 31:262–64.

Solomon, J. 1994. The rise and fall of constructivism. In *Studies in Science Education* 70:1–19.

Spiegelberg, H. 1956. Husserl's and Peirce's phenomenologies: Coincidence or interaction? In *Philosophy and Phenomenological Research* 17:164–85.

Stachowiak, Herbert, ed. 1983. *Modelle—Konstruktion der Wirklichkeit*. Munich: Fink.

Steffe, L. P., and J. Gale, eds. 1995. *Constructivism in education*. Hillsdale, N.J.: Erlbaum.

Tanner, Laurel N. 1997. *Dewey's laboratory school: Lessons for today*. New York: Teachers College Press.

Terhart, E. 1999. Konstruktivismus und Unterricht. In *Zeitschrift für Pädagogik*, Heft 45:629–47.

Tiles, J. E. 1995. Applying the term "mental" in a world without withins: Dewey's realism. *Transactions of the Charles S. Peirce Society* XXXI, No. 1: 137–66.

Tobin, K., ed. 1993. *The practice of constructivism in science education*. Hillsdale, N.J.: Erlbaum.

*Transactions of the Charles S. Peirce Society*. 1992. 28:161–215.

Uslucan, Haci-Halil. 2001. *Handlung und Erkenntnis: Die pragmatistische Perspektive John Deweys und Jean Piagets Entwicklungspsychologie*. Münster: Waxmann.

Von Glasersfeld, Ernst. 1995. *Radical constructivism: A way of knowing and learning*. London: Falmer Press.

Voß, Reinhard. 1997. *Die Schule neu erfinden*. Neuwied: Luchterhand.

Voß, Reinhard, ed. 1998. *Schul-Visionen*. Heidelberg: Auer.

Vygotsky (Wygotsky), Lew Semjonowitsch. 1977. *Denken und Sprechen*. Frankfurt am Main: Fischer.

Waldenfels, Bernhard. 1999. Vielstimmigkeit der Rede. *Studien zur Phänomenologie des Fremden* 4. Frankfurt am Main: Suhrkamp.

Wallner, Friedrich. 1992a. *Konstruktion der Realität*. Vienna: WUV-Universitätsverlag.

————. 1992b. *Acht Vorlesungen über den Konstruktiven Realismus*. Vienna: WUV-Universitätsverlag.

Watzlawick, Paul, Janet H. Beavin, and Don D. Jackson. 1967. *Pragmatics of human communication: A study of interactional patterns, pathologies, and paradoxes.* New York: W. W. Norton.

Weinert, F., and H. Mandl, eds. 1997. *Psychologie der Erwachsenenbildung.* Vol. 4 of *Enzyklopädie der Psychologie: Pädagogische Psychologie.* Göttingen: Verlag für Pyschologie.

Welchman, Jennifer. 1995. *Dewey's ethical thought.* Ithaca, N.Y.: Cornell University Press.

Welsch, Wolfgang. 1992. Transkulturalität: Lebenformen nach der Auflösung der Kulturen. In *Information Philosophie,* Heft 2:5–20.

Westacott, Emrys. 1996. Relativism and autonomy. In *Philosophical Forum* 27:127–45.

Westbrook, Robert B. 1991. *John Dewey and American democracy.* Ithaca, N.Y.: Cornell University Press.

Westmeyer, H. 1999. Konstruktivismus und Psychologie. In *Zeitschrift für Erziehungswissenschaft,* Heft 4:507–26.

Wittgenstein, Ludwig. 1953. *Philosophical investigations.* Trans. by G. E. M. Anscombe. New York: Macmillan.

# Contributors

Jim Garrison is Professor of Philosophy of Education at Virginia Tech in Blacksburg, Virginia. His work concentrates on philosophical pragmatism. Jim is a past winner of the Jim Merritt award for his scholarship in the philosophy of education as well as the John Dewey Society Outstanding Achievement Award. He is a past president of the Philosophy of Education Society and current president of the John Dewey Society. His most recent book is an edited work: *Reconstructing Democracy, Recontextualizing Dewey* (2008).

Larry A. Hickman is Director of the Center for Dewey Studies and Professor of Philosophy at Southern Illinois University Carbondale. His most recent book is *Pragmatism as Post-Postmodernism: Lessons from John Dewey* (2007). He is also the editor of the electronic edition of *The Collected Works of John Dewey, 1882–1953* and *The Correspondence of John Dewey, 1871–1952*.

Stefan Neubert teaches in the Faculty of Human Sciences at the University of Cologne and is Co-Director of the Cologne Dewey Center. His publications include *Erkenntnis, Verhalten und Kommunikation— John Dewey's Philosophie des "experience" in interaktionistisch-konstruktivistischer Interpretation* (1998) and "Konstruktivismus, Demokratie und Multikultur" (2002).

Kersten Reich is Professor of Education in the Faculty of Human Sciences at the University of Cologne and Co-Director of the Cologne

Dewey Center. His books include *Systemisch-konstruktivistische Päda-gogik* (2000) and numerous other works in the philosophy of education.

**Kenneth W. Stikkers** is Professor of Philosophy at Southern Illinois University Carbondale. His research involves the historical and the-matic connections between American pragmatism and continental thought, especially phenomenology and the sociology of knowledge. He is the editor and co-editor of several works by Max Scheler, co-editor of *Wealth and Well-Being* (1986), and author of the forthcom-ing *Economics as Moral Philosophy* and numerous articles on philoso-phy of economics, contemporary continental thought, and American philosophy.

# Index

James, William, 7, 36, 68, 71, 76, 73–74,
92
his concept of real, 189
dynamic psychology of, 6
and fallibilism, 145
and habit, 5–6
and imperialism, 188
influence on Dewey, 5
Jerusalem and, 70–72
and knowledge, 77
paradigm of observation of, 132
reflex arc model, 7
on sociology of knowledge, 70
Jerusalem, Wilhelm, 70–73
judgments, 146
absolute, 147
import of, 149
intermediate, 159
relative, 147
in social sciences, 153
techno-scientific, 144, 150–51, 154, 157
truth of, 160
universalizable, 148–50, 153, 156
warranted assertibility, 151–52

Kaplan, Robert, 148
Kelly, George, 50
knowing-known events, 141
knowledge, 51
constructivist critique of, 191
functionalization of, 77
objects of, 90, 92, 97, 99, 101
perspectival character of, 160
restrictions of, 132
sociology of, 70–72, 78–80, 82
techno-scientific, 151
theory and logic of, 24–25
and truth, 239
Kuhn, Thomas S., 151, 206

Laboratory School, 9–10, 30–31
Laclau, Ernesto, 56, 176–77
Language and meaning, 97–98, 105
language games, 139, 140
learning, 6–9, 31
analysis of, 7–12, 25
constructive notion of, 63–64

liberalism, 29, 30
linguistic transactions, 102–3
Locke, John, 20
*Logic*, 24–25, 87–88
and language, 105
logical forms, 96

Marxism, 30, 56
Mead, George Herbert, 26, 36, 60, 100
culture theory of, 162
and interaction, 218
meaning, 102, 104, 227
and language, 97
as social construction, 101, 105
theory of, 97, 102
means-consequence, 87, 90, 97–98
means-end relations, 88, 126
Meier, Deborah, 10–11
metaphysics, 22, 58, 79, 85, 244n4
naturalistic, 221–22
and Pragmatism, 58–60
methodischer Konstruktivismus, 43,
208, 249n2
methods, 42, 43, 155
denotative, 152–53
techno-scientific, 150, 151, 205
universalizable, 150
modernity, 215
morality, 27–28
Mouffe, Chantal, 56, 176–77
multiculturalism, 178

nature, concept of, 25, 193
naturalism, 20, 51, 192
neo-Pragmatists, 160
Neubert, Stefan, 144–45

observation, 116, 137
and education, 134
and participation, 128, 135
in scientific research, 138
theory of, 132–33
observer, participant, and agent, 168,
200–1
in constructivism, 115, 218
perspectives of, 109–14, 119, 200–1
roles of, 117, 119–23, 125–27

AMERICAN PHILOSOPHY SERIES
*Douglas R. Anderson and Jude Jones, series editors*

Kenneth Laine Ketner, ed., *Peirce and Contemporary Thought: Philosophical Inquiries.*

Max H. Fisch, ed., *Classic American Philosophers: Peirce, James, Royce, Santayana, Dewey, Whitehead,* second edition. Introduction by Nathan Houser.

John E. Smith, *Experience and God,* second edition.

Vincent G. Potter, *Peirce's Philosophical Perspectives.* Ed. by Vincent Colapietro.

Richard E. Hart and Douglas R. Anderson, eds., *Philosophy in Experience: American Philosophy in Transition.*

Vincent G. Potter, *Charles S. Peirce: On Norms and Ideals,* second edition. Introduction by Stanley M. Harrison.

Vincent M. Colapietro, ed., *Reason, Experience, and God: John E. Smith in Dialogue.* Introduction by Merold Westphal.

Robert J. O'Connell, S.J., *William James on the Courage to Believe,* second edition.

Elizabeth M. Kraus, *The Metaphysics of Experience: A Companion to Whitehead's "Process and Reality,"* second edition. Introduction by Robert C. Neville.

Kenneth Westphal, ed., *Pragmatism, Reason, and Norms: A Realistic Assessment—Essays in Critical Appreciation of Frederick L. Will.*

Beth J. Singer, *Pragmatism, Rights, and Democracy.*

Eugene Fontinell, *Self, God, and Immorality: A Jamesian Investigation.*

Roger Ward, *Conversion in American Philosophy: Exploring the Practice of Transformation.*

Michael Epperson, *Quantum Mechanics and the Philosophy of Alfred North Whitehead*.

Kory Sorrell, *Representative Practices: Peirce, Pragmatism, and Feminist Epistemology*.

Naoko Saito, *The Gleam of Light: Moral Perfectionism and Education in Dewey and Emerson*.

Josiah Royce, *The Basic Writings of Josiah Royce*.

Douglas R. Anderson, *Philosophy Americana: Making Philosophy at Home in American Culture*.

James Campbell and Richard E. Hart, eds., *Experience as Philosophy: On the World of John J. McDermott*.

John J. McDermott, *The Drama of Possibility: Experience as Philosophy of Culture*. Edited by Douglas R. Anderson.

Larry A. Hickman, *Pragmatism as Post-Postmodernism: Lessons from John Dewey*.

Dwayne A. Tunstall, *Yes, But Not Quite: Encountering Josiah Royce's Ethico-Religious Insight*.